ALSO BY

AMY LATTA

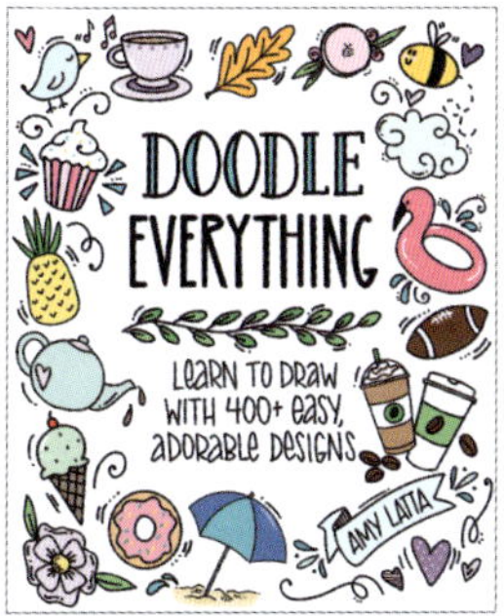

Doodle Everything

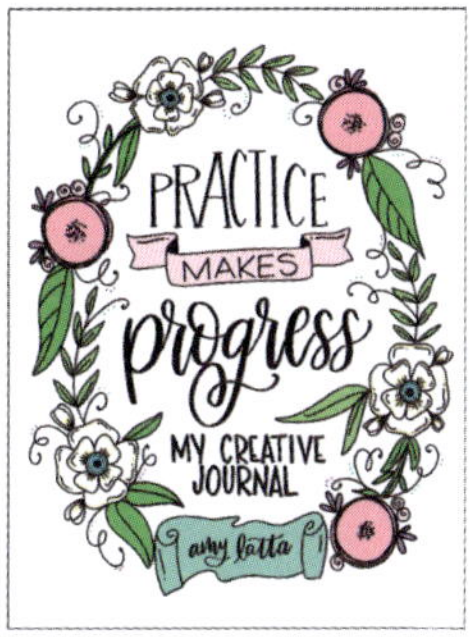

Practice Makes Progress: My Creative Journal

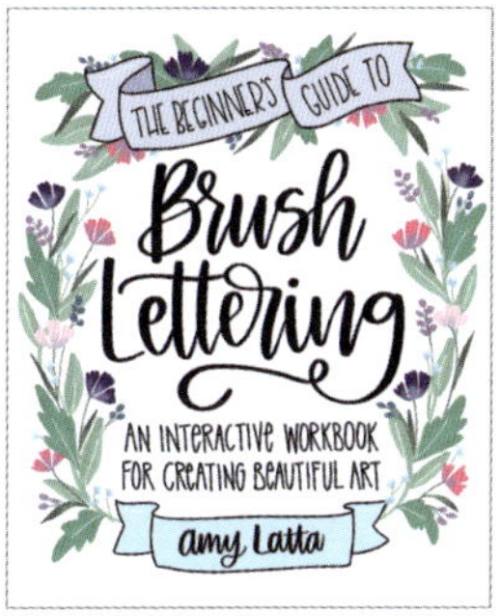

The Beginner's Guide to Brush Lettering

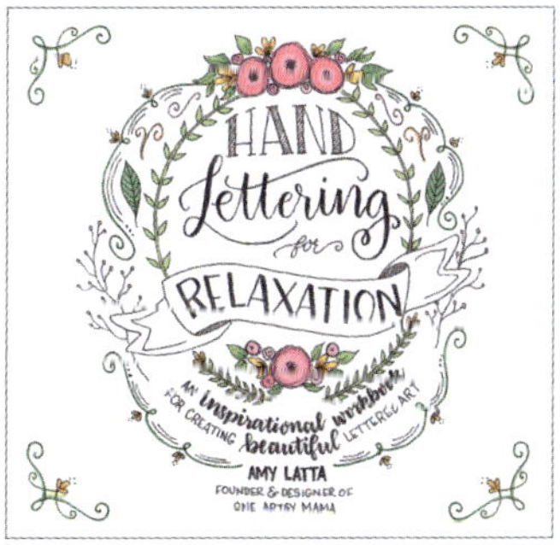

Hand Lettering for Relaxation

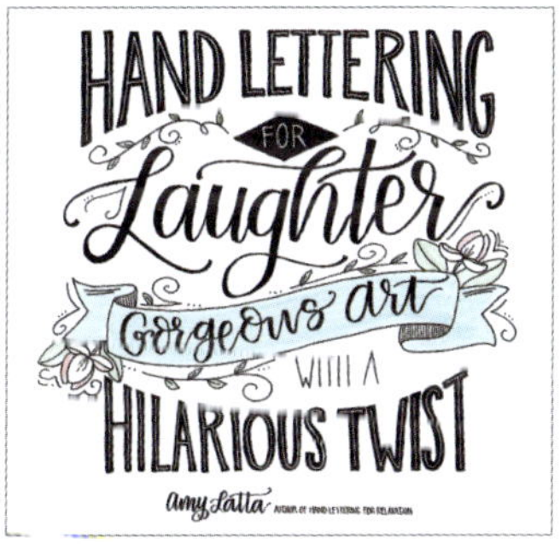

Hand Lettering for Laughter

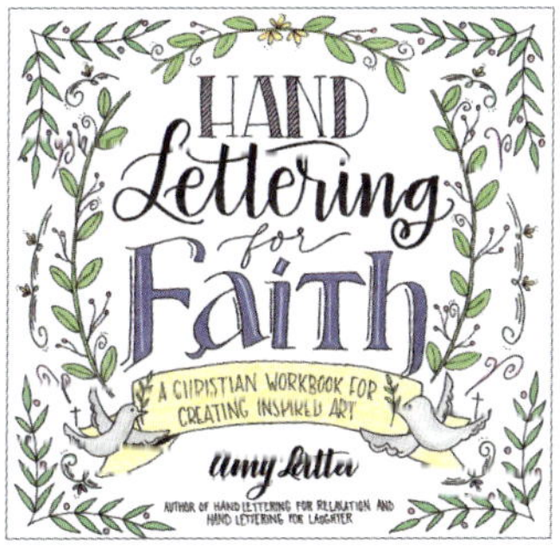

Hand Lettering for Faith

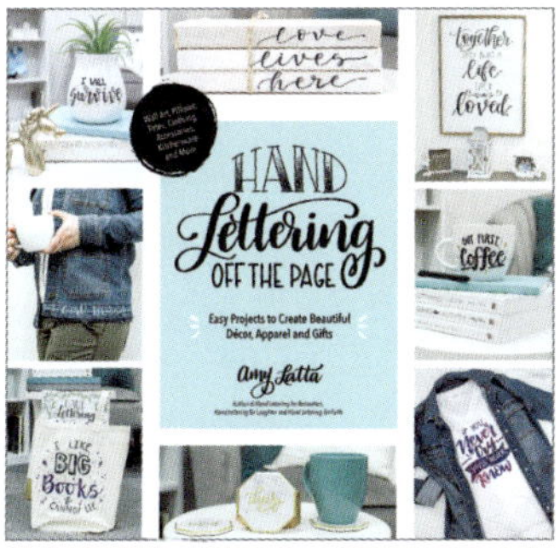

Hand Lettering Off the Page

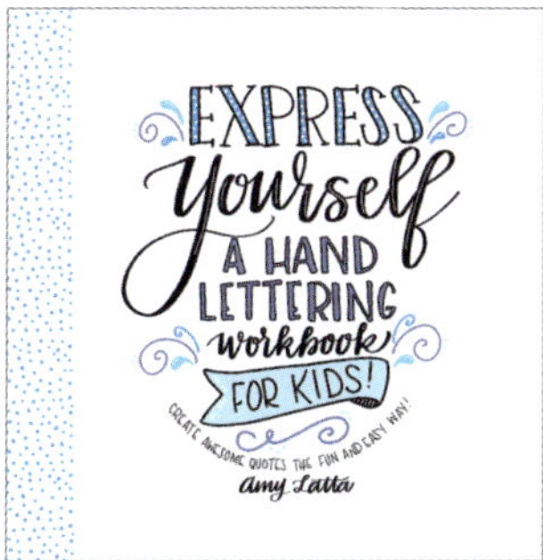

Express Yourself: A Hand Lettering Workbook for Kids

DOODLE ALL THE ANIMALS

LEARN TO DRAW
200+ CUTE CRITTERS

AMY
LATTA

PAGE STREET
PUBLISHING CO.

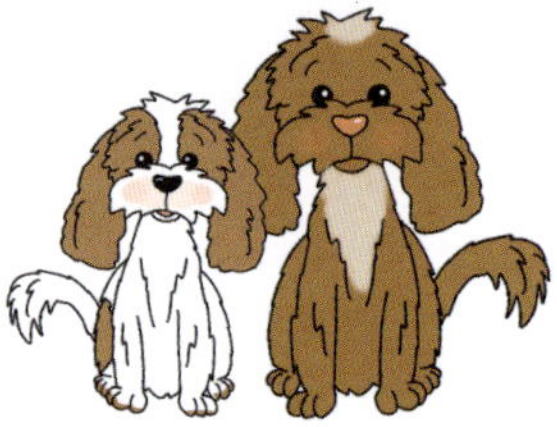

**FOR PUMPKIN AND PEANUT—
MY FAVORITE DOODLES.**

First published in 2024 by
Page Street Publishing Co.
27 Congress Street, Suite 1511
Salem, MA 01970
www.pagestreetpublishing.com

Distributed by Macmillan, sales in Canada by The Canadian Manda Group.

28 27 26 25 24 1 2 3 4 5

ISBN-13: 979-889003-035-1

Cover by Amy Latta and book design by Meg Baskis for Page Street Publishing Co.
Illustrations by Amy Latta

Printed and bound in China

Page Street Publishing protects our planet by donating to nonprofits like The Trustees, which focuses on local land conservation.

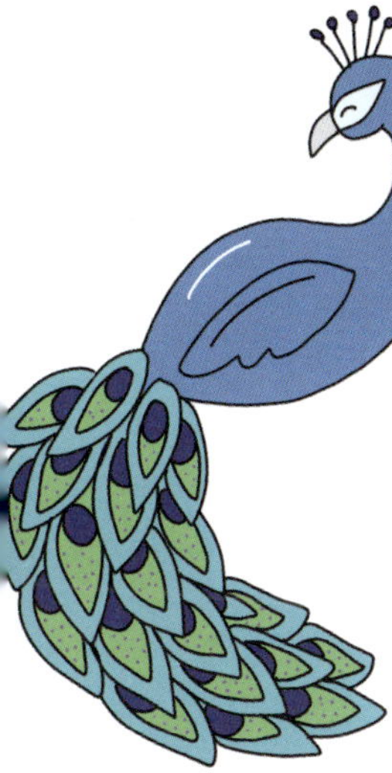

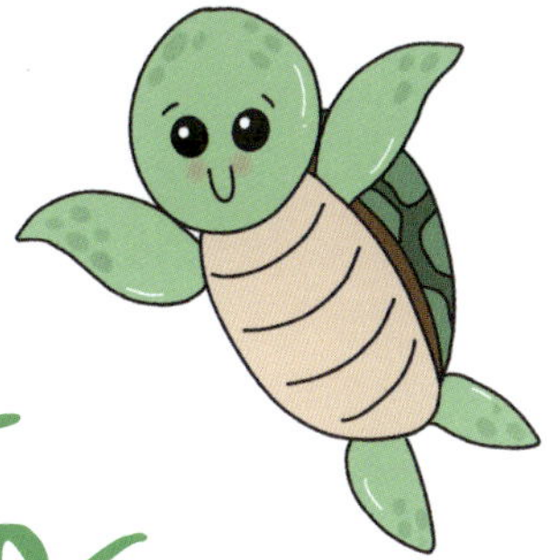

Contents

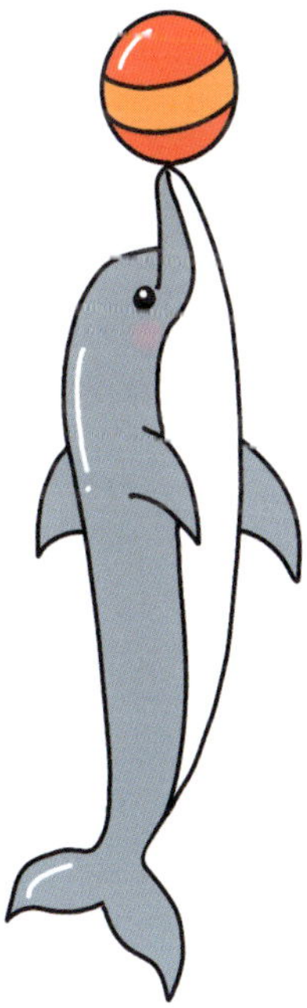

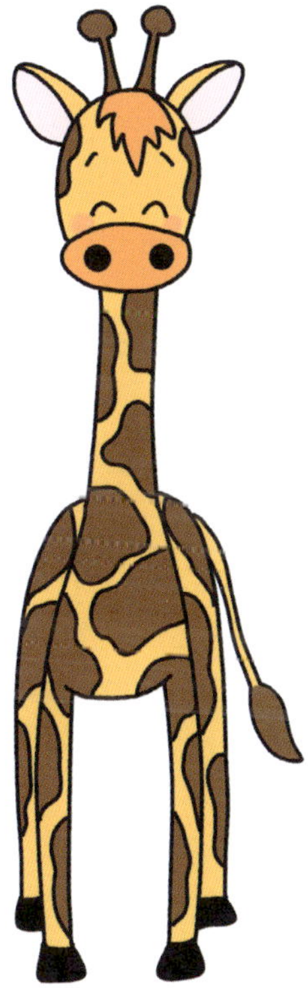

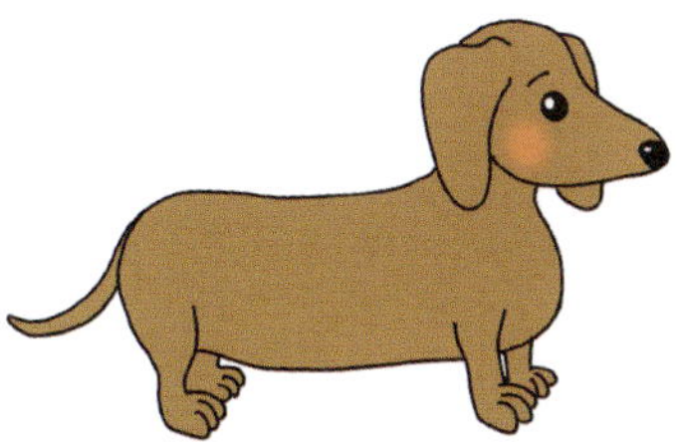

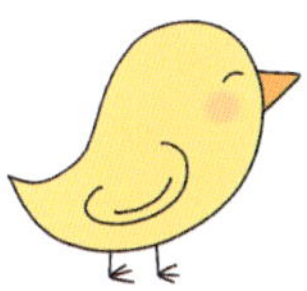

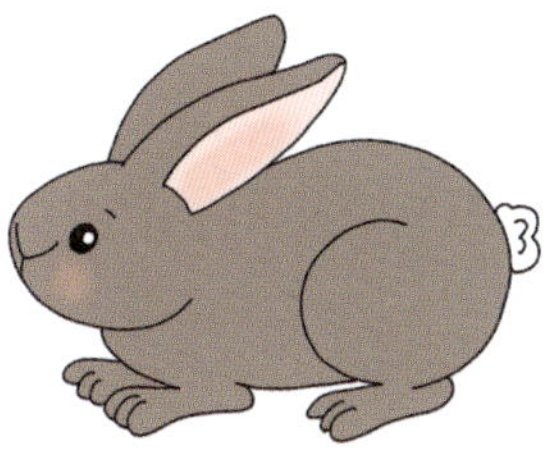

INTRODUCTION

Did you know that doodling is good for you? It's true! Not only is it just plain fun to sketch whimsical pictures, it has a ton of other benefits too. Doodling relaxes us, lowering our stress level, our anxiety and our blood pressure. It boosts our creativity and can cause our brains to release serotonin, boosting our mood as well. Not only do our doodles benefit us physically, they can also bring joy and offer opportunities for connection with others, like when we create a handmade card for someone we love. The best part is that since doodles aren't meant to be realistic, there's absolutely no pressure to draw them perfectly! We can take a deep breath, relax and just enjoy creating.

There are millions of things in the world that we can doodle, many of which I included in my previous book, *Doodle Everything*. In this book, we're going to focus on animals, which are my favorite things to doodle—and I'm guessing they might be yours too! We're going to explore some of the world's habitats and ecosystems together, learning about the animals who live there and how to draw them. As I did my background research, I quickly realized that there are incredibly fascinating facts about every living creature, and I hope you'll enjoy discovering them as much as I did.

In each section, I also included a few bonus doodles for things found in the natural habitats of the animals, like plants and landforms. This way, not only can you draw individual animals, you can also put several of them together and create a whole illustrated scene! I've given an example of this at the beginning of each chapter as extra inspiration.

As we begin, let me offer this encouragement: Whether you feel like you have artistic ability or not, you truly can doodle. Please don't be intimidated by a finished drawing that looks "too hard." The reality is that all doodles are just combinations of basic shapes and lines, put together in a particular way. I've broken down each animal doodle into clear steps, both visually and with written instructions, so that no matter what type of learner you are, you can follow them. You can even place your paper on top of the book and do some tracing while you're learning to help you get the hang of things. You can mimic my doodles exactly or you can put your own spin on them, making them uniquely yours.

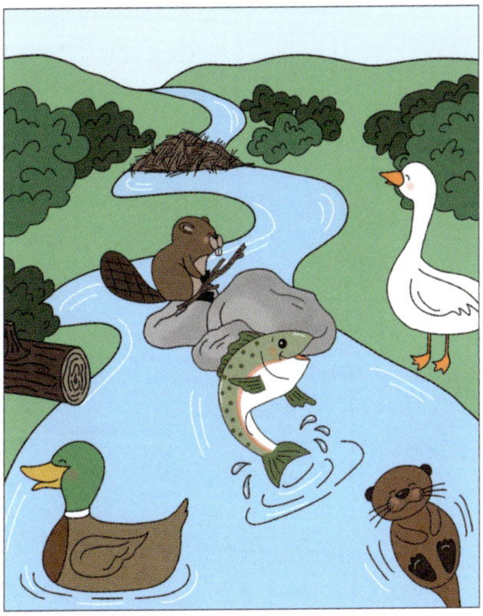 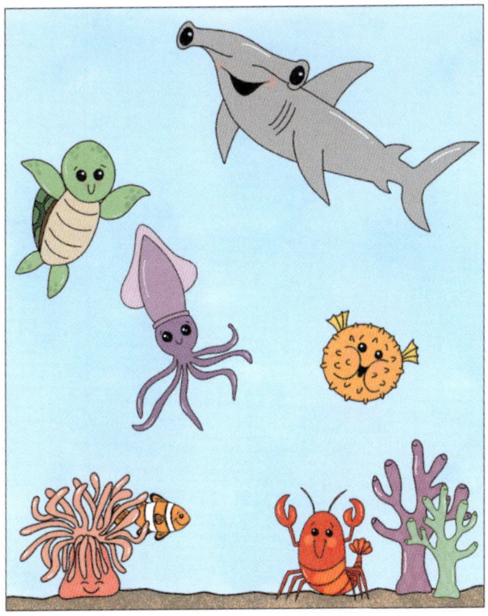 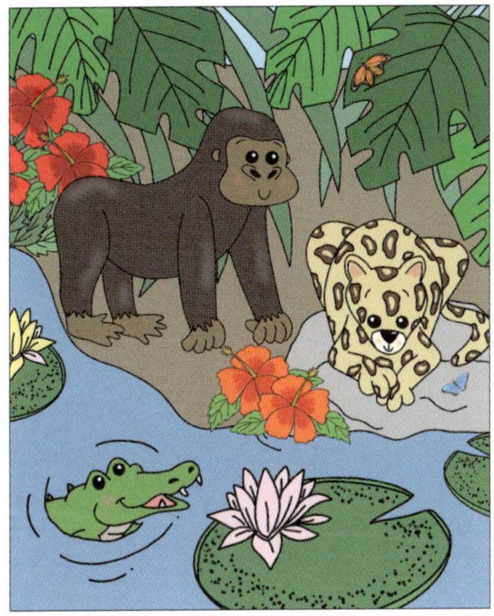

So, what additional supplies do you need besides this book? Just paper and a pencil! Of course, doodles are more fun when you add color, so you'll probably also want to grab your favorite markers, crayons or colored pencils. Personally, I like to sketch with a pencil first so that I can erase any mistakes, as well as any lines that overlap each other as I go through the various steps of drawing my animals. Then, I trace my pencil lines with a fine-tip drawing marker like a Tombow MONO Drawing Pen or Sakura® Pigma® Micron™. Finally, when the outline is dry, I color my doodle. Sometimes, I like to add highlight lines with a white gel pen like the Uniball™ Signo™. Another option is to doodle digitally, using an app like Procreate® along with an Apple Pencil. Just remember, there's no wrong way to doodle!

One of my favorite things as an author is to see what you choose to do with the things you learn from these pages. When you create something, I'd love for you to share it with me. You can tag me on social media @amylattacreations or post your pictures in my Facebook group, Amy Latta & Friends. I'd also love for you to visit amylattacreations.com for more art and craft ideas. Let's stay in touch! For now, grab your supplies, turn to the first chapter and let's doodle all the animals!

Amy Latta

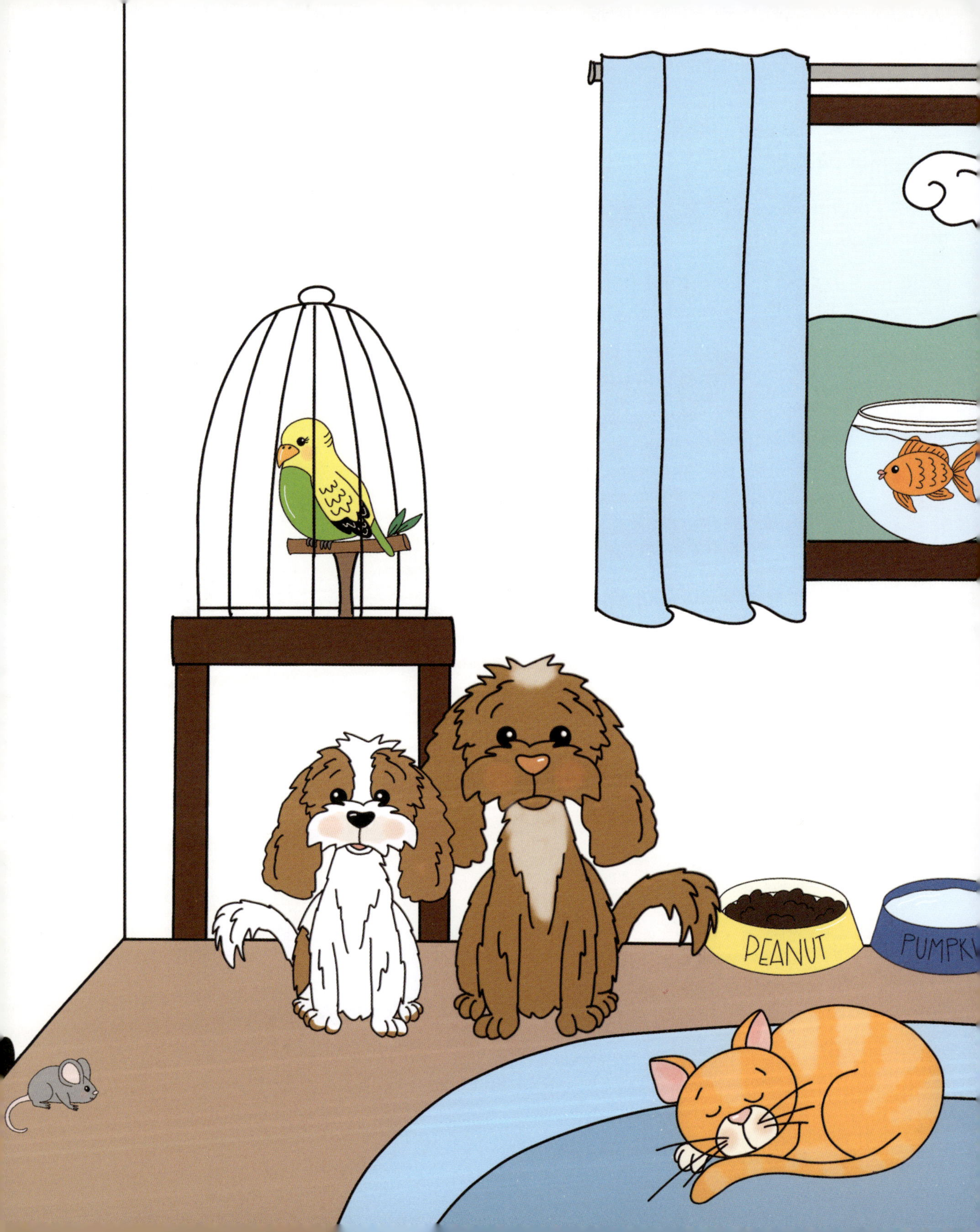
PEANUT
PUMPKI

IN THE House

Whether you live in an apartment, a condo or a single-family house, animals make it feel like home. Pets are found in almost every culture and society, creating a relationship that's beneficial to both the humans and the animals. Not only do pets provide us with companionship, they have a positive impact on our overall health and well-being. Interacting with animals can lower our blood pressure and stress and boost our mood. Some studies even suggest that pet owners tend to live longer than people who don't own an animal. The most common types of household pets in America are cats and dogs, but there are lots of other types of pets too. Let's look at some of them and learn how to doodle our favorites!

SLEEPING DOG

Dogs make wonderful companions for humans—so much so that approximately one-third of all households around the world have a pet dog. Their intelligence is often compared to a two-year-old child.

Let's draw a sleeping dog together. Start with an upside-down, egg-shaped head on an angle. Next, add a pair of short, floppy ears and erase the spots where they overlap the head. Now, draw a long, curving line for the body that ends in a pointed tail. Add a curving line for the back leg, then draw a pair of paws below the head. Finish by giving your dog a face, including a nose and muzzle, eyebrows and closed eyes. All that's left to do is color your doodle.

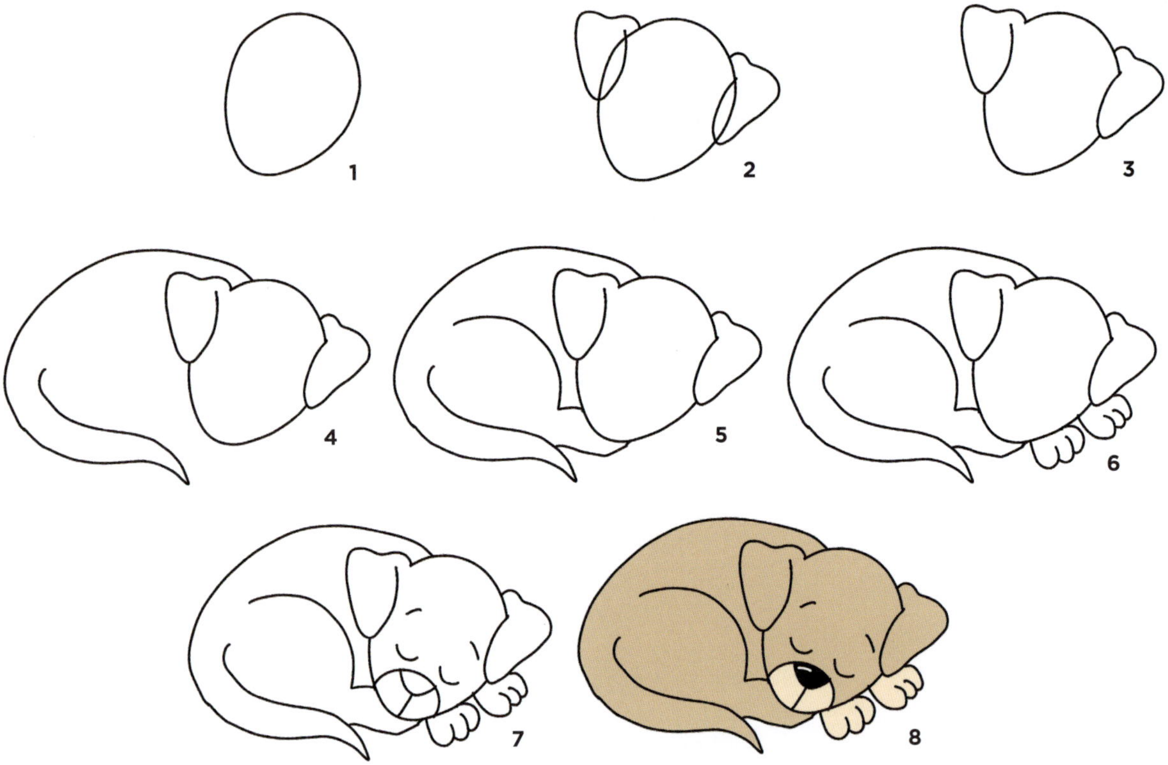

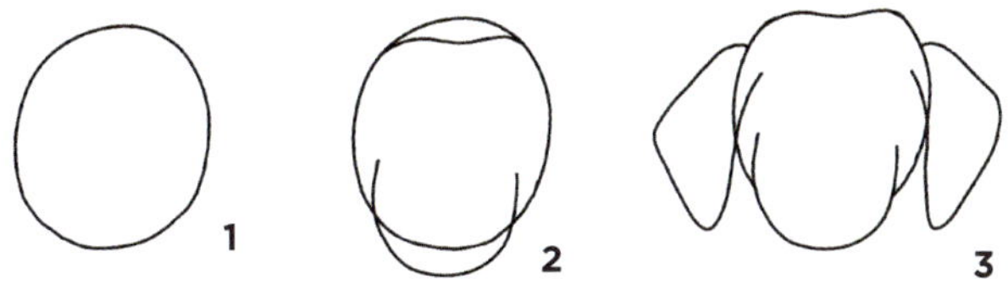

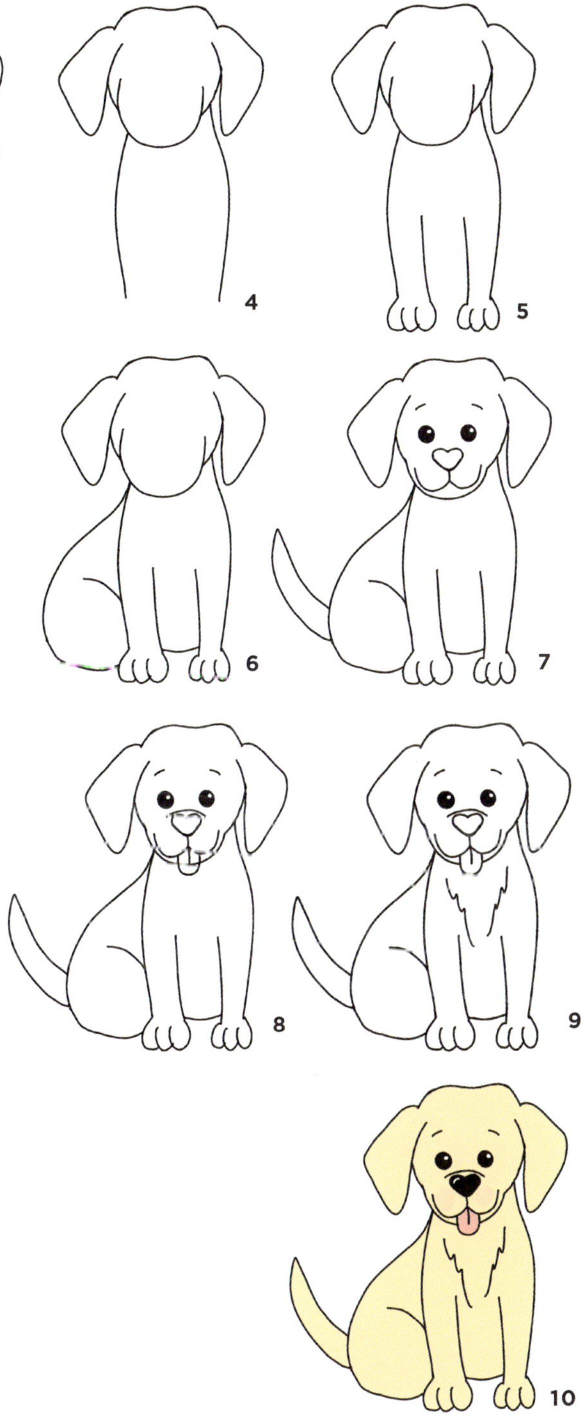

RETRIEVER

There are six types of retrievers, all of which are extremely intelligent, sweet-tempered and athletic. Their gentle personalities and ability to bond well with humans make them a great choice for a family pet. Retrievers also make excellent guide dogs, therapy dogs and search-and-rescue dogs.

Start your retriever sketch with a circle. Draw a wavy "m" shape across the top and a "u" shape at the bottom, erasing the extra lines to form the head shape. Next, add a pair of floppy ears. Draw two lines for the front of the body and add front legs and paws. Next, sketch the back end of the body, along with a curving line for the back leg. Give your dog a large tail and a face. If you like, add a tongue and erase the lines where it overlaps the jaw. Finally, add a pair of zigzag lines on the chest to show the furry texture. Color your retriever to complete your doodle.

practice here

LABRADOODLE

Labradoodles are a cross between a Labrador retriever and a poodle. They were bred as guide dogs for people with allergies, because they have hair rather than fur. Lovers of company, labradoodles hate to be alone and want to be lapdogs, even when they're too big! They're highly trainable, as well as energetic, making them great family pets.

To draw a labradoodle, we're going to primarily be using zigzag lines to show the texture of this breed's hair. Start with a semicircle and add a heart-shaped nose. Draw the fluffy muzzle around the nose, then add a small lower jaw under it. Give your doodle eyes, eyebrows and a pair of long ears. Draw the front of the body, front legs and paws. Connect the front legs to form the lower body. Add a back leg and a paw on each side, then draw a tail that gets even more fluffy at the tip. Draw additional zigzag lines throughout to emphasize the ever-growing hair. Finish your doodle by coloring your . . . doodle!

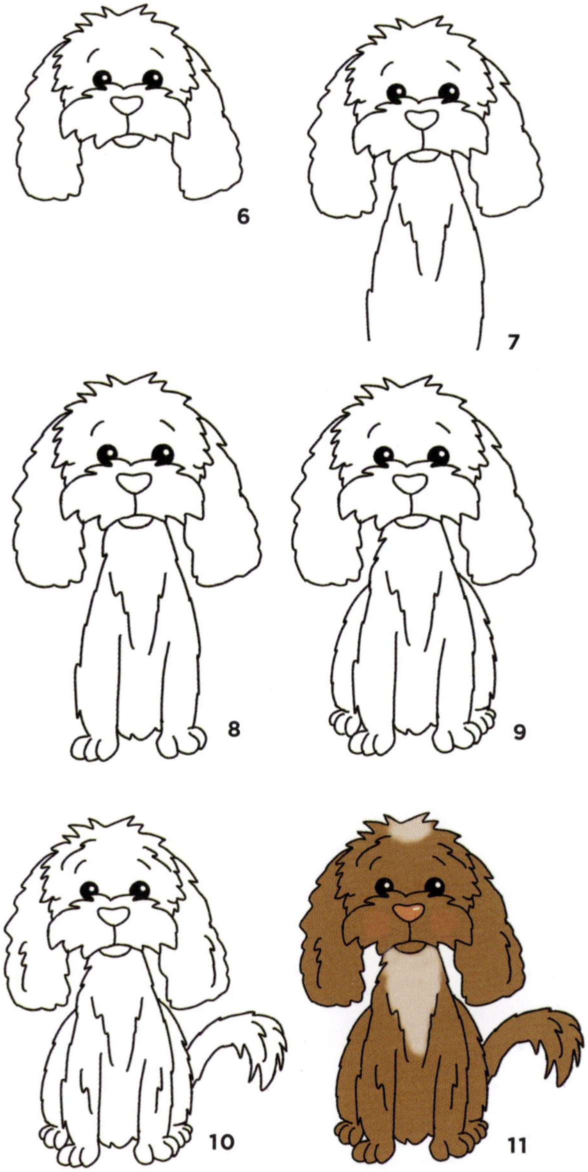

practice here

POODLE

Poodles are highly active dogs that were originally bred to hunt ducks and other waterfowl. Unlike many dog breeds, poodles have hair rather than fur. This hair grows continually and doesn't shed like fur does. Poodles have been ranked as the second-most intelligent dog breed after border collies.

Start your doodle with a long, thin face topped with a scalloped oval. Next, add a pair of scalloped ears. Use scalloped lines to form a pair of front legs, then add a tiny paw at the end of each one. Draw the back portion of the body and sketch another tiny paw below it. Connect the front legs with a scalloped line to complete the body. Add more scallops to show the curly hair on the ears, body and head. Finally, add a face, then color your drawing.

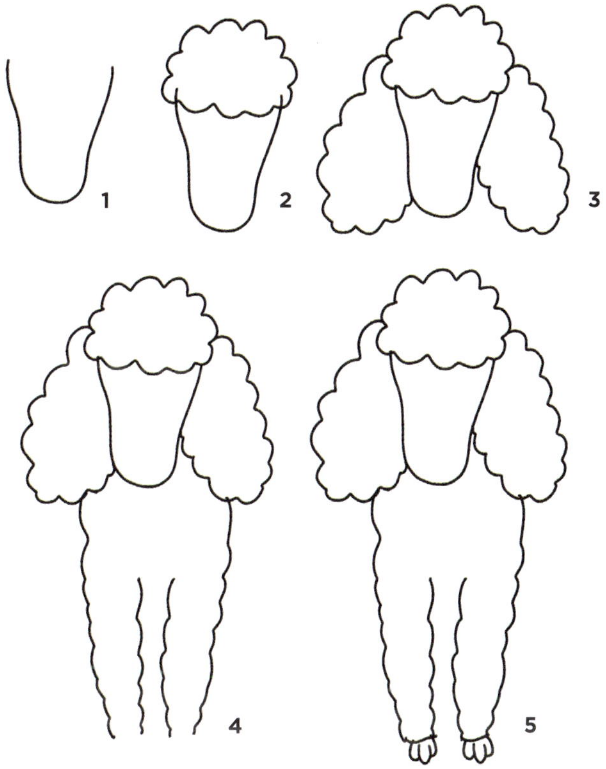

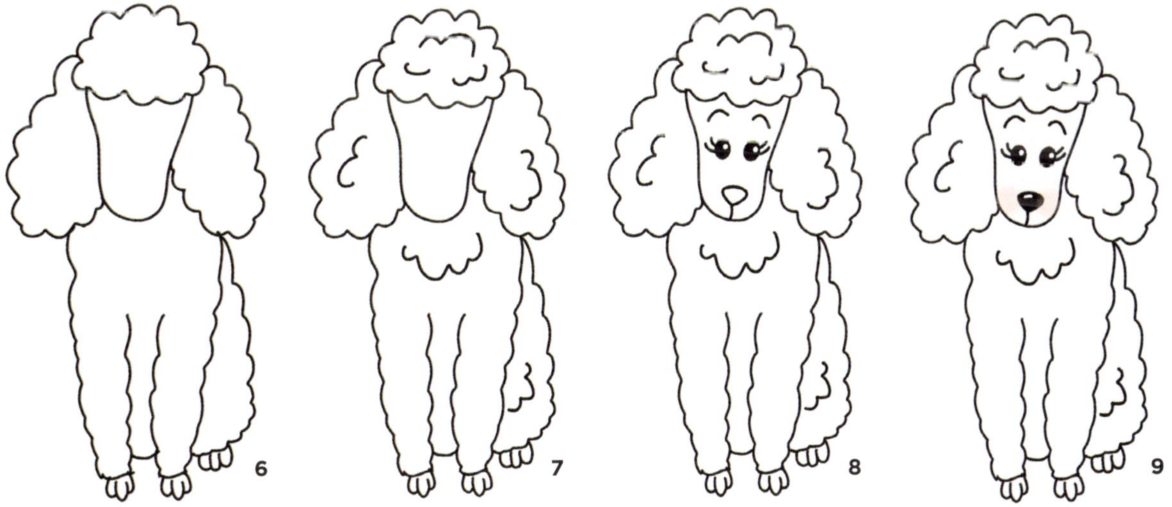

HUSKY

Siberian huskies are friendly, athletic, high-energy dogs that love running long distances. They're known for their work as sled dogs, cooperating as a team to pull sleds through the ice and snow where other modes of travel aren't possible.

Draw your own husky by sketching a small arch with a large, pointed ear on each side. Draw a rounded "v" shape for the rest of the face, then divide the ears into two parts, adding zigzags where they meet the head. Doodle the front legs and paws and add a back leg and a paw on each side of the body. Connect the front legs with a short zigzag. Draw two jagged lines to separate the center of the body from the legs. Add a tail, with pointed details to show the furry texture. Add zigzags to the sides of the face and give your husky a nose and a pair of eyes. Divide the top portion of the head from the rest of the face with a rounded "m" shape. Add a smiling mouth and a tongue, erasing the line where the tongue overlaps the chin. Add detail lines inside the ears, then color your husky.

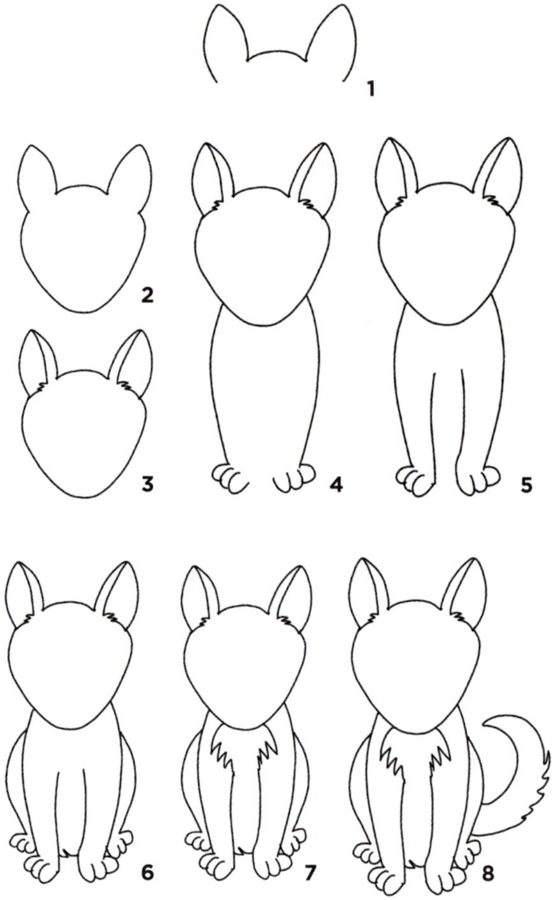

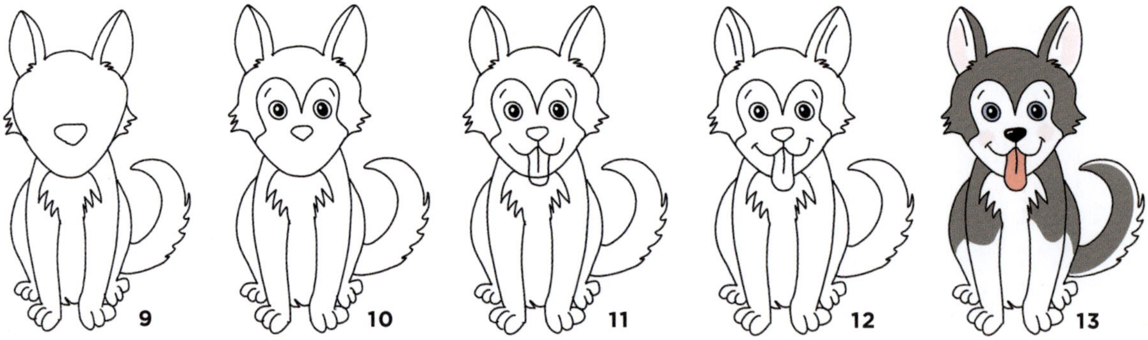

BULLDOG

Bulldogs are known for their adorable wrinkly skin, large heads and short, stocky build. They're one of the five most popular dog breeds in America and have been the pet of choice for two presidents and many celebrities. Bulldogs are the official mascot of more than 35 American colleges, thanks to their tenacity and courage.

To draw your own, start by sketching a pear-shaped face that's open at the bottom. Add a pair of short, floppy ears, erasing the spots where the lines overlap the head. Add a nose with a curved line above it, a pair of droopy jowls and a small chin. Draw dots inside the jowls and add a pair of eyes and brows. Sketch a pair of front legs and paws, then add a back leg and a paw on each side. Connect the front legs to form the rest of the body. Add a short, thick tail and divide off any sections of the body that you want to color differently to give your dog spots. Finally, color your doodle.

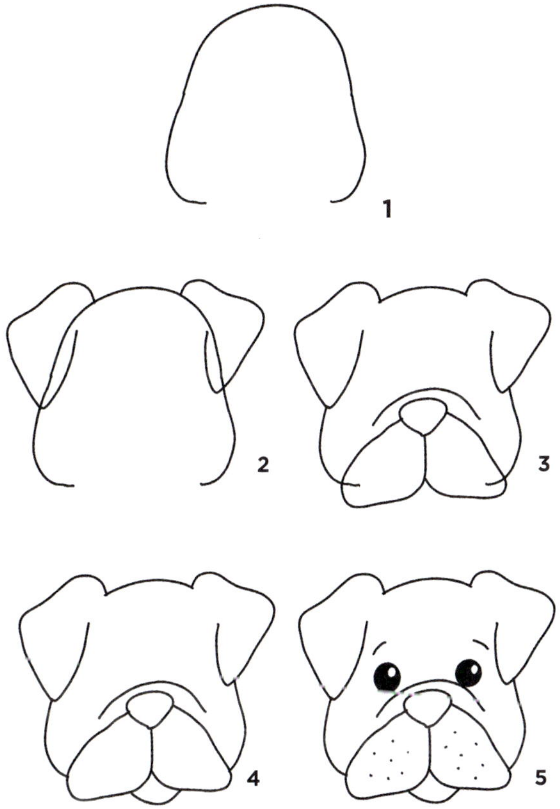

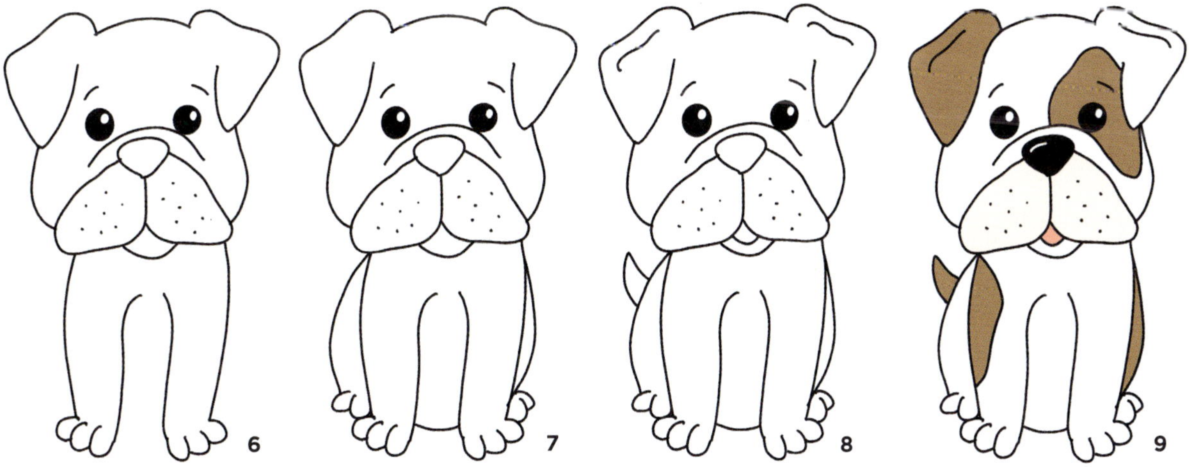

CORGI

Corgi means "dwarf dog" in Welsh and seems to be a fitting name for this compact dog breed. They're the smallest of all the herding dogs, measuring only 10 to 13 inches (25 to 33 cm) in height. Corgis are among the smartest dogs and enjoy mental stimulation like puzzle toys.

Start your corgi drawing with an arch for the top of the head and a large ear on each side. Draw the inner ear, including a few zigzags to show fur. Sketch the rest of the oval-shaped face, adding that same fur texture on the sides. Draw a jagged "v" shape for the furry chest, then add curving lines for the back and two legs. Continue drawing the other front leg and a pair of front paws. Give your corgi a back paw, then connect the paws to form the lower body. Add a tiny tail, along with a face. Divide the face into three sections, using two "w" shapes, then color your dog.

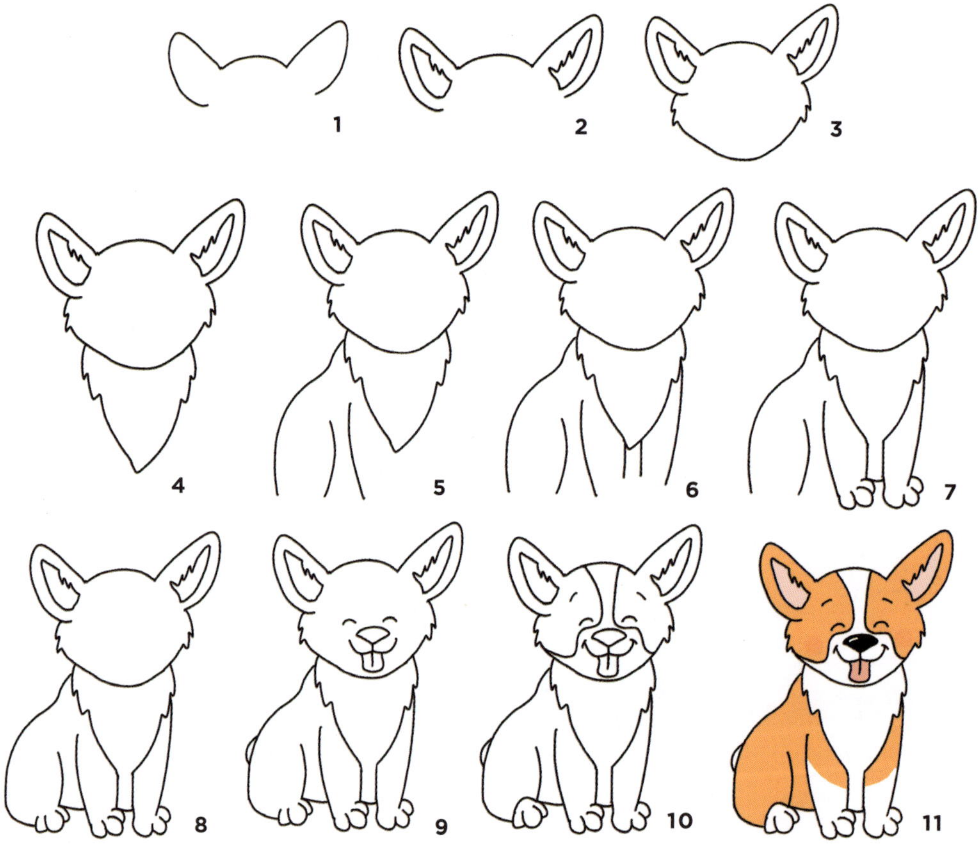

DACHSHUND

Also known as "wiener dogs," dachshunds are the smallest hounds. They were originally bred to hunt badgers and their large ears were designed to keep grass and debris out of their ear canals while crawling into burrows on the hunt. Did you know that hot dogs were named after these pups, not the other way around?

To draw this recognizable dog, start with a long, thin face and add a floppy ear. Then, sketch the other ear behind the face. Next, draw curving lines for the chest and back, making sure to elongate the body. Add a pair of short front legs and paws, then add the back legs and paws. Connect the legs to form the belly. Draw a thin tail and give your dachshund an eye, an eyebrow and a nose. Finally, add color to your sketch. You can stick with a solid color or use a combination of colors to make your drawing resemble your own pup.

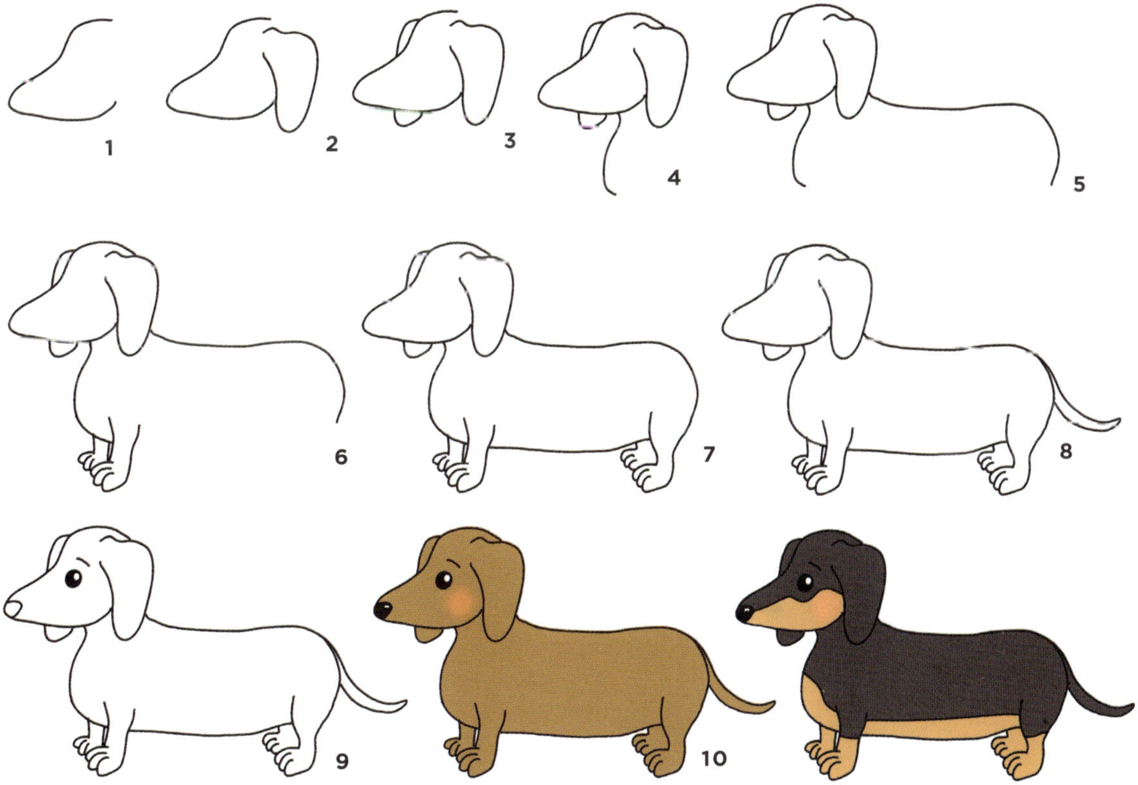

TERRIER

Terriers are small, energetic dogs that were originally bred to hunt small game and kill pests. There are many specific terrier breeds, as well as mixes, but all of them are highly intelligent. If a terrier gets bored, it will bark incessantly, so pet owners need to provide plenty of exercise and activities for their pup.

Start your terrier drawing with an egg-shaped head and a pair of short, floppy ears. Erase the areas where the ears overlap the head. Draw a pair of front legs and paws, then add a back leg on each side. Connect the front legs to form the belly. Then, add a back paw at the base of each back leg. Give your terrier a simple face and a short tail. Finally, add any lines where you want your dog's coloring to change. Color your terrier any mixture of colors you like.

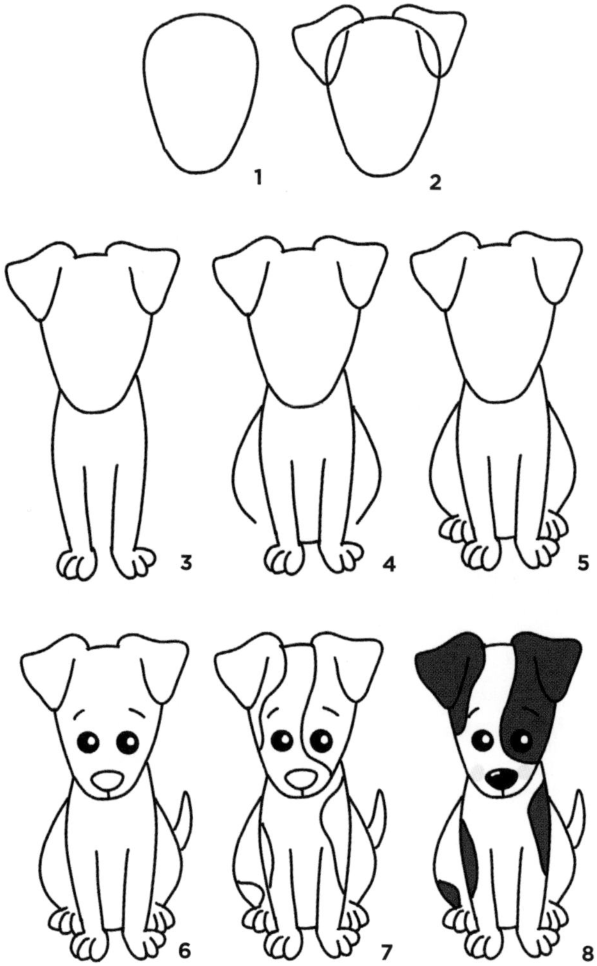

practice here

CHIHUAHUA

Chihuahuas are tiny dogs that typically weigh less than 6 pounds (3 kg). In fact, they're so small that some owners carry them around in a purse. Despite their small stature, chihuahuas have big personalities. Loyal and loving to their owners, they're wary of strangers and enjoy being in charge.

To doodle this miniature pup, start with a round face and draw a "u" shape at the bottom, erasing the area where the lines overlap. Sketch a large pair of pointed ears and divide them into two sections. Add curving lines for the front and back of the body, then draw a pair of short legs with small paws. Draw a curving line for the back leg that extends behind the front paws. Divide the front section of the body from the rest and add a thin, pointed tail. Divide the face, making a stripe in the center that extends at the bottom to cover the muzzle. Finally, add eyes, brows, a nose and detail lines to finish your sketch. Color your chihuahua in any combination of tan, cream, black, brown, red and white.

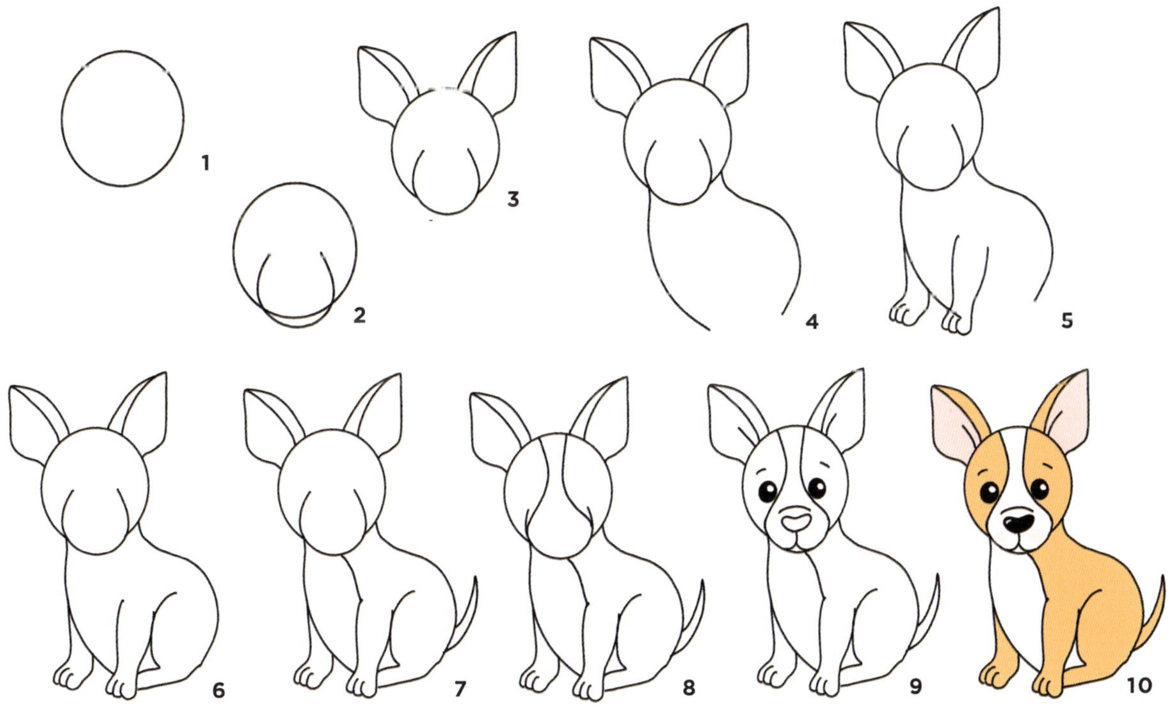

SLEEPING CAT

There are 88 million household cats in the United States, making them the most popular pet in the country. Cats spend 70 percent of their time asleep, and when they're awake, they spend up to half of that time grooming themselves. When they're hungry, cats can change their meows to sound more like a human baby in order to manipulate their owners.

Let's start our feline doodles by drawing a sleeping cat. First, draw an oval that's tilted to one side. Add a pair of pointed ears that are divided into two parts. Sketch a large curve for the cat's curled-up body and draw a tail that extends underneath its head. Add a front paw below the head and curving lines on the body to indicate where the legs are. Give your cat a face that includes a nose, a muzzle, whiskers and closed eyes. Finally, color your cat in any way you like.

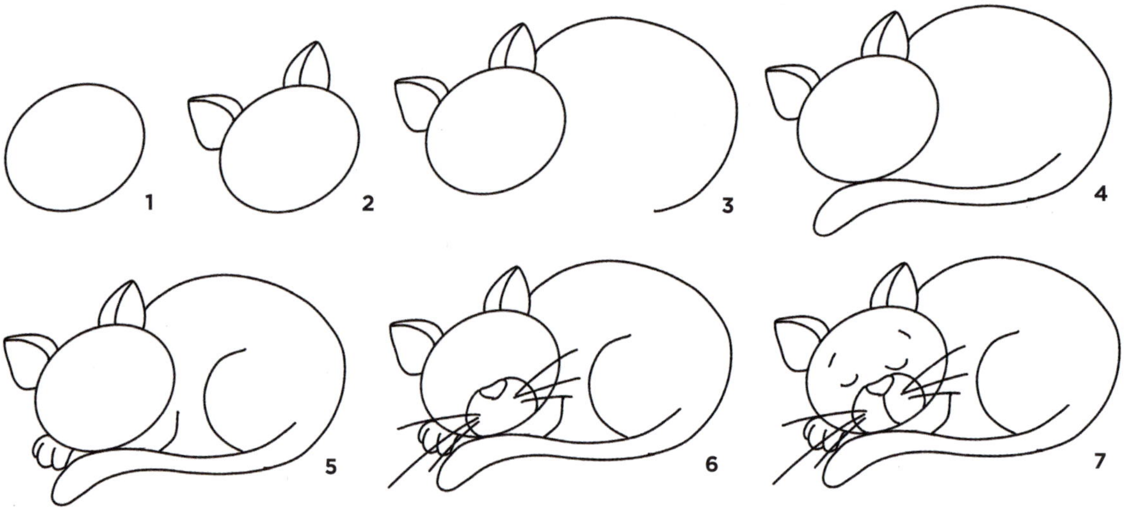

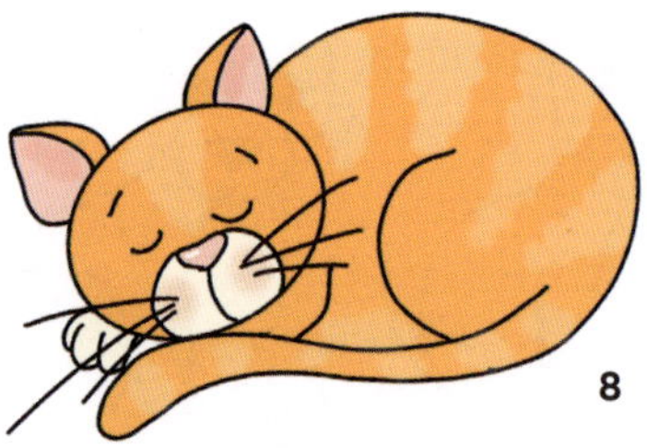

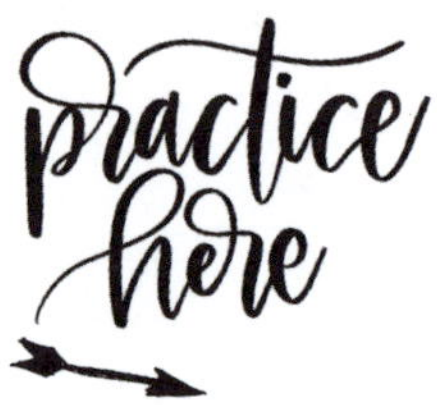

CALICO/SHORTHAIR CAT

American shorthair cats were brought by settlers in the 17th century to help eliminate rats on ships and in homes. Known for their intelligence and adaptability, these felines are also excellent hunters.

To doodle this cat, start with a round head and a pair of pointed ears that are divided into two parts. Sketch a pair of curving lines below the head to form the front of the body and draw a "v" to create the front legs. Add a line on each side of the body for the back legs. Next, sketch a tail that wraps around the front of the body, erasing where the lines overlap. Draw a pair of zigzag lines on the chest to show the furry texture, then give your cat a face, including a nose, a muzzle, eyes, eyebrows and a smile. To personalize your doodle, feel free to add stripes or spots on the cat's head and body. Finally, color your drawing. You can combine any colors you like, including or omitting the stripes to make your drawing resemble your favorite feline friend.

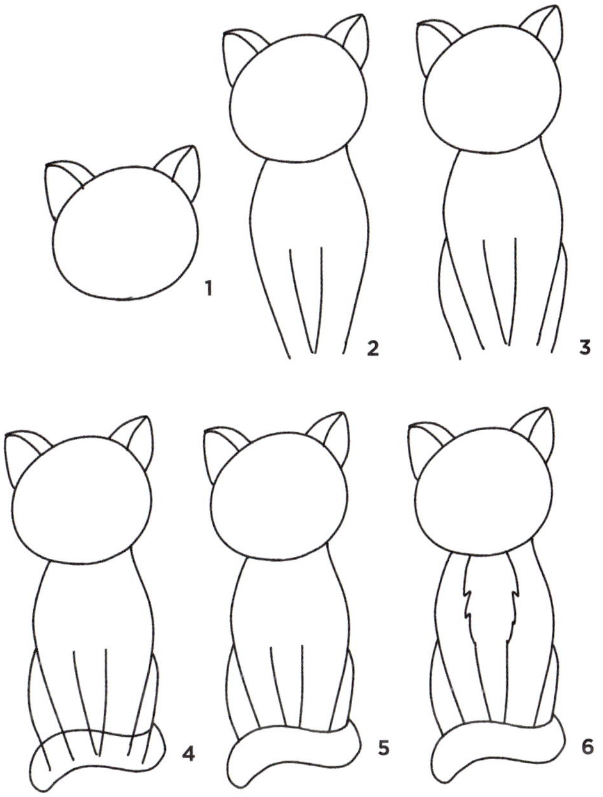

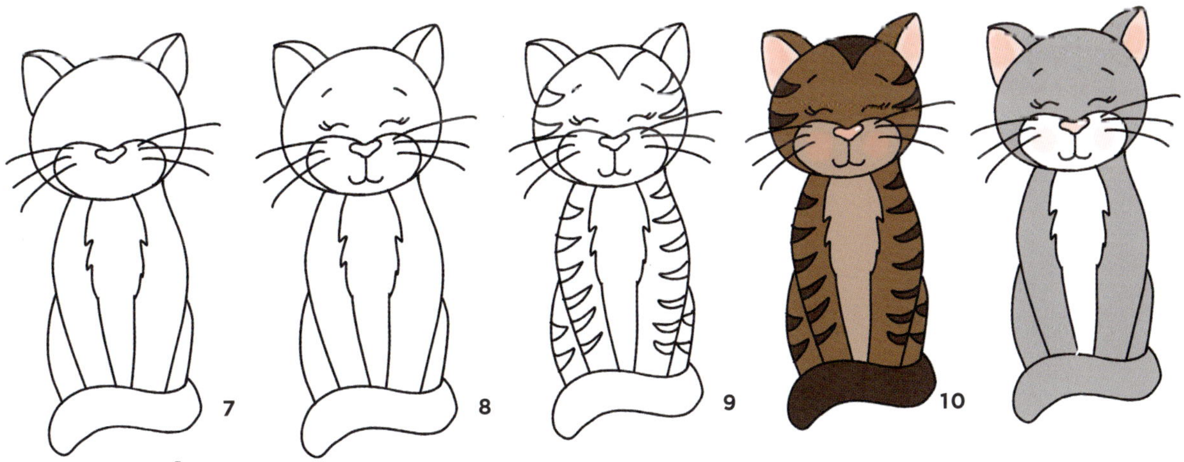

PERSIAN CAT

Persian cats are known for their thick, luxurious coats and their round, flat faces. While we often think of this breed of cat as being white, they can actually be a variety of colors and patterns, including cream, brown, red, black and blue.

To draw this type of cat, start with a curving line that has a pointed ear on either end. Divide each ear into two parts. Add zigzag lines curving down from each ear to form the sides of the face. Draw a large oval shape made of zigzags around the head. Sketch two small paws below the oval. Add a large, fluffy tail on the side. Next, finish the head by drawing a nose and the lower portion of the face. Give your cat eyes and eyebrows and draw detail lines inside the fur to show the fluffy texture. Finally, add color to finish your doodle. By changing the angle of the eyebrows, you can give your cat different moods!

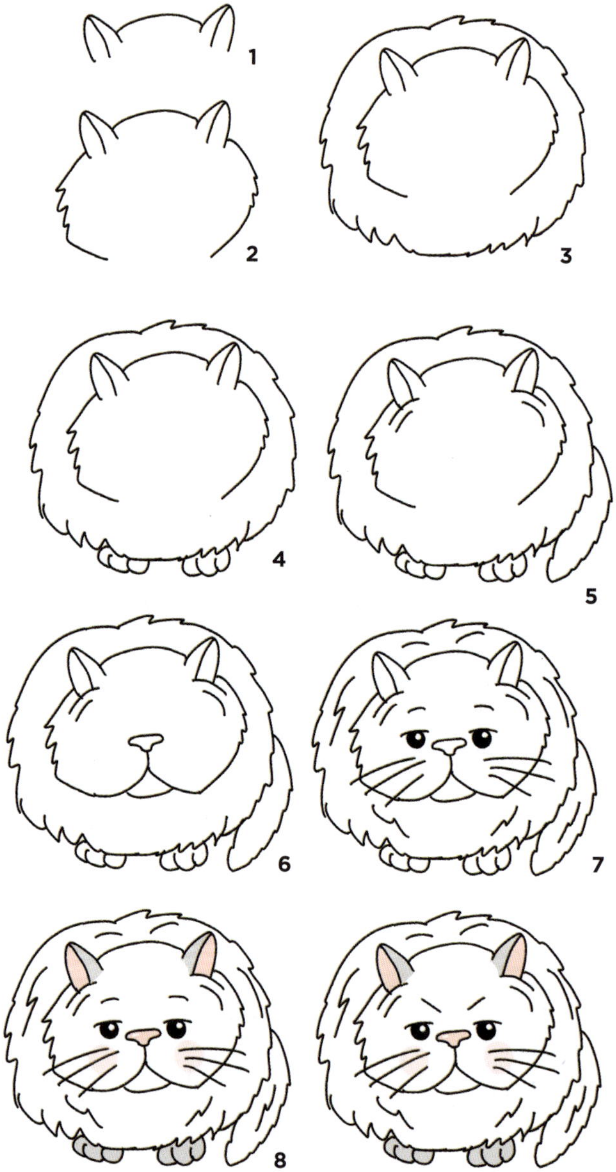

practice here

RABBIT/BUNNY

Did you know that a happy rabbit will purr like a cat? Another behavior of a joyful rabbit is a "binky," which is an athletic jump that includes midair kicks and twists. Although we often associate carrots with rabbits, they're not part of a rabbit's natural diet and can actually cause a stomachache.

To sketch a rabbit, start with a slightly pointed "c" shape for the face, then draw a pair of long ears. Next, make a curved line for the back of the body, then add another curve for the back leg and draw a foot at the base. Sketch a short chest and draw a pair of front feet. Connect the front and back feet and divide the front ear into two parts. Finally, add a fluffy, round tail and a simple face. Color your rabbit in any way you like.

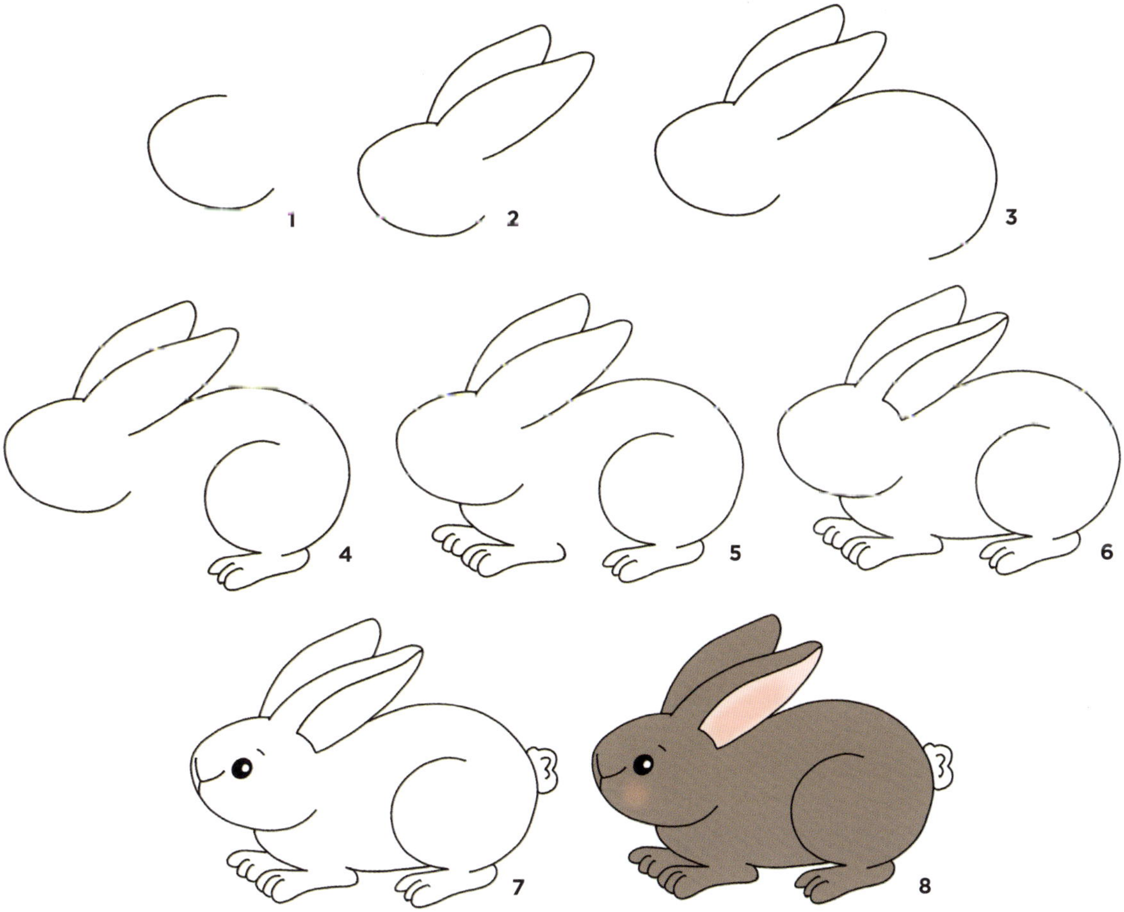

HAMSTER

Hamsters are small, furry mammals with pretty incredible cheek pouches. One purpose of these pouches is storing as much food as their own body weight in their cheeks to eat later. Also, if they fill up their cheeks with air, hamsters can float in water!

Start your hamster drawing with an arch for the top of the head and a "c"-shaped cheek on each side. Sketch a pair of small, egg-shaped ears and draw a smaller shape inside each ear. Draw a rounded body and add small arms and hands reaching up toward the mouth. Erase any overlapping lines, then draw a pair of feet under the body. Separate the hands from the arms with short lines. Add zigzag lines to divide the sides of the body from the stomach and show a furry texture. Draw a long, thin tail extending out to the side and give your hamster eyes, eyebrows and a nose. Add a smile and draw an egg-shaped seed in your hamster's hands. Finish your doodle by adding color.

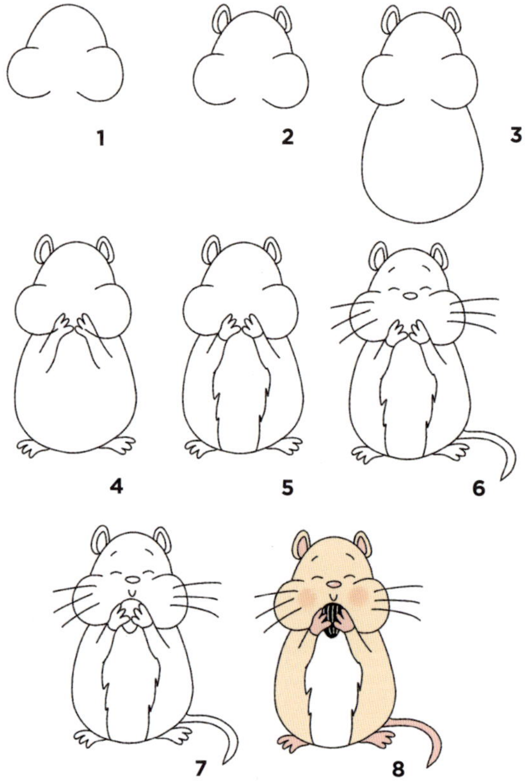

MOUSE

Did you know that mice can navigate obstacles with their whiskers? These agile rodents are social and prefer to live in pairs. Mice don't actually prefer cheese; they also enjoy fruits, vegetables, insects, nuts and sweets.

Start your mouse doodle with an arch for the body, then add a curving line for the back leg and a foot. Add the rest of the body shape and a front leg and foot. Then, sketch a pair of large, rounded ears, erasing the overlapping lines. Draw an egg shape inside the front ear. Give your mouse a long, thin tail and finish your sketch by adding an eye, a nose and a smile. Finally, add color to complete your drawing.

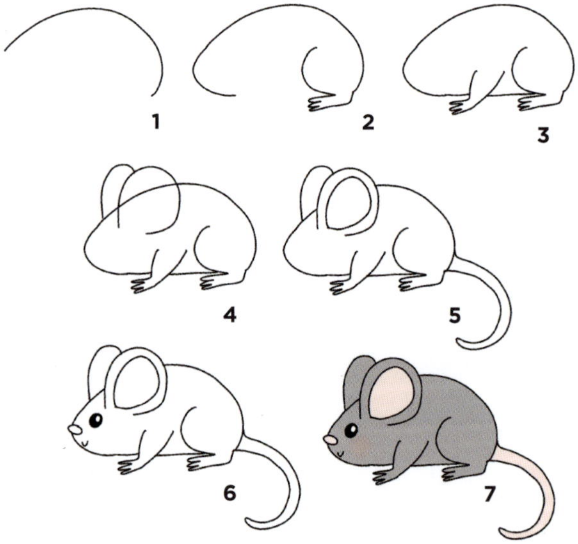

GERBIL

Gerbils love friends! In fact, gerbil owners are strongly encouraged to always have at least two at a time, because a lone gerbil will become depressed and anxious. Although we can hear some of a gerbil's squeaks, many of their vocalizations are so high frequency (50 kilohertz) that they aren't detectable to human ears!

Start your gerbil doodle with a rounded "v" shape for the face and a pair of small ears. Give your gerbil a long, pear-shaped body. Use a curving line to divide the stomach from the rest of the body and add a short arm and hand. Add a second arm and separate the hands from the arms with short lines. Give your gerbil an eye, a nose and whiskers. Draw a leaf shape inside the front ear. Sketch a long, thin tail, then color your doodle.

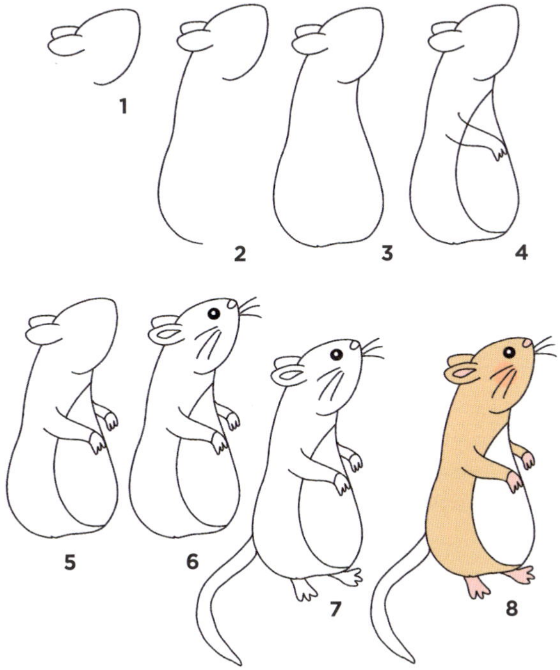

GUINEA PIG

Guinea pigs are social rodents with teeth that grow continually, so they need to munch on lots of hard things to file them down. When guinea pigs are excited, they'll jump in the air, sometimes doing a little twist. This is called popcorning!

Ready to doodle your own guinea pig? Start by forming the basic body shape, which is a lot like a potato. Add a pair of ears and two tiny feet. Give your guinea pig a face with an eye, a nose, a mouth and an eyebrow. Divide the front ear into two parts. Draw a line to divide the back part of the body from the front and another line separating a section around the eye and ear. Finish by coloring your drawing.

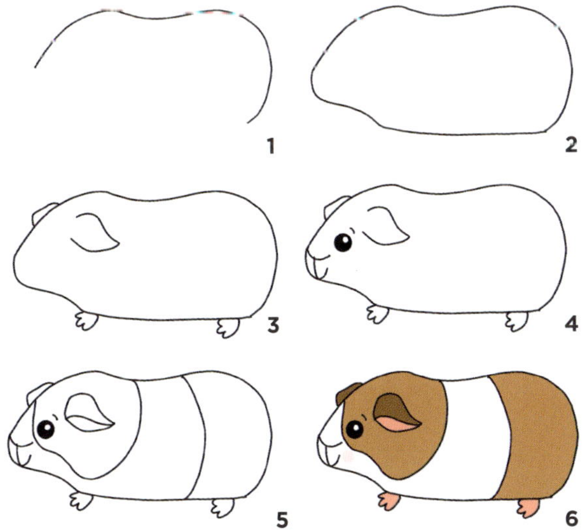

FERRET

The scientific name for a ferret, Mustela putorius furo*, literally means "stinky little thief." Ferrets are notorious for grabbing any and every small object around the house and stashing it in their favorite hiding spots. They're quite intelligent, as well as extremely flexible, and can be trained to do tricks.*

To doodle a ferret, start with an oval-shaped head and a pair of small, rounded ears. Draw an inner section in each ear and separate the top of the head from the rest of the face with a wavy "m"-shaped line. Sketch eyes, a nose and a mouth, then outline the eye section to separate it from the rest of the face like a mask. Draw curving lines for the front and back of the body and add a pair of short arms. Finish drawing the body shape and sketch a pair of small feet below it. Add a long, thick tail and draw a line to divide the top and bottom halves of the body. Finally, color your ferret.

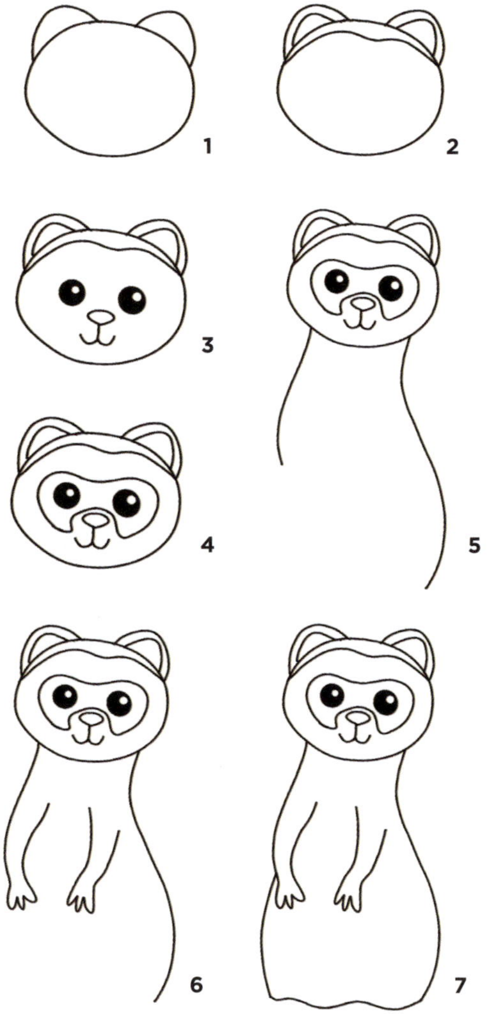

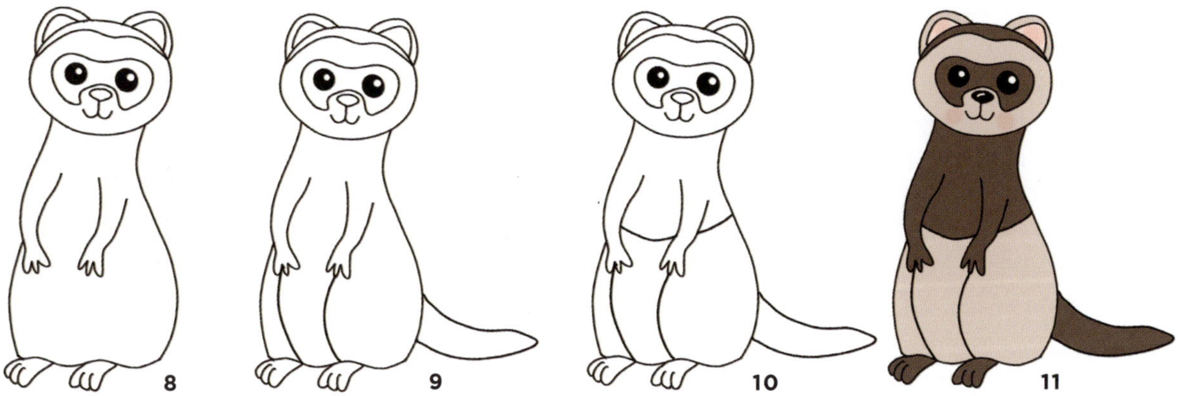

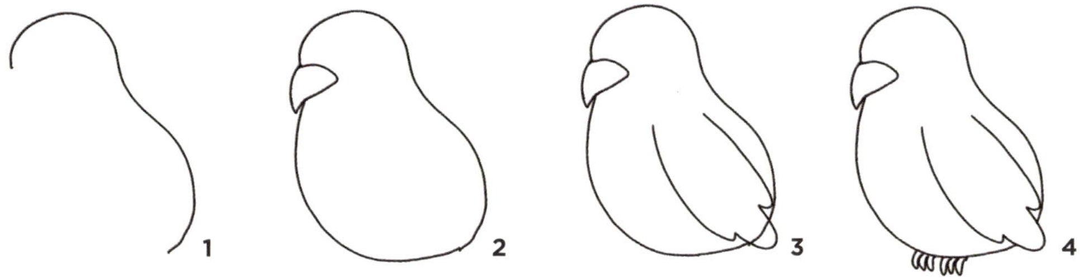

PARAKEET

Parakeets are incredibly intelligent birds that can learn to perform tricks. Many parakeets can be trained to talk, learning as many as 1,700 words! They also communicate using body language, which is helpful for owners to learn.

To draw a parakeet, start with a curving line for the head and the bird's back. Add a triangle beak that points downward and another curving line for the front of the body. Give your parakeet a wing and a pair of tiny feet. Sketch a long, thin tail. Add an eye, as well as some bumpy lines for texture on the wing and a few detail lines on the back of the head. Give your parakeet a branch to stand on, with a few leaves as accents. Finally, add two small markings inside the beak. Color your parakeet using green and yellow or blue and white.

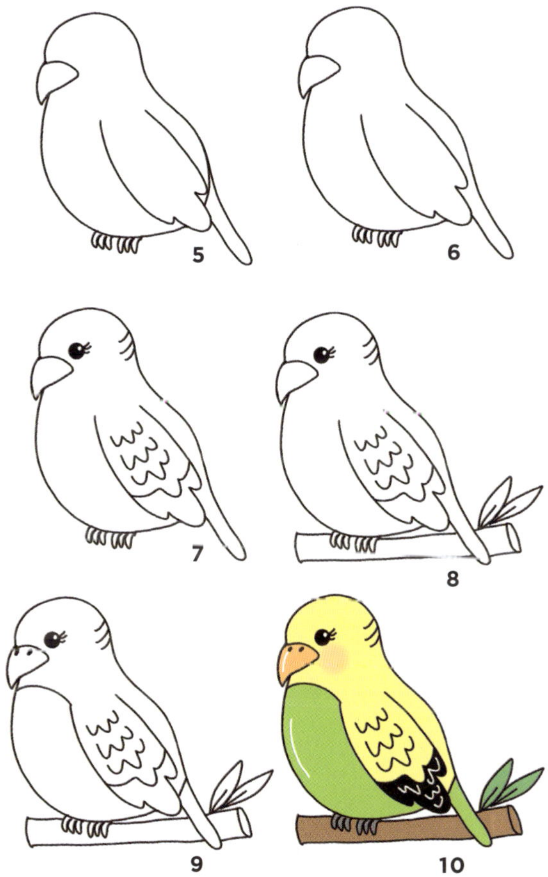

practice here

TURTLE

Turtles carry their homes with them at all times; their shells are actually part of their skeletons! The shell grows along with the rest of the turtle's body, so it's always just the right size. Turtles have a long life span; they're able to live more than 50 years when they're cared for well.

Doodle your own turtle by starting with a "c" shape for the head. Draw an arch next to it for the shell, then extend the top of the "c" down to form the shell's base. Extend the bottom of the head to create a neck and a tummy. Add a rim to the shell and give your turtle four legs. Sketch a face with eyes, eyebrows, and a smile and add a few oval spots on top of the head. Draw a geometric pattern inside the shell and don't forget to give your turtle a short, pointed tail. All that's left to do is color your turtle in shades of green and brown.

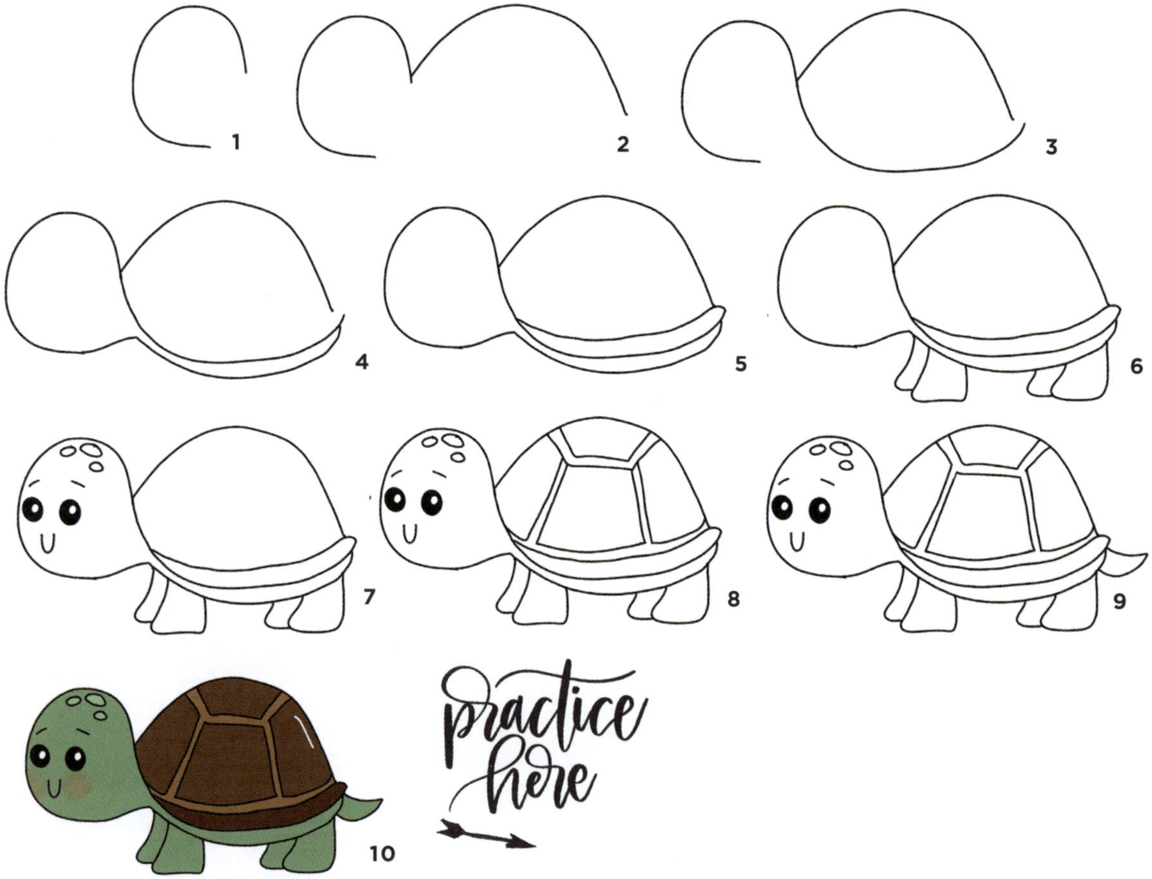

CHAMELEON

Chameleons are known for being masters of disguise, with the ability to change their colors and even their patterns as a form of camouflage, but did you know they also shift colors as a form of communication with one another? These fascinating creatures have eyes that move independently in their sockets and long, sticky tongues that can be up to almost three times the length of their bodies! Although they're a type of lizard, the name "chameleon" actually means "ground lion."

Let's draw a chameleon together, starting with a sideways "v" shape that has a short smile line on the lower end. Sketch a pointed head that curves around and ends below the "v" to form the lower jaw. Next, add a curved line for the back that ends with a spiral tail. Draw a front leg and two short lines to form the chest and belly. Add a second front leg, then draw a back leg and connect it to the tail to complete the body. Draw a large eye and add a series of triangle stripes along the back. As you add color to your doodle, remember that chameleons can become any combination of colors, so feel free to be as creative as you like.

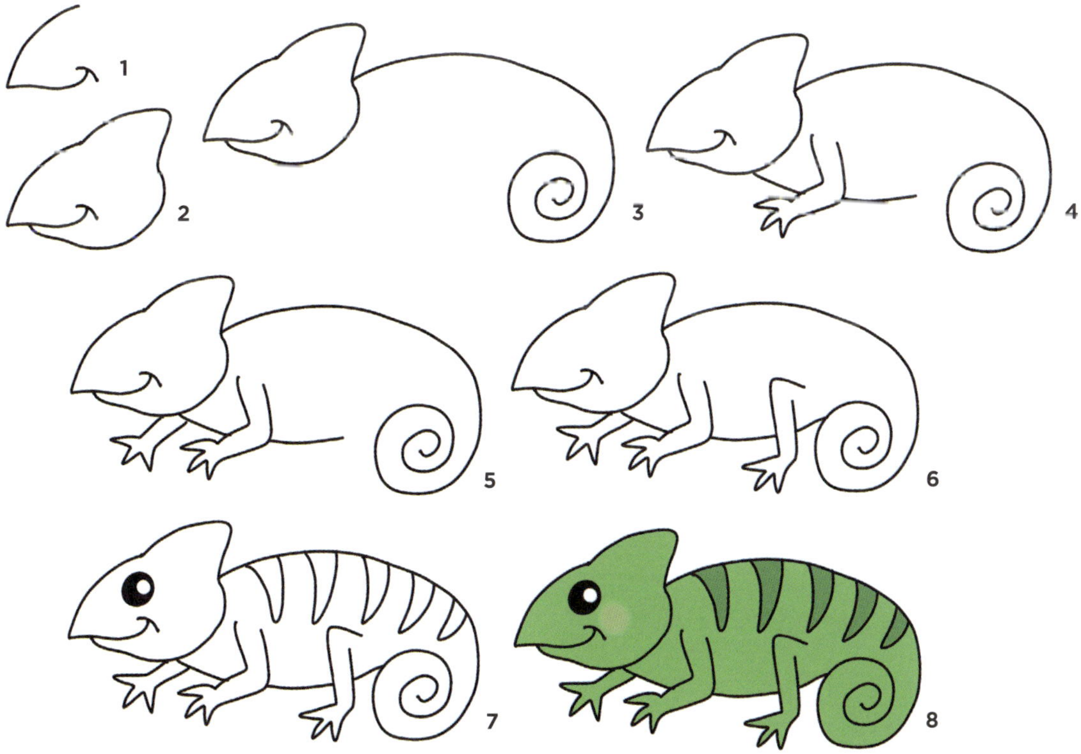

BEARDED DRAGON

Bearded dragons are easy to care for, as well as very interactive, which is why they're one of the most popular pet reptiles. Although you'll typically see them lounging on all fours, they're able to run on two legs and can even sleep standing up by locking their hind legs! Bearded dragons are known for two particularly interesting behaviors: a head bob and the ability to wave with one arm. An occasional, slow head bob shows submission, while fast, aggressive ones are a show of dominance. There are several reasons why a bearded dragon might wave, including submission, stress or just acknowledging the presence of their owner.

Let's start our bearded dragon doodle with a wavy "m" shape for the top of the head. Then, add zigzags on both sides to form the famous beard. Connect the bottom of the head and draw a curving line for the chest. Add a pair of arms, then draw a curving line for the back that extends into a thin, pointed tail. Sketch a line for the belly and a curving line extending down from the side of the arm. Draw a back leg and a foot. Now, add details, like stripes on the tail, small zigzags along the side of the body and a detail line on the chest. Add a face, with large eyes, a wavy mouth, eyebrows and a pair of nostrils. Sketch a "v" shape on the forehead and stripes on the bearded dragon's back. Finally, color your doodle.

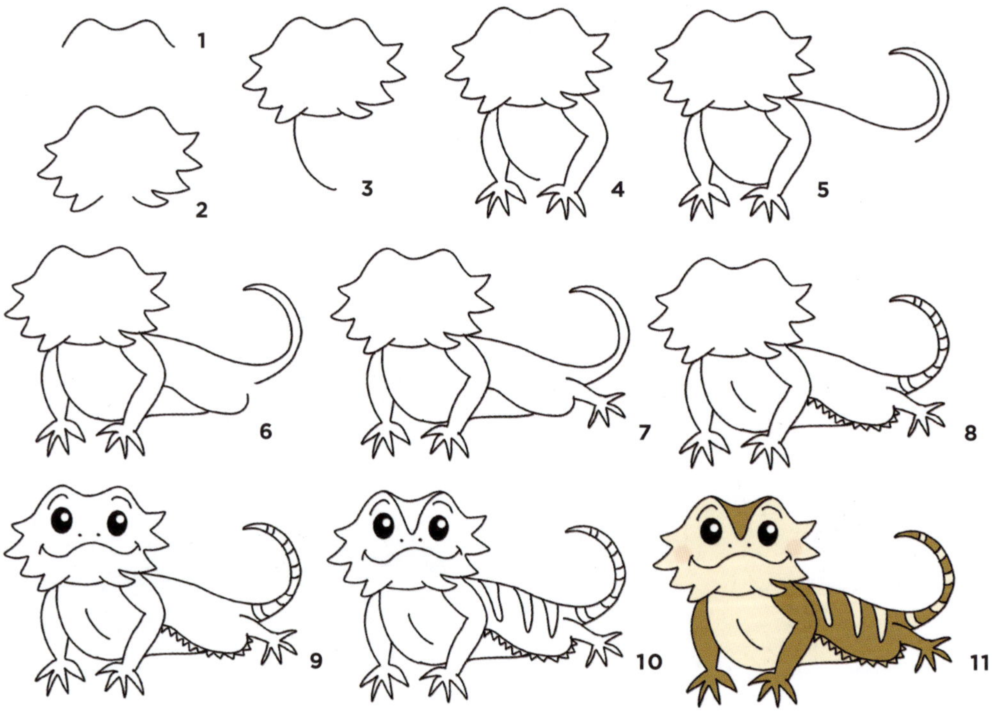

HERMIT CRAB

Hermit crabs are crustaceans that are born without shells. In order to protect their bodies, they take up residence inside the abandoned shells of other creatures. These nocturnal creatures enjoy climbing, hiding in dark spaces and exploring.

To sketch your own, start with an oval and add two leaf shapes with wavy lines inside for claws. Add two more legs on each side of the body, then draw the first layer of the shell on top of the crab. Erase the lines where the shell overlaps the legs. Add three more sections of shell, each one decreasing in size as you get to the top. Draw a pair of eyes extending up from the body, erasing the overlapping lines, and add a smile. Finally, color your hermit crab to complete your masterpiece.

practice here

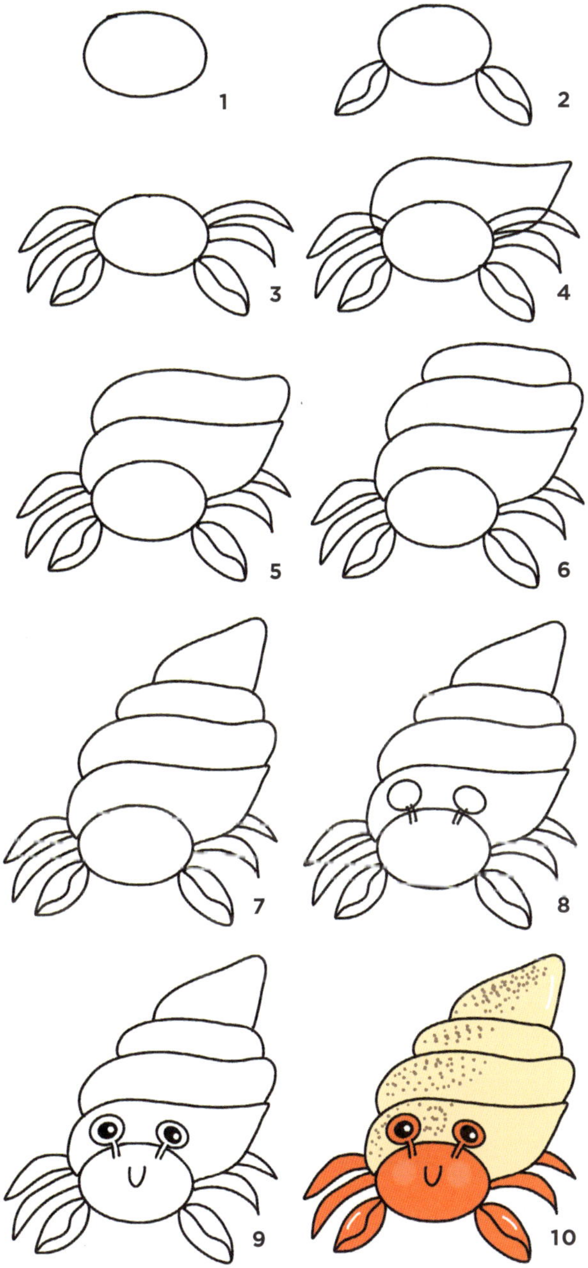

BETTA FISH

Bettas are beautiful tropical fish with ornate, colorful fins. Unlike many types of fish that travel in schools, betta fish prefer independence. Males, in particular, are incredibly territorial and may attack other fish living in the same tank. In fact, they're so aggressive that they sometimes try to attack their own reflections!

To doodle your betta, start with two curving lines to form the basic body shape. The lower line should extend slightly longer to form the mouth. Next, add two long, thin fins on the lower body. Sketch a larger fin next to them and draw detail lines inside of it. Give your betta a large, curving fin on the top of its body and draw detail lines inside that as well. Add a fan-shaped tail, also with a series of lines inside. Sketch an eye and a gill, then use your favorite vibrant colors to finish your betta doodle.

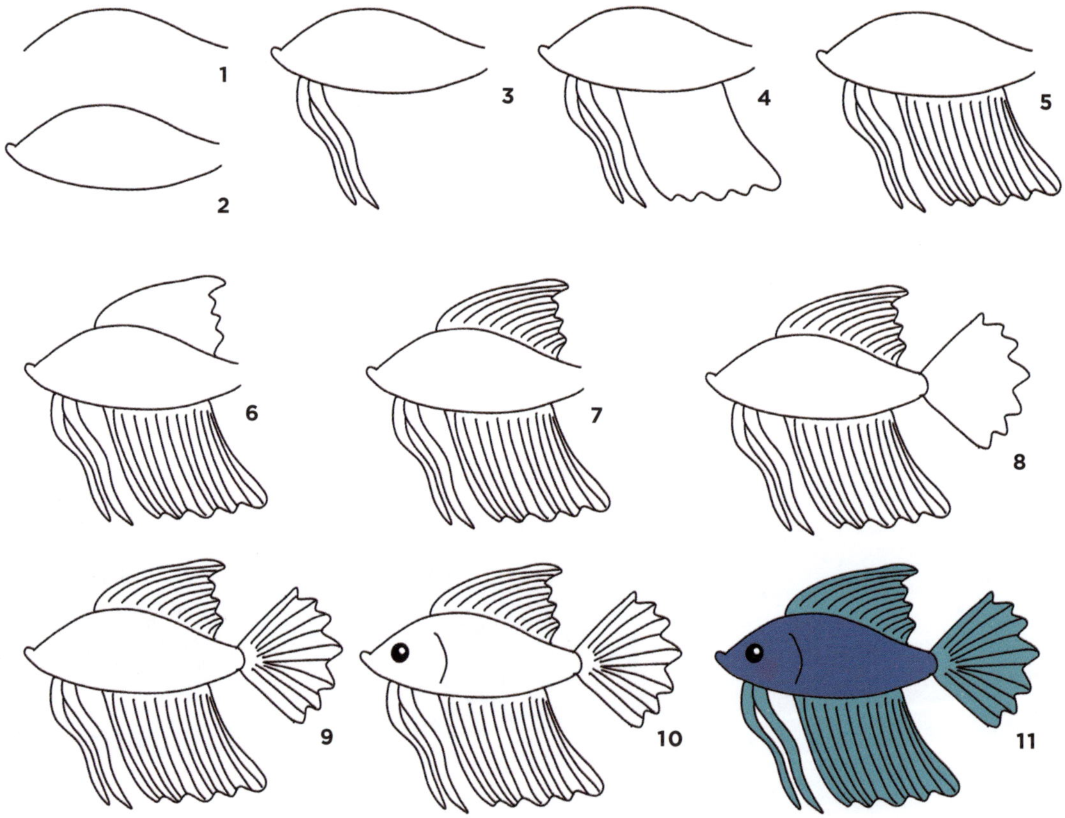

GOLDFISH

The goldfish has been a favorite pet for more than 1,000 years, starting in ancient China. Goldfish get used to humans and can even distinguish between different faces. They're omnivores without stomachs, so they need to eat in many small feeding sessions rather than a few large ones.

Doodle your goldfish by starting with an oval-shaped body. Add three fins: one on the top and two on the bottom. Then, sketch a tail. Draw a series of detail lines inside the tail and each of the fins. Give your fish a set of heart-shaped lips, an eye and a gill. Finally, add scalloped lines on the body to give the illusion of scales. Color your goldfish orange, adding pink lips and cheeks.

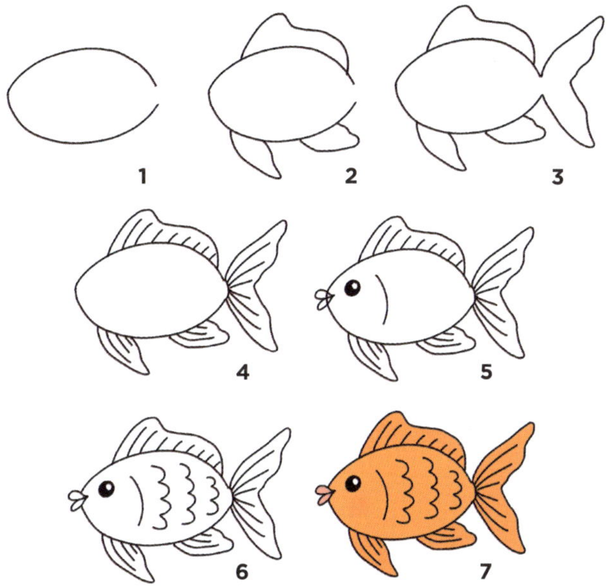

FOOD & WATER BOWL

One of a pet owner's big responsibilities is to make sure their animals are properly fed and have access to fresh water. Here is a quick doodle you can create to give your illustrated pets those basic necessities too!

Begin your bowl sketch with an oval, then draw a diagonal line extending down from each side. Connect your lines with a semicircle to form the bottom of the bowl. Then, draw an arch inside the oval to show dimension. To fill your bowl with food, sketch bumpy lines inside the oval. Or, draw a wavy line inside the bowl instead to represent water. Erase any spots where the lines overlap, then add color to finish your doodle. You can personalize the bowl by adding your pet's name on the front!

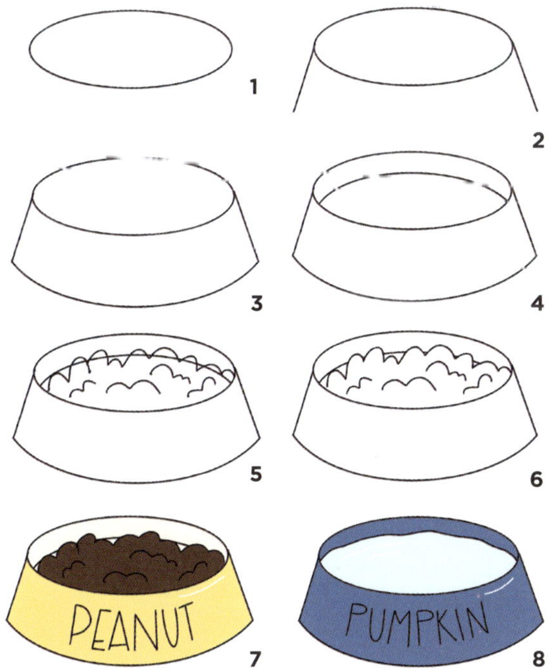

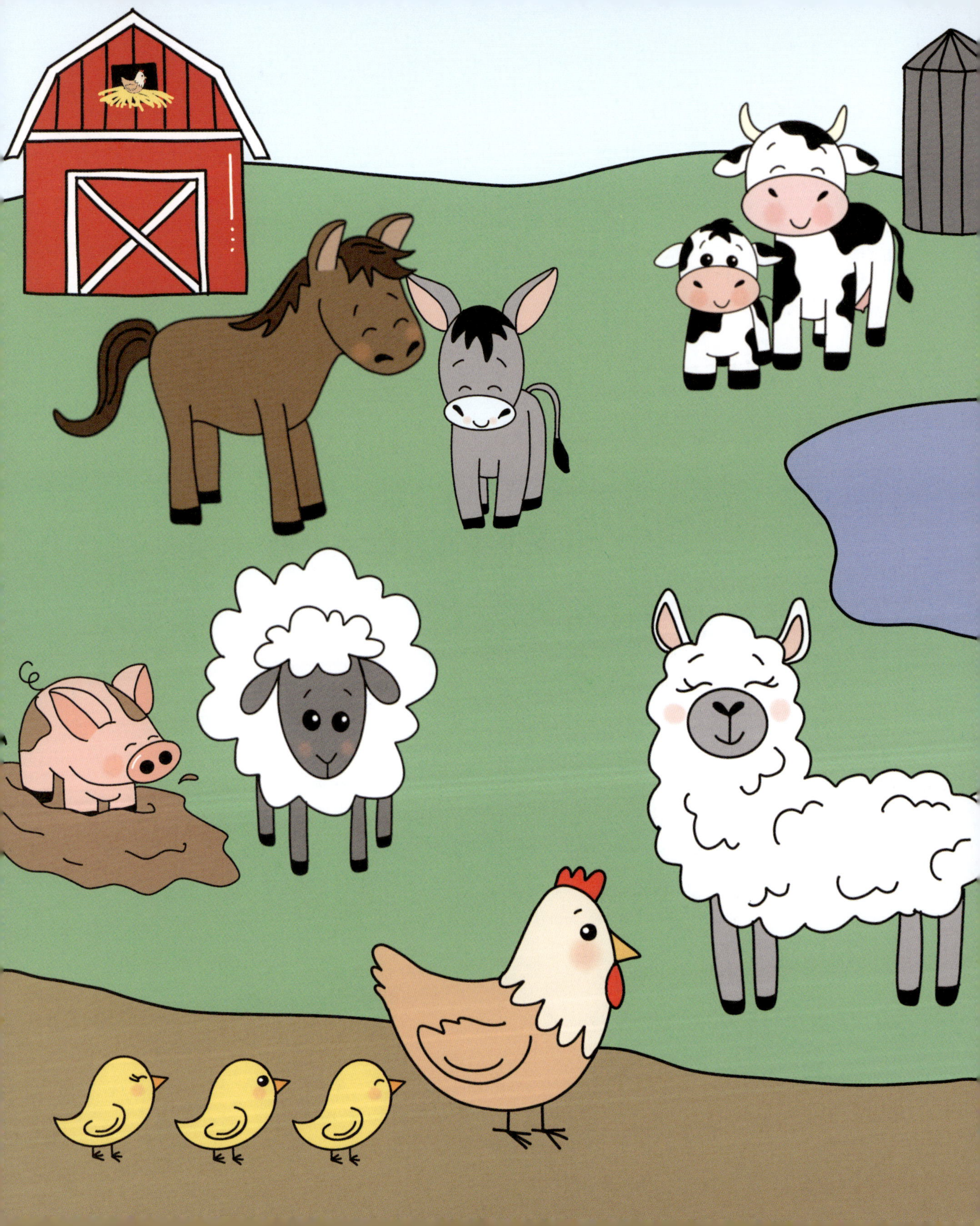

ON THE Farm

Farms are essential to our lives in many ways. They produce food, fiber for clothing and even renewable fuel. In the United States, the farming industry contributes more than $100 billion to the economy each year. There are many types and sizes of farms, and they're located all over the country. Texas has more than 246,000 farms, the most of any state. Let's take some time to learn to draw the animals commonly found on a farm, like cows, sheep, pigs, chickens and more!

CHICKEN

We all know that chickens lay eggs, but did you know one hen can lay more than 300 per year? Maybe that's why there are more chickens on the planet (25 billion) than people! Chickens with red earlobes lay brown eggs and chickens with white earlobes tend to lay white eggs.

Doodle your chicken by starting with a paisley shape and dividing the head area from the rest of the body with a series of "u" shapes. Add a few bumps to the tail area for feathers. Draw a comb on top of the head and give your chicken a wing on the side of its body. Sketch a triangle beak and a teardrop-shaped wattle, as well as an eye and a detail line on the wing. Give your chicken legs and feet, then color it to complete your drawing.

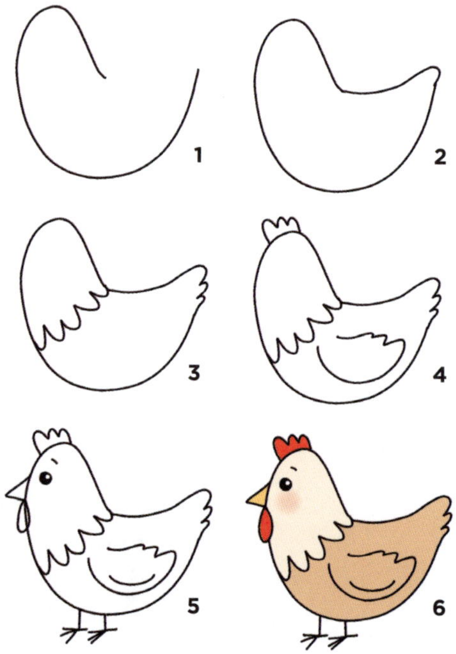

CHICK

Did you ever wonder how a baby chick is able to crack the shell of its egg so that it can hatch? Chicks actually have an "egg tooth" located on their beaks that's specially designed just for that purpose! They use this tooth to break the hard shell, then a few days later, the tooth falls out on its own.

Let's doodle an adorable baby chick together. Start by drawing a paisley shape, then add a "c"-shaped wing inside. Draw a triangle beak and give your chick an eye. Add legs and feet, as well as a detail line inside the wing. Finally, color your chick to bring it to life.

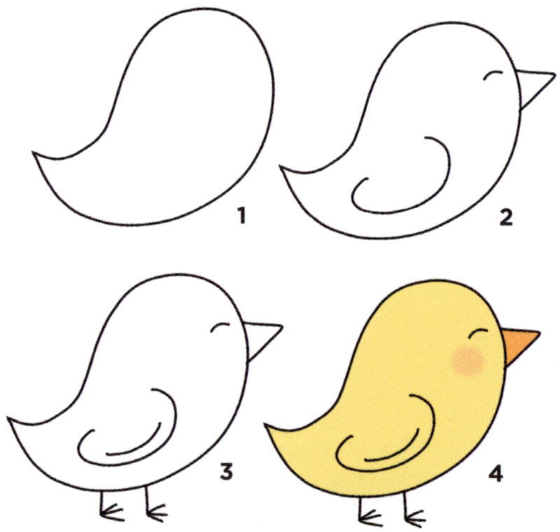

ROOSTER

A rooster's job is to protect the flock of hens, always keeping an eye out for danger. The lead rooster is also responsible for waking the flock each morning at dawn with his loud crow of "cock-a-doodle-doo." Another job for the rooster is to maintain the flock's pecking order, or social hierarchy.

To draw this fascinating farm animal, start by sketching the head, with a comb on top and a zigzag line at the bottom to separate it from the rest of the body. Next, draw the comb on top of the head. Add a beak and wattle, then add a sideways "U" shape in the area where the eye will go. Just below that, add a small circle. Draw two curving lines to form the body and sketch a wing inside. Then, add a tail, composed of seven to eight individual feathers. Sketch legs and feet and give your rooster an eye. Finally, color your rooster.

Bonus: Now that you can draw roosters, chickens and chicks, try combining them to form a little scene! You can sketch the mama leading a line of her babies or even the whole family together.

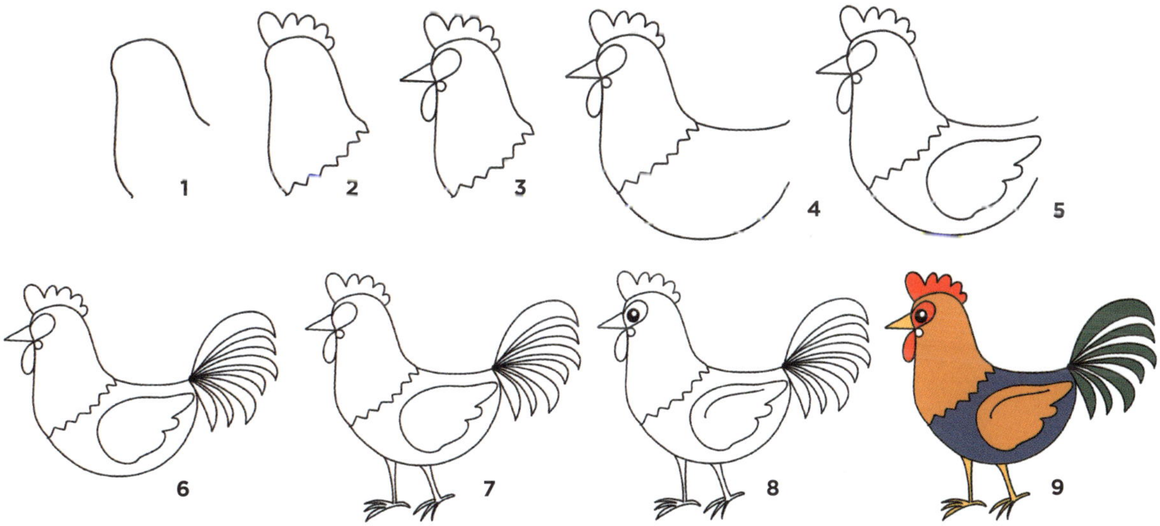

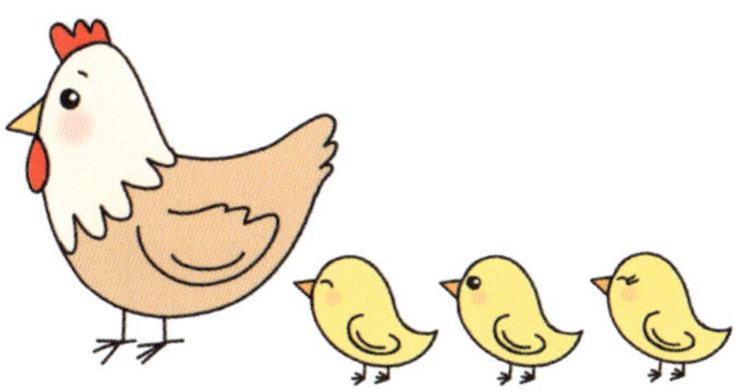

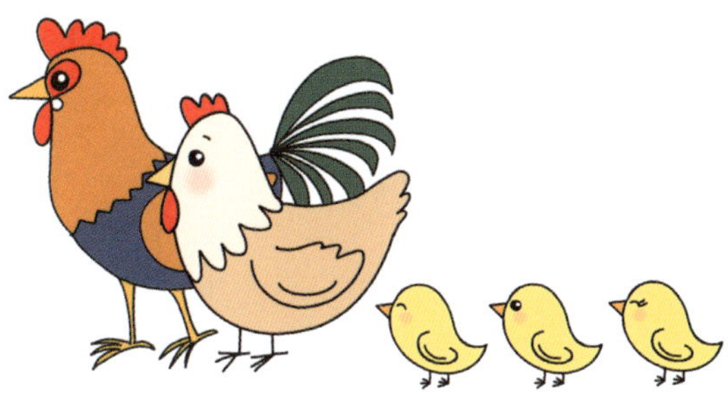

COW

Cows can eat a tremendous amount of food. Their stomachs are divided into four parts, which can hold a total of 50 gallons (189 L) of food at a time. The average cow spends about eight hours a day chewing cud, on top of six hours of eating. A female is called a heifer until she gives birth to her first calf, after which she's called a cow.

Doodle your own cow by starting with a semicircle and an oval to form the head. Add a pair of ears and a smile, then draw small horns on top of the head. Sketch eyes, eyebrows and nostrils, then draw a pair of front legs. Draw a curving line for the back and extend it down to form the back leg. Connect the front and back leg to form the completed body. Add a fourth leg behind the front two. Give your cow hooves and a tail, along with an udder between the front and back leg. If you'd like your cow to have spots, sketch them all over the body. If not, you can skip to the final step. Color your cow in any way you like. Holstein cows are typically white with black patches, while Jersey cows are brown.

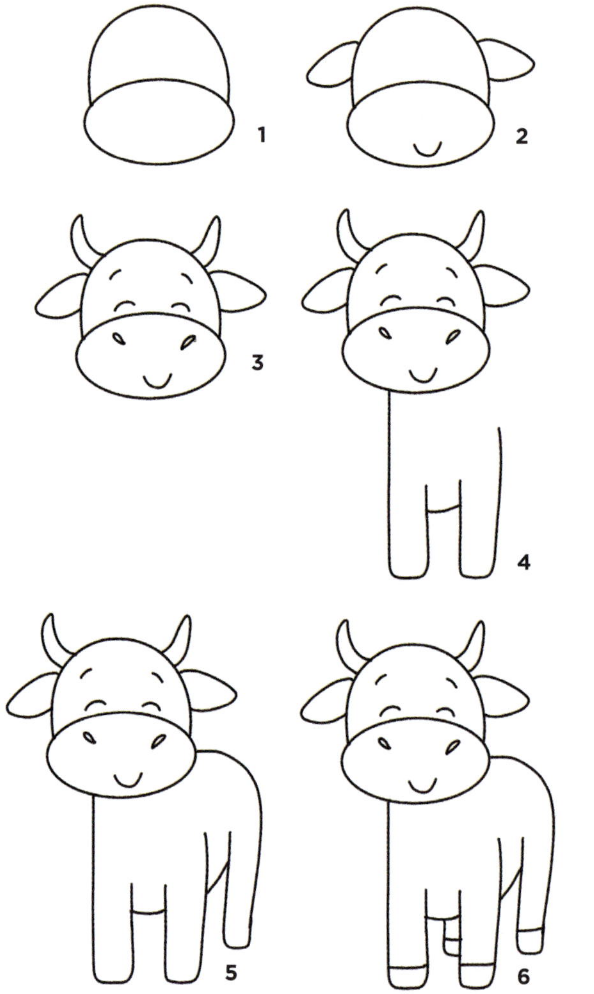

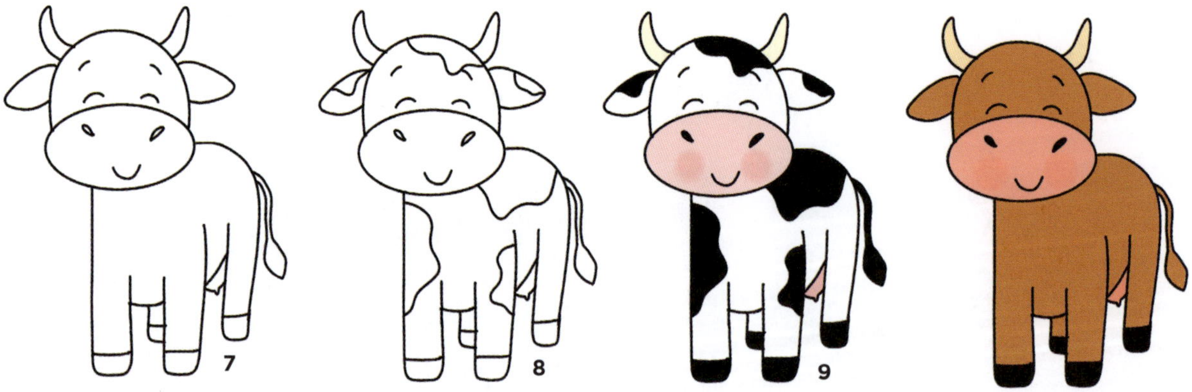

CALF

Within an hour of being born, calves are able to stand and begin walking. A baby calf weighs between 65 and 100 pounds (29 and 45 kg) and has thin baby teeth that can feel sharp if they bite.

To draw this adorable animal, start with a semicircle and draw an oval directly below it to form the head. Add a pair of ears and a smile, then draw the front legs. Sketch the back legs, then add a hoof at the bottom of each leg. Draw a line with a leaf shape at the end for the tail. Give your calf eyes and nostrils to complete the face, and draw spots all over the body. Next, add a patch of hair on top of the head and erase the area where the lines overlap. All that's left to do is color your calf.

practice here

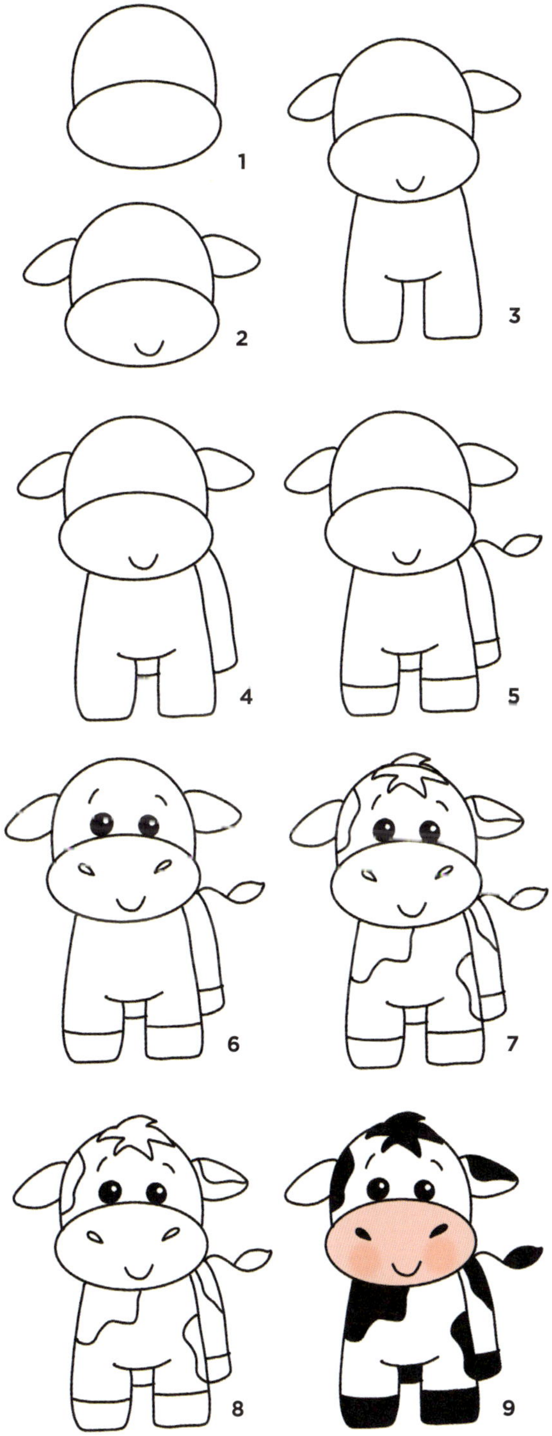

BULL

Male cattle are known as bulls, and they're much stronger and more muscular than female cows. An adult bull weighs between 1,100 and 2,200 pounds (499 and 998 kg)! Bulls can be aggressive, so it's important for farmers to learn how to safely handle them to protect the humans and other animals on the farm.

To draw this powerful animal, start with a wide upside-down "u" shape and add a kidney bean shape below it to form the head. Draw a pair of horns and add a set of nostrils. Sketch an oval-shaped body, then draw the front and back legs. Add a hoof to each leg and draw a pair of ears. Divide the ears into two parts and give your bull eyes. Sketch a patch of hair on top of the head. Finally, add eyebrows and a mouth. The way you draw these features will determine if your bull is happy or angry! Finish your doodle by coloring your bull.

Bonus: Now that you've learned to doodle a bull, a cow and a calf, why not draw them together?

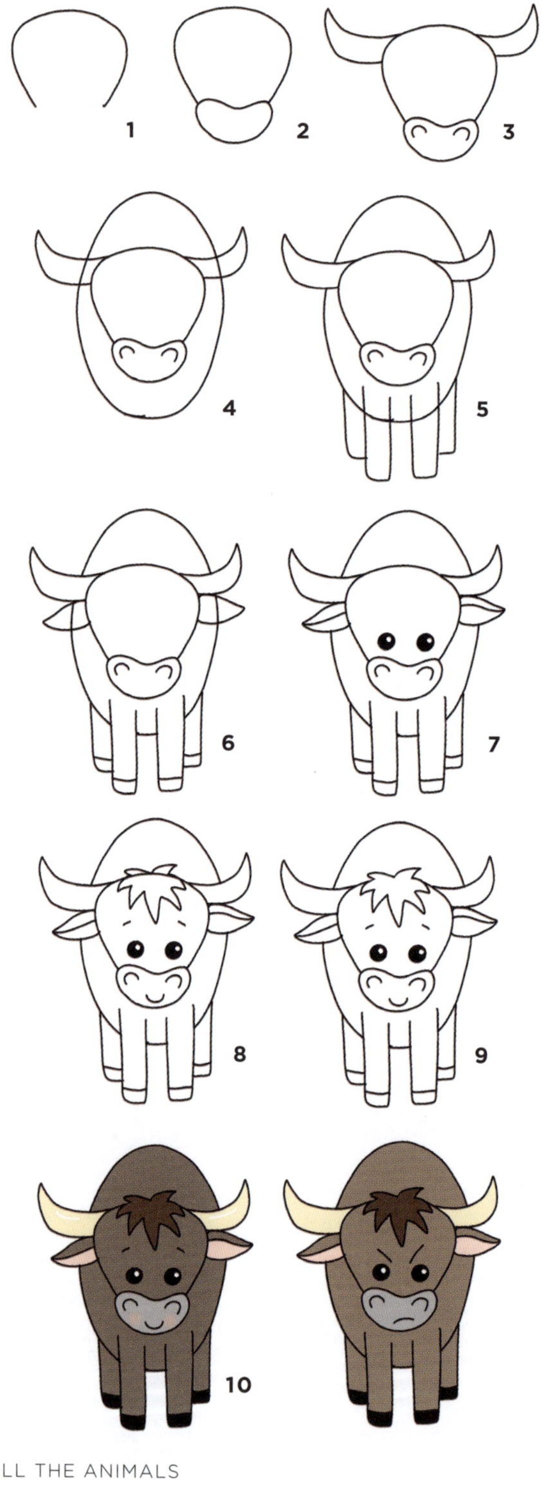

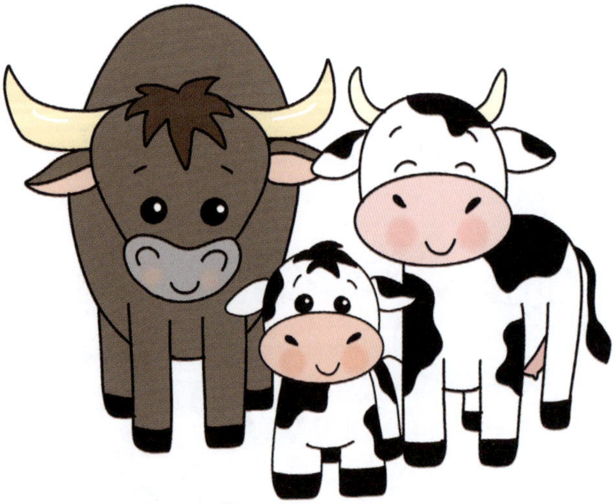

LONGHORN CATTLE

Texas Longhorns are American beef cattle named for their long horns, which can span a distance of 8 feet (2 m). This particular breed of cattle was the one around which "cowboy culture" was born. Today, they're a symbol of Texas, but they originally came to the New World with Christopher Columbus, who acquired them from the Canary Islands.

The first step in doodling your own is to sketch a tall, thin arch with an oval below it to form the face. Add eyes, nostrils and a pair of pointed ears. Next, draw two long horns extending from the top of the head in both directions. Sketch a tuft of hair and divide the ears into two parts. Then, draw the front of the body and legs and add a back leg on either side. Give your steer a hoof at the end of each leg. Add a smile, then color your drawing.

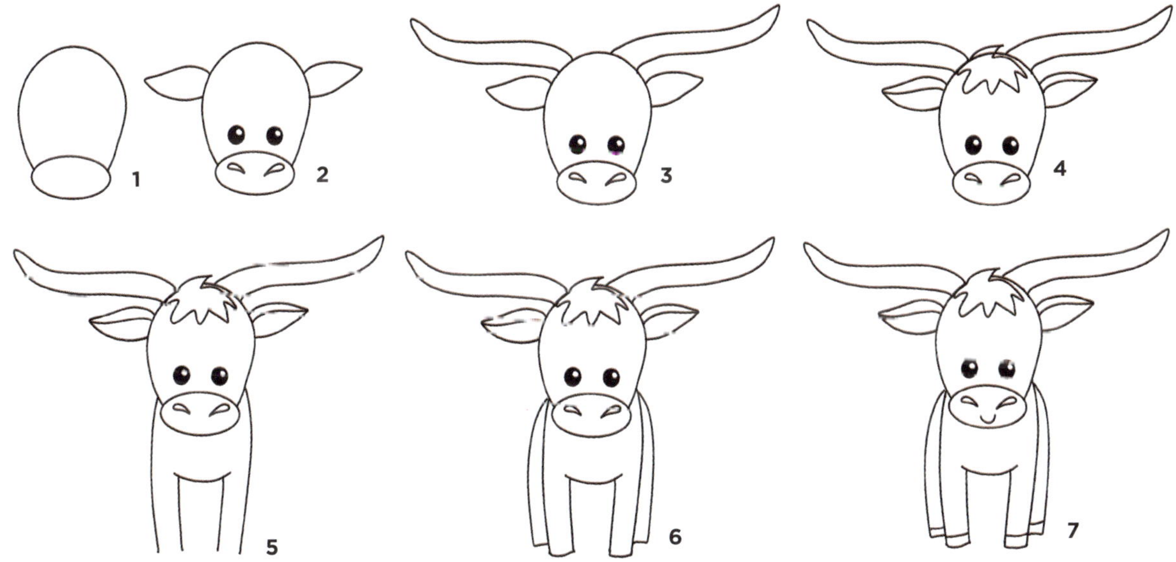

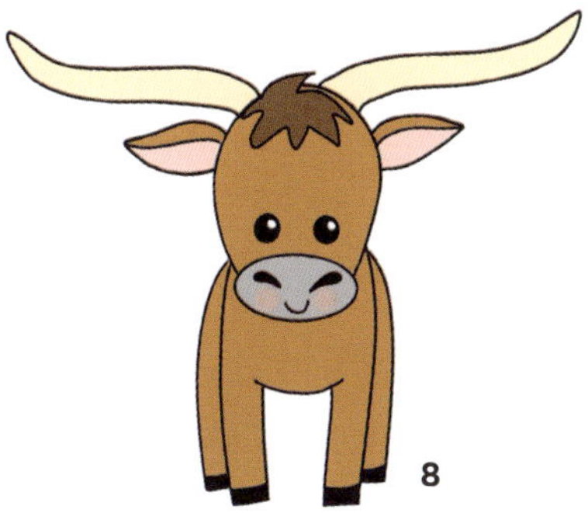

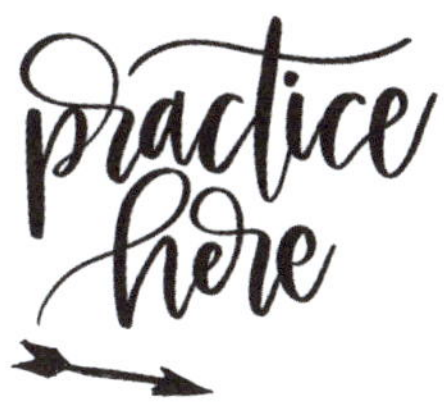

HORSE

Horses are fascinating animals. They have a field of vision that's almost 360 degrees and their eyes are able to work independently, focusing on two different things at the same time. Unlike most mammals, horses are physically incapable of vomiting or burping. Their teeth are huge, taking up more space in their heads than their brains do!

To doodle a horse, start with the head shape and add a pair of ears that curve slightly forward. Add a line for the chest and a pair of front legs. Draw the horse's back and back legs. Sketch a patch of hair on top of the head, as well as a mane going down the back, erasing overlapping lines. Give your horse a tail, then add detail lines and a simple face. Finally, color your horse brown, black, gray, white or any other color you choose.

Bonus: Changing your color pattern can easily create the look of different breeds.

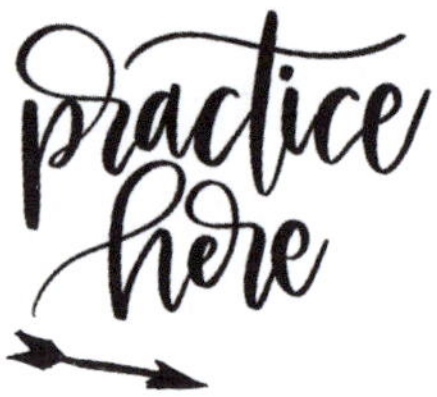

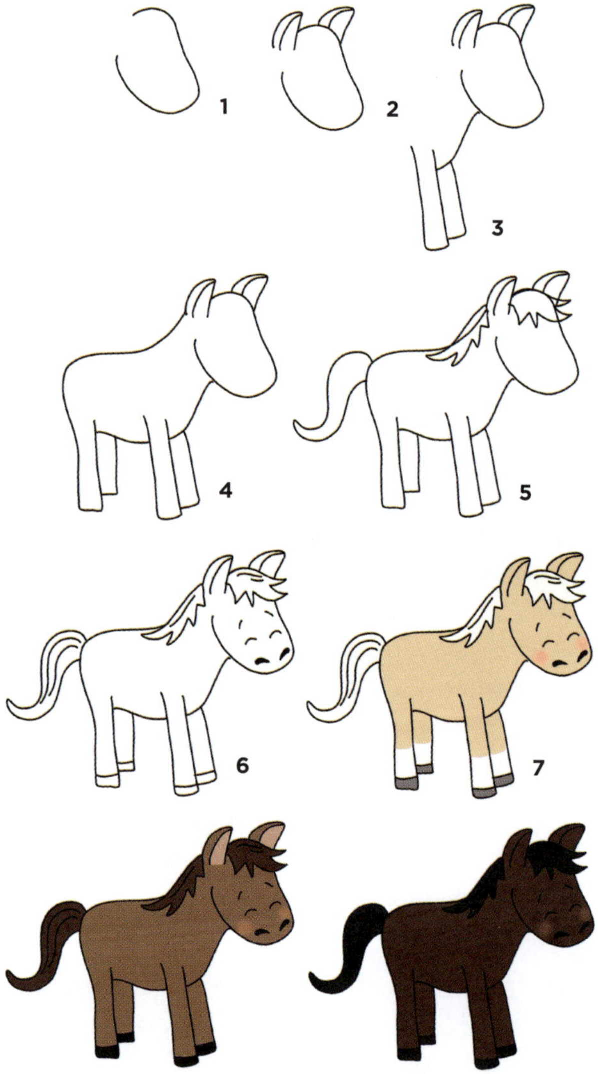

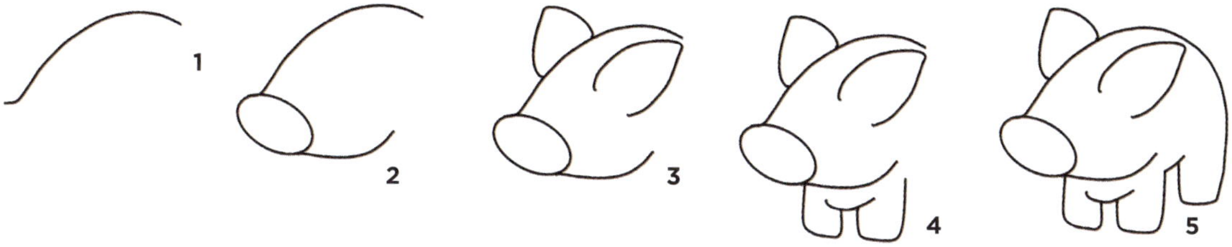

PIGLET

Piglets only weigh about 2.5 pounds (1.1 kg) when they are born, but they double that body weight in their first week of life! Newborn piglets quickly learn to recognize their mother's sounds and run to them. Although their eyesight is poor, they make up for it with an excellent sense of smell, which helps them to search for food.

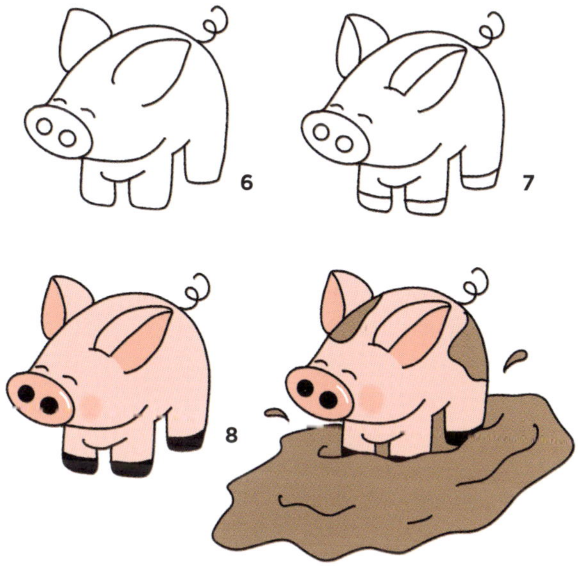

To doodle a piglet, start with a curving line for the upper head and draw a large oval for the snout. Make another curving line for the base of the head. Draw a pair of ears, then a pair of front legs below the head. Extend the upper body down to form the back leg and connect it to the front legs. Add details like nostrils, eyes and a curly tail. Divide the ears into two parts and add a hoof on each leg. Finally, color your piglet. For a fun variation, draw a wavy circle around your piglet to form a mud puddle! Add spots on the body to represent areas where he got muddy.

Bonus: Try combining adult pigs from the next page and piglets to create a family!

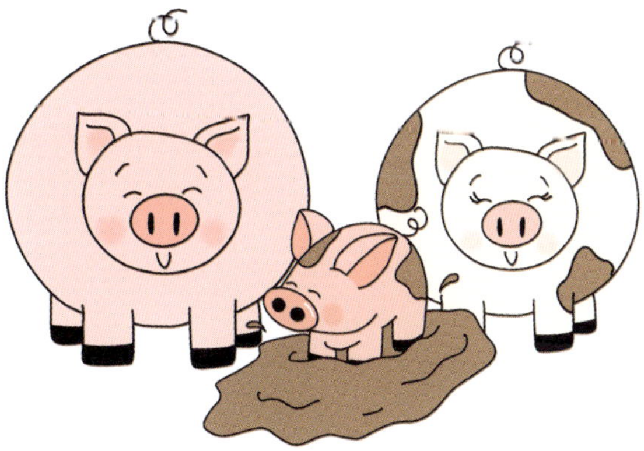

practice here

PIG

Despite the stereotypes, pigs are actually very clean animals. They're incredibly smart, with great memories, and studies have suggested that their intelligence is greater than that of dogs and human toddlers! Pigs are unable to sweat, which is why they love cooling off in mud baths.

To draw a pig, start by making a circle for the head and drawing a larger semicircle around it for the body. The farther apart these are, the fatter your pig will be! Add a pair of front legs, add a pair of back legs and finish off the body circle. Draw an oval inside the head for the snout and give your pig a hoof at the end of each leg. Sketch a curly line for the tail and give your pig a face. Finally, add short, pointed ears. To finish your doodle, color your pig. Remember, not all pigs are pink! They can also be white, black, gray, brown or a mixture of colors.

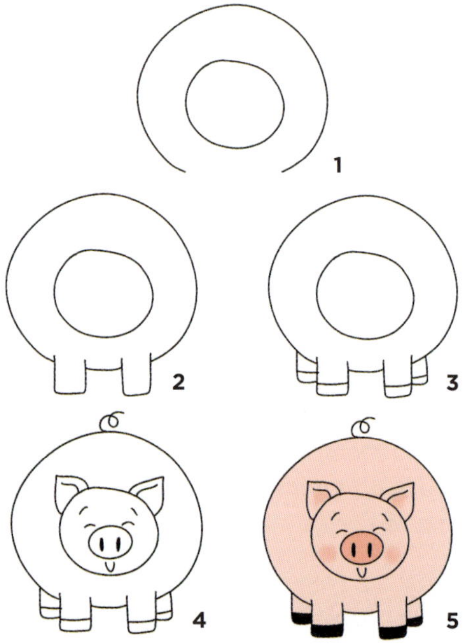

DONKEY

Donkeys can live for up to 50 years and their excellent memories allow them to remember places and animals they knew decades ago. These intelligent animals are known for being stubborn, but it's typically a form of self-preservation. Donkeys resist doing anything they feel isn't in their best interest.

To draw your own, start with a tall, thin upside-down "u" shape with an oval at the bottom. Add a pair of large, pointy ears. Sketch a patch of hair in the center of the head and draw nostrils inside the oval. Draw a pair of front legs, then add a curving line for the back and back leg. Add the other back leg, and draw a hoof at the bottom of each leg. Give your donkey a tail as well as eyes, eyebrows and a smile. Finally, color your doodle.

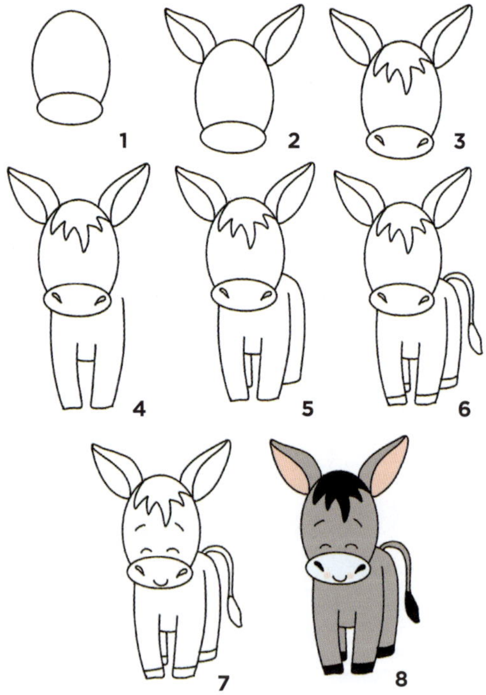

GOAT

Goats first came to the United States with European settlers in the 17th century, and may have been on board the Mayflower. *They're extremely agile animals and can even climb trees if the need arises. Myotonic goats are a species known as "fainting goats," because when they're excited or frightened, their muscles freeze and cause them to topple over as if they've fainted.*

To draw your goat, start with an oval head and a pair of horns. Draw large, pointed ears extending out to the sides and a jagged goatee. Sketch a pair of front legs, then add a curving line for the back. Add the back legs and draw a hoof at the bottom of each leg. Give your goat a face including eyes, a heart-shaped nose and a smile and add a patch of hair. Erase overlapping lines, then sketch a short tail. Finish your doodle by coloring your goat.

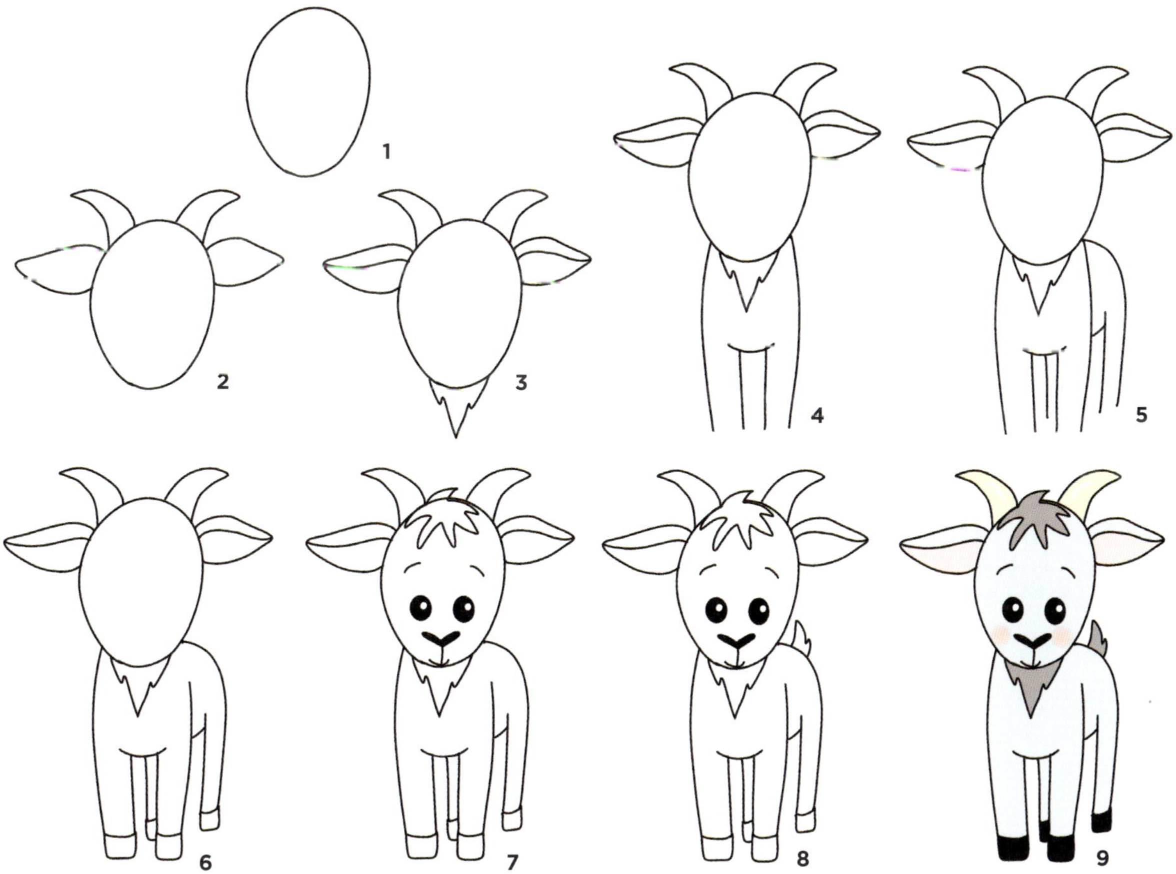

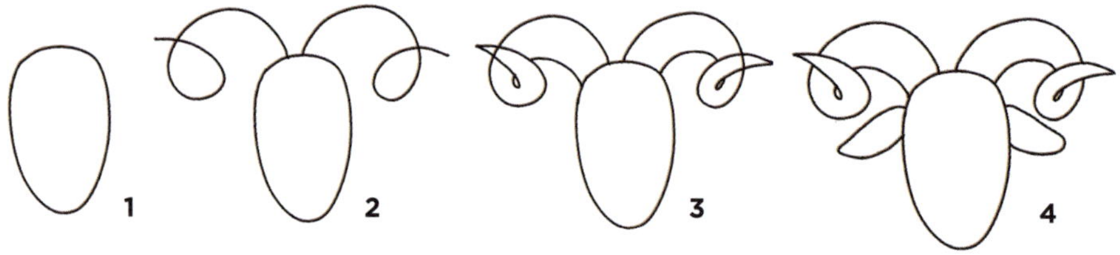

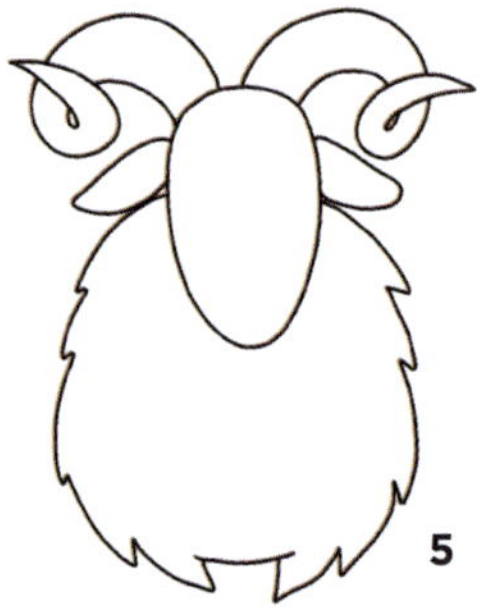

RAM

Male sheep are called rams and can be distinguished by their curling horns, which are coated in keratin (the same substance as human fingernails)! Each mating season, the ram's horns form a new growth ring, so it's possible to tell the age of the ram by counting the rings, just like you would with a tree.

To sketch a ram, start with an oval and draw two looping lines extending from the top. Add lines below and inside the loops to create the spiral horns. Draw a pair of ears, then create an oval-shaped body using zigzag lines to show the furry texture. Sketch four legs with hooves below the body. Divide the ram's face into two sections using an arch, then add eyes, eyebrows and a nose. Finally, add detail lines on the horns and inside the body to show texture. Color your ram to finish the drawing.

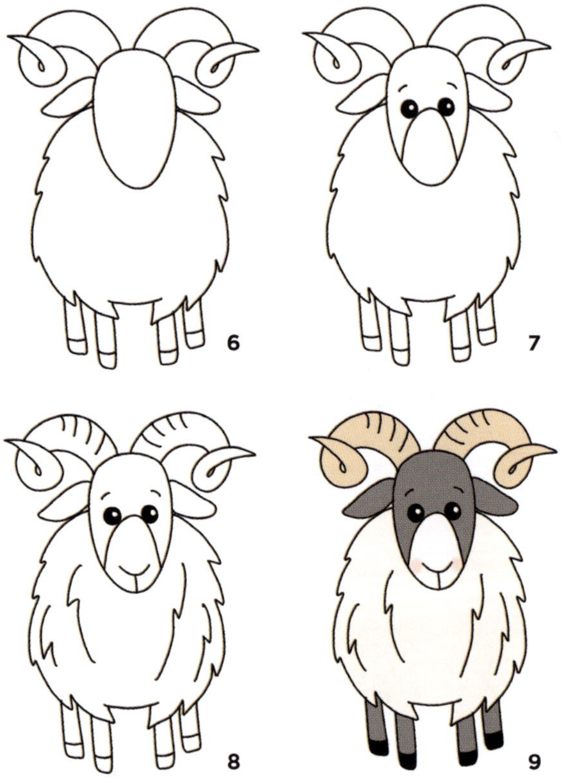

practice here

SHEEP

Sheep were one of the first animals to be domesticated by humans. They're very social and will form strong friendships with other sheep in their herd. They also have a wide range of emotions, including happiness, fear, anger, sadness, loneliness and disgust, all of which they display with a variety of facial expressions.

To draw your own sheep, start with a "u" shape for the face and add a bumpy oval on top for wool. Sketch a pair of ears, then draw a bumpy oval around the entire head to form the body. Give your sheep four legs with hooves, then add eyes, eyebrows and a nose. Color your sheep however you like. While many sheep are white, they can also be black or shades of cream.

Bonus: Try putting your ram and sheep doodles together. To draw a baby sheep, just follow the same steps but make your drawing smaller than the adult sheep.

practice here

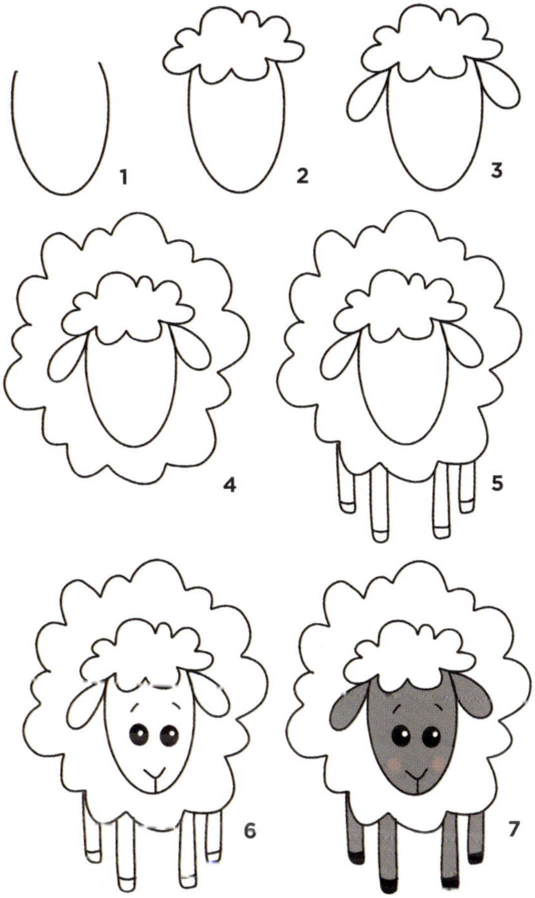

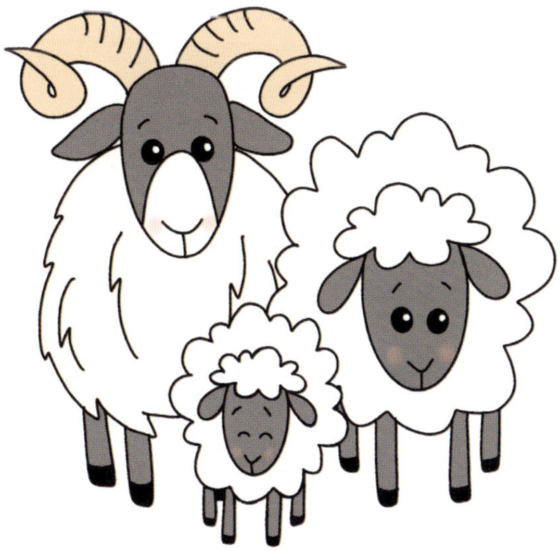

LLAMA

Llamas are native to South America and are actually the distant cousins of camels. Although they're typically agreeable, if llamas get annoyed, they'll stick out their tongues as a warning. If that doesn't work, they'll spit (which can travel up to 15 feet [5 m])!

To begin your llama doodle, use bumpy lines to draw an open "L" shape for the body. Add tall, pointed ears, then draw an oval inside the head. Give your llama a face, including eyes, eyebrows, a heart-shaped nose and a smile. Then, draw four legs and a short, fluffy tail. Finally, sketch a series of "u" shapes inside the body to represent the texture of the fur. Color your llama to finish your drawing.

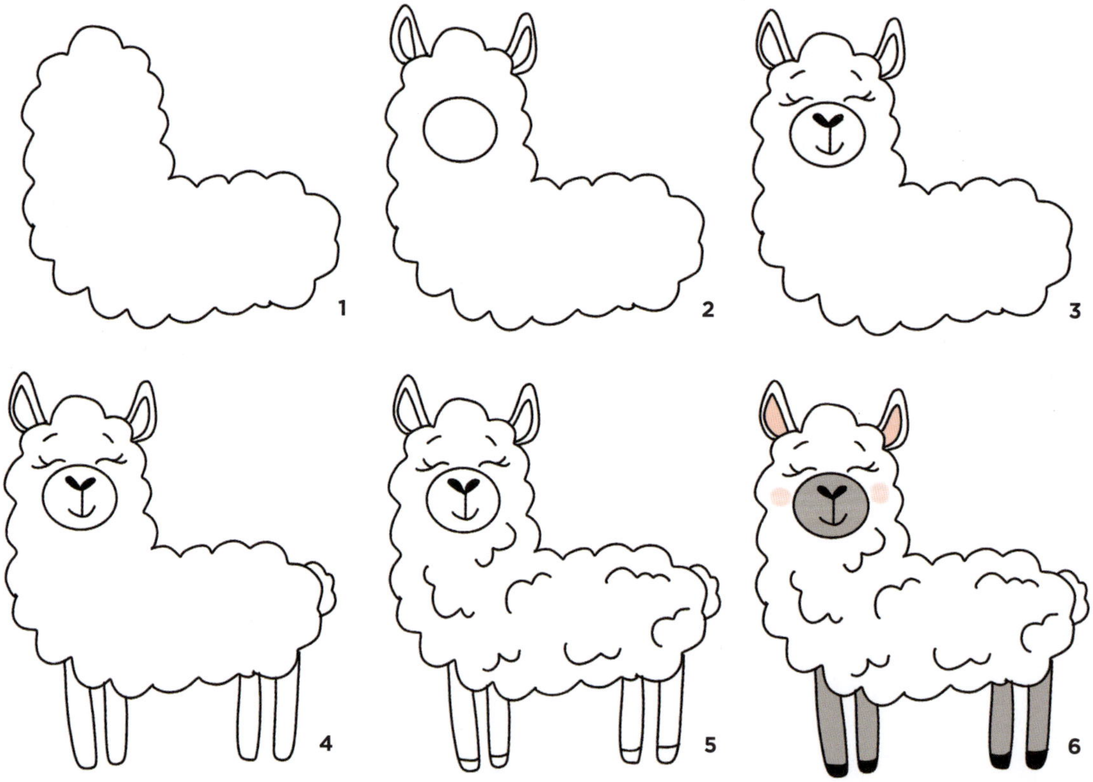

TURKEY

Did you know you can tell a turkey's gender by its droppings? Male turkey droppings are shaped like the letter "J," while females leave spiral-shaped poop. Turkeys primarily eat berries, nuts and insects but sometimes add small reptiles to their diet as well.

Start your turkey doodle with a shape that resembles a bowling pin. Add a large wing on each side of the body and erase the areas where the wings overlap it. Sketch detail lines to divide each wing into feathers and add the beak and snood. Give your turkey eyes and eyebrows to finish the face. Add a series of rounded feathers behind the body. You can draw as many feathers as you like. Finish your sketch by drawing legs and feet, then add color to complete your doodle.

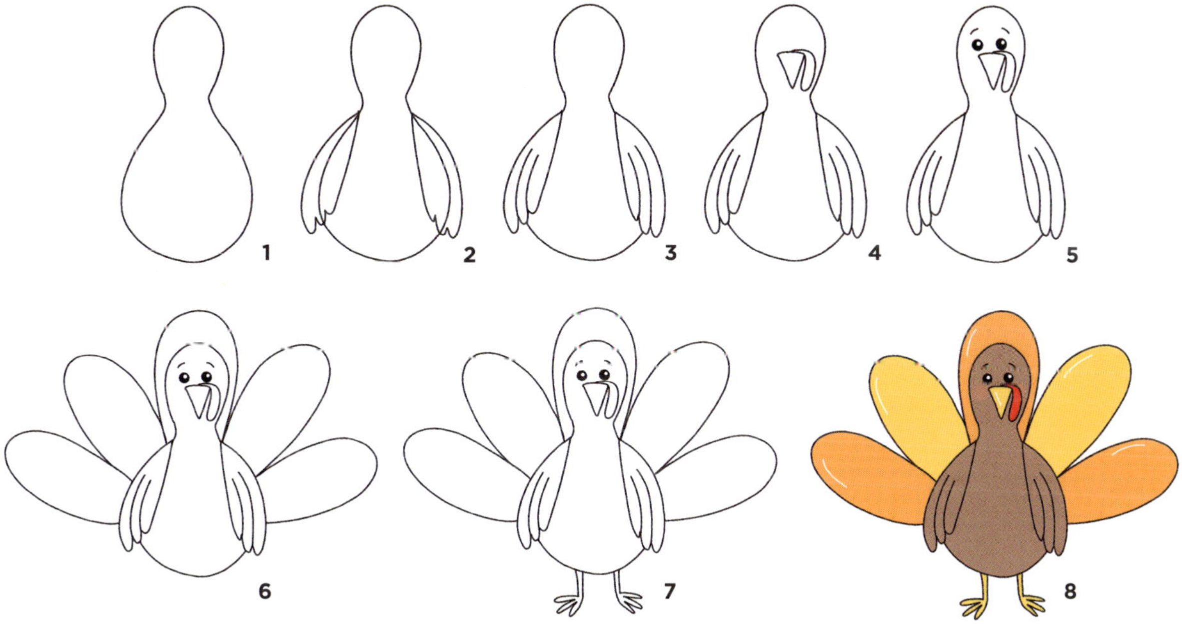

practice here

IN THE HABITAT

BARN

Barns are important wooden or steel buildings on the farm that hold livestock, equipment and grain. Although they can be any color, the most common color associated with barns is red, because historically it was an affordable option when farmers had to mix their own paint. They'd combine linseed oil with skimmed milk, lime and rust, which gave the paint a red hue.

To doodle a barn, start with a "v"-shaped roof peak that has a diagonal line extending down from each side. Draw a second slightly smaller roof shape below the first. Add a double line inside the roof shape, then sketch lines for the sides and bottom of the barn. Draw a large square barn door with an "x" running through it and a small square in the upper section of the building. Add vertical lines in the roof section. Finally, color your barn. Feel free to add some hay coming out of the square opening as an extra detail.

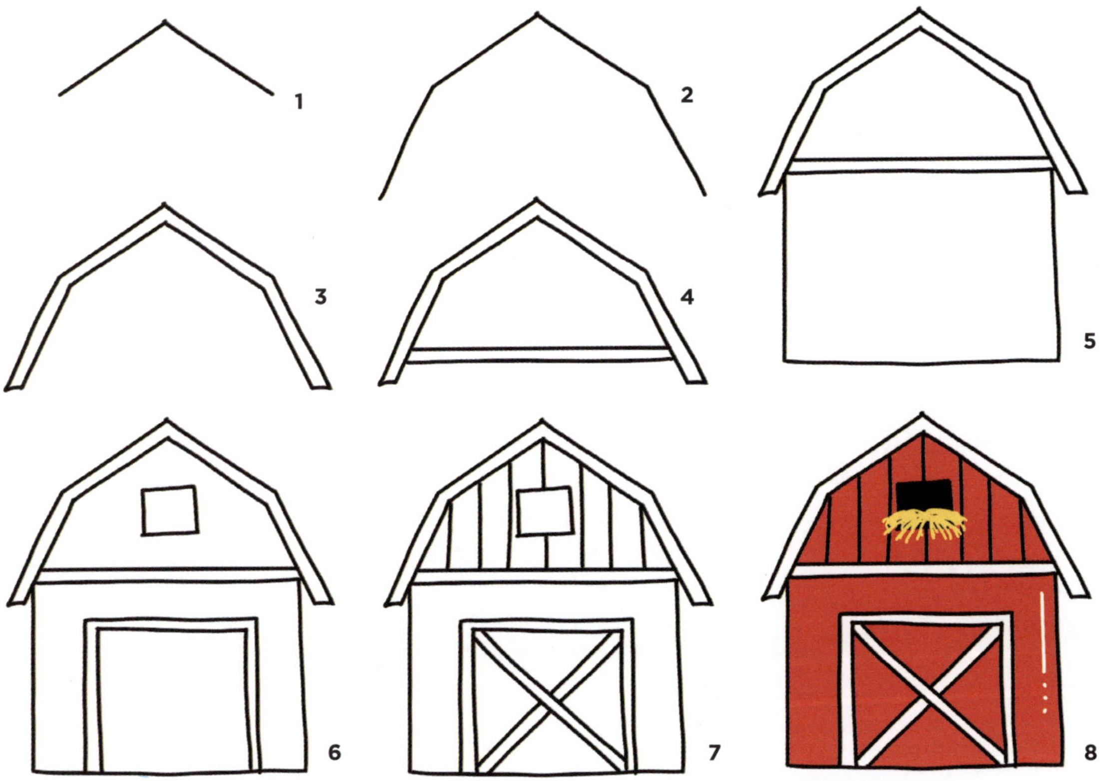

SILO

A silo is a tall, typically cylindrical structure on a farm that holds large amounts of silage. Silage is fodder made from green foliage crops—basically, it's pickled grass. It ferments in the silo, which causes it to keep most of its nutrients. Then, it serves as feed for cattle and other livestock in the winter when there's little natural pasture.

To draw your silo, start with two vertical lines connected by a pair of arches. Add a "v" shape on top. Then, sketch lines running from the peak all the way down the tower. Color your silo to finish your drawing.

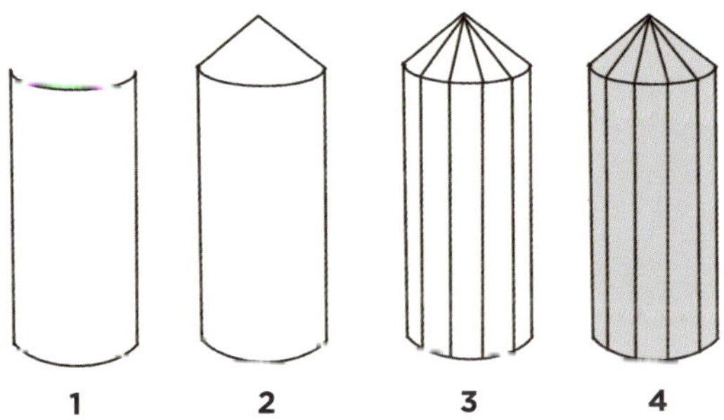

SUNFLOWER

Sunflowers, which can reach an impressive 30 feet (9 m) in height, bloom from June through September. Some varieties are annual, only surviving for one growing season, but others are perennial and will return to bloom year after year. These lovely flowers are heliotropic, meaning they tilt their faces throughout the day to follow the sun.

To draw a sunflower, start with an oval for the center. Add rounded "v" shapes all around it for the petals. Draw a long, curving stem and add a leaf. Place some dots in the oval to show the texture. Finally, color your sunflower yellow, brown and green.

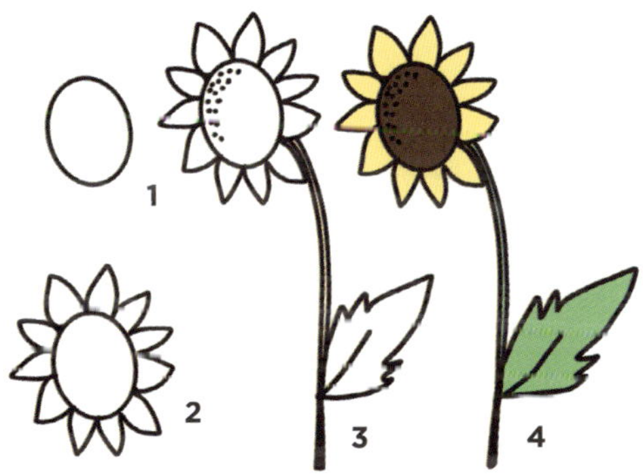

FENCE

Fences are necessary for separating farmland into sections and keeping different types of animals safe in their proper locations. Wood, vinyl, metal and wire can all be used for building fences.

We'll be drawing a wooden one, starting with four thin vertical rectangles. Make sure to leave plenty of space in between. Then, draw two long, thin horizontal rectangles that cross through the vertical ones. Erase the areas where the lines overlap, then color your fence. Wooden fences are typically either brown or painted white.

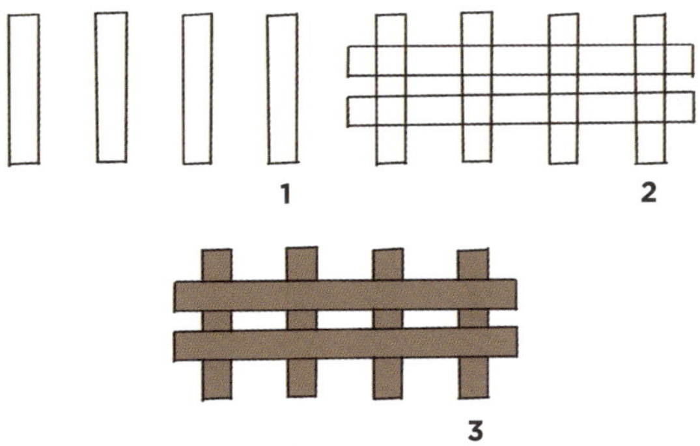

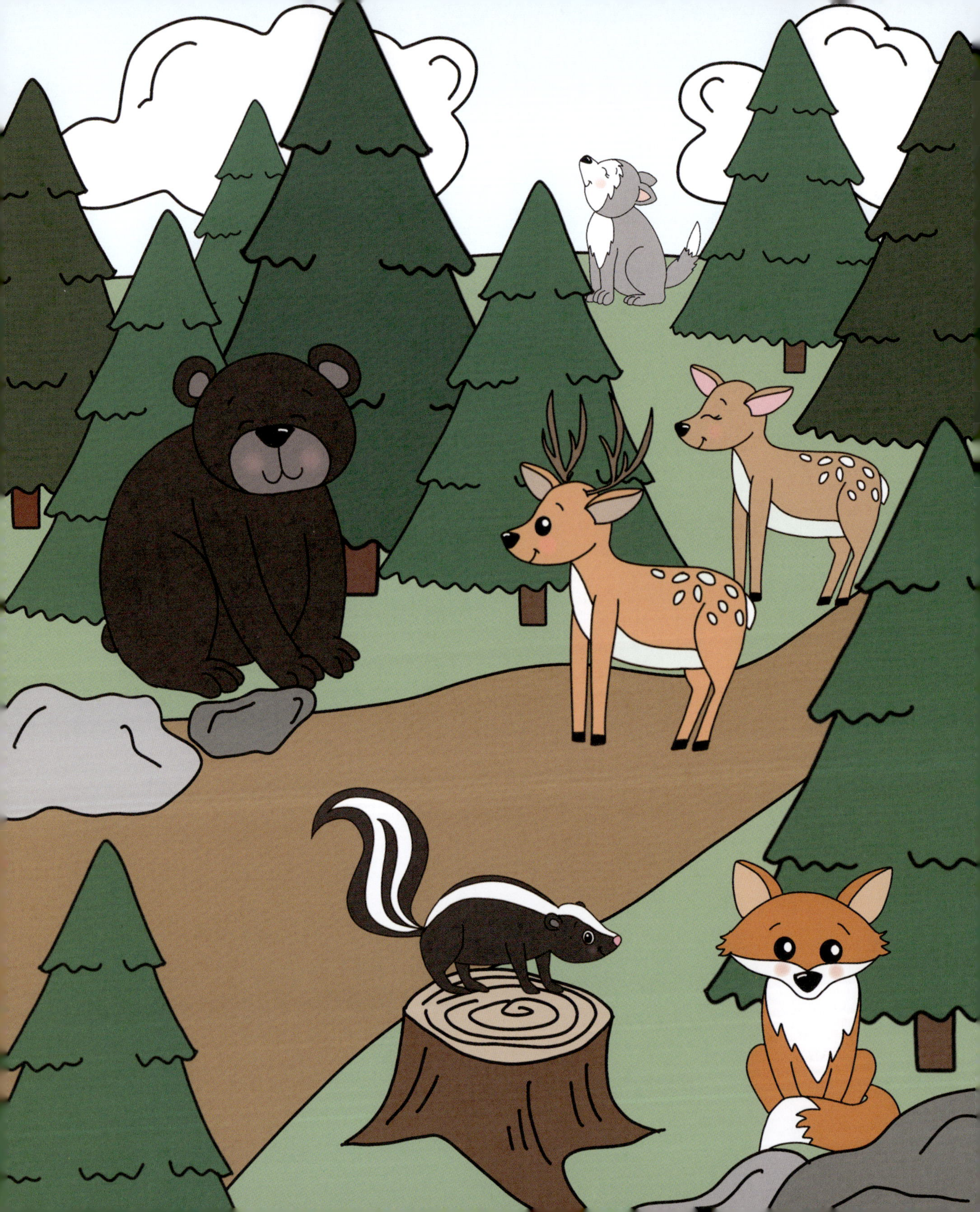

IN THE Woods

Woods, also known as temperate forests, are characterized by the fact that most of the ground is covered by trees. Some trees are evergreens, with needles that remain on the branches year-round, while others are leaf-shedding trees that experience the effects of all four seasons. The animals living in the forest also experience the changing seasons, so they need to be incredibly adaptable. In addition to temperate forests, bamboo forests can be found in Asia, Central Africa and South America. They're particularly recognized among the natural beauties of southern China along the Yangtze River, where they're surrounded by mountains. Did you know that more than 80 percent of the plants, animals and insects on land call forests their home? Let's explore some of the wildlife found in this type of habitat.

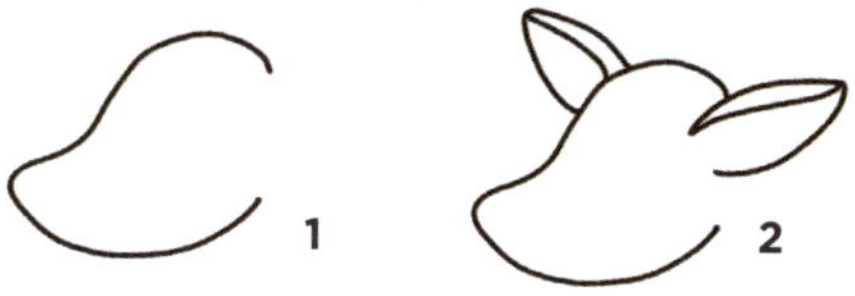

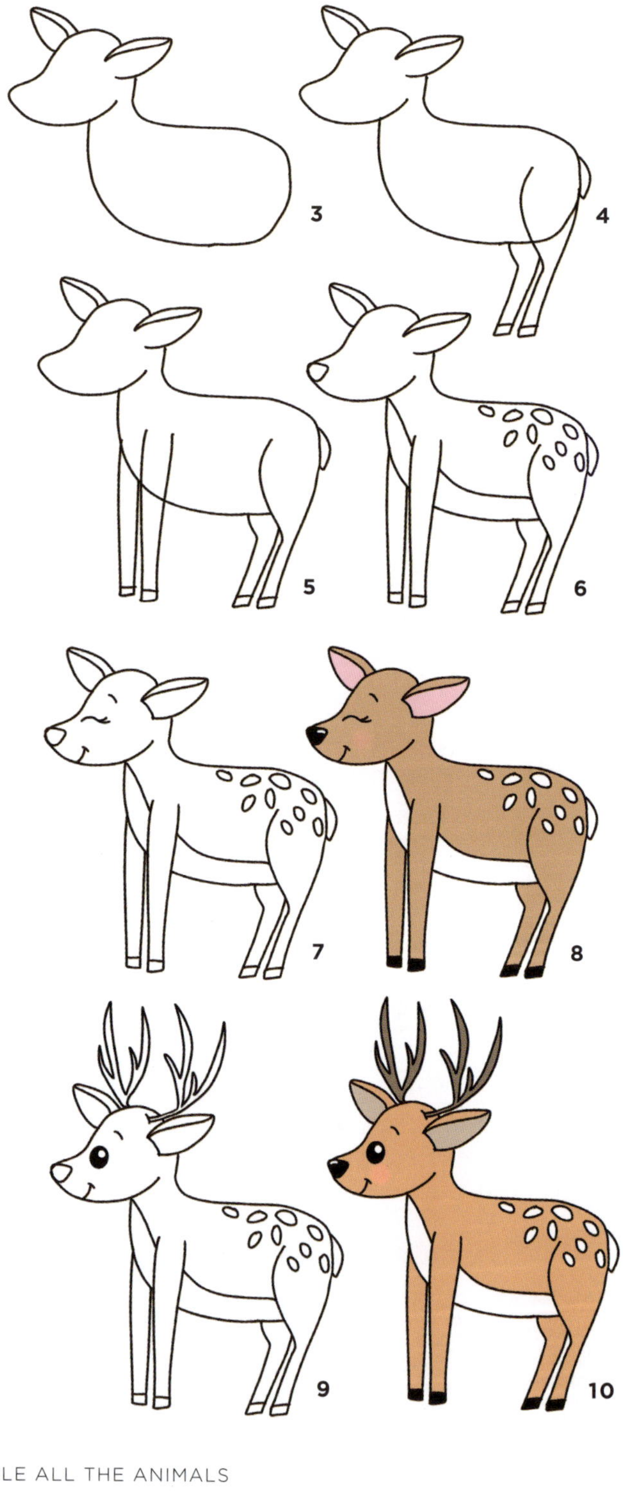

DEER

There are more than 40 million deer living in the United States and Canada today. They're excellent jumpers, able to bound more than 28 feet (9 m) in one jump. Many deer are able to "stot," which means they can take off and land from all four feet instead of just two.

We're going to draw both a doe and a buck. The process is the same, except that we'll give the male a pair of antlers at the end. The first step is to draw a head shape, as seen from the side. Draw a pointed ear on each side of the head that's divided into two sections with a curving line. Then, add a basic body shape that's connected to the head with a neck. Draw two back legs and a tail, followed by a pair of front legs. Draw lines just above the bottom of each leg for the hooves. Divide the chest/stomach section from the rest of the body with curving lines and add details like a nose and spots on the back.

For a doe, add facial features like a closed eye with eyelashes and a smile. For a buck, add the face, as well as a pair of antlers. For a realistic look, color the main part of the body a light reddish brown, then use pink or light brown for the inside of the ears. The antlers will be dark brown, while the stomach, tail and spots can stay white. Or, use any colors you like to create your own version of this animal.

MOOSE

The antlers of a male moose can grow up to 6 feet (2 m) in length, which female moose "cows" find very attractive. Females will often choose a mate based on who has the largest set of antlers, because it's an indication of good health and strength. Moose are among the most solitary animals, spending their time alone except for calves, which stay with their mothers until they're able to be independent.

Let's learn to doodle our own moose, starting with a wide "u" shape for the face and snout. Add a zigzag shape at the top for a tuft of hair, then draw an antler on each side of it. Sketch a pair of small, pointed ears above the antlers next to the hair. Next, draw a curving line for the neck and back and a tufted "V" shape for the chest. Sketch lines for the front and back legs, then add hooves. Give your moose a short tail and a face, then finish your doodle by adding color.

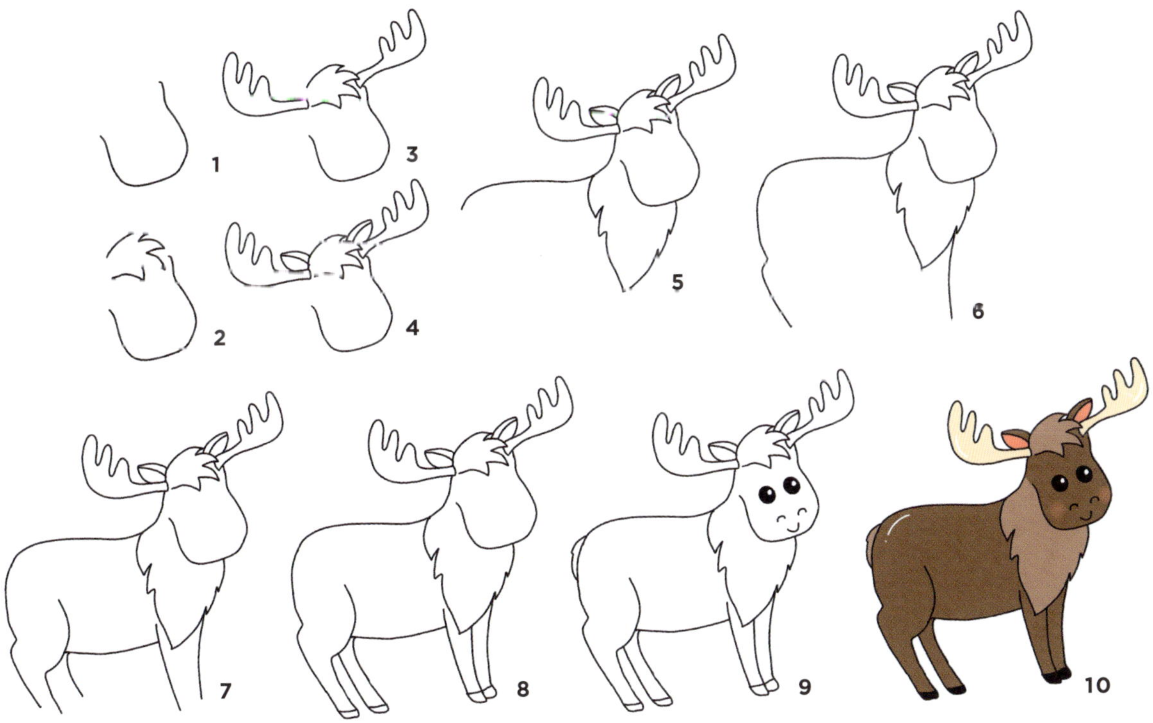

FOX

The red fox is the most common type of fox found in North America. Although red foxes are canines, they share more traits with cats than with dogs. Like cats, they have very fine hairs (spines) on their tongues to help them groom their fur. Foxes are scavengers and they enjoy visiting areas inhabited by humans to rifle through the garbage for good leftovers.

Doodle this furry friend, starting with an arch and a pair of large, pointed ears. Add lines to divide the ears into outer and inner sections and draw a zigzag on each side of the arch for a fuzzy texture. Draw the bottom of the head, then add curving lines to indicate the body. Sketch a "v" shape in the chest area with zigzags to show texture. Draw a curving line on each side of the body for the legs and sketch a thick, pointed tail wrapping around the body from the right side. Divide the tip of the tail from the rest with a zigzag line and add short lines for the front legs. Finally, form the face by drawing a nose, large eyes, eyebrows and a line separating the top of the head from the bottom section. Color the fox reddish-brown, leaving the chest area, the tip of the tail and the bottom of the face white.

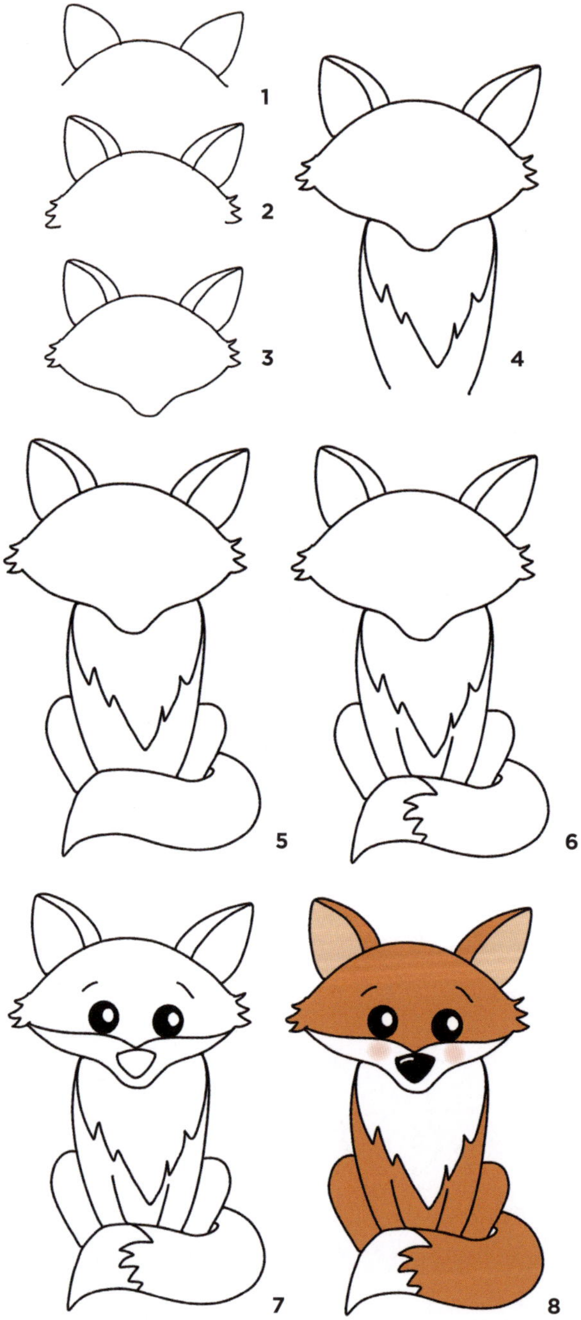

RACCOON

This fascinating animal gets its name from the Powhatan tribe; the word "raccoon" means "he scratches with the hands." Raccoons have whiskers on their hands and their sense of touch is the primary way they explore the world. They're crepuscular creatures, meaning they're most active at dawn and dusk.

To doodle your own raccoon, start by sketching a shape that looks like a lemon for the head. Add short, pointed ears on top and draw curving lines inside to divide the inner and outer ears. Sketch two teardrop shapes coming in toward the center of the face from the points of the sides of the head. Add a semicircle with a nose inside underneath. Draw eyes, eyebrows and a smile, then sketch two curving lines below the head for the body. Add lines for the arms and a tufted "v" shape just below the head. Draw a tail wrapping around the body from right to left, erasing the lines that overlap, and draw two short curved lines for the legs. Divide the tail into stripes, then color your raccoon.

practice here

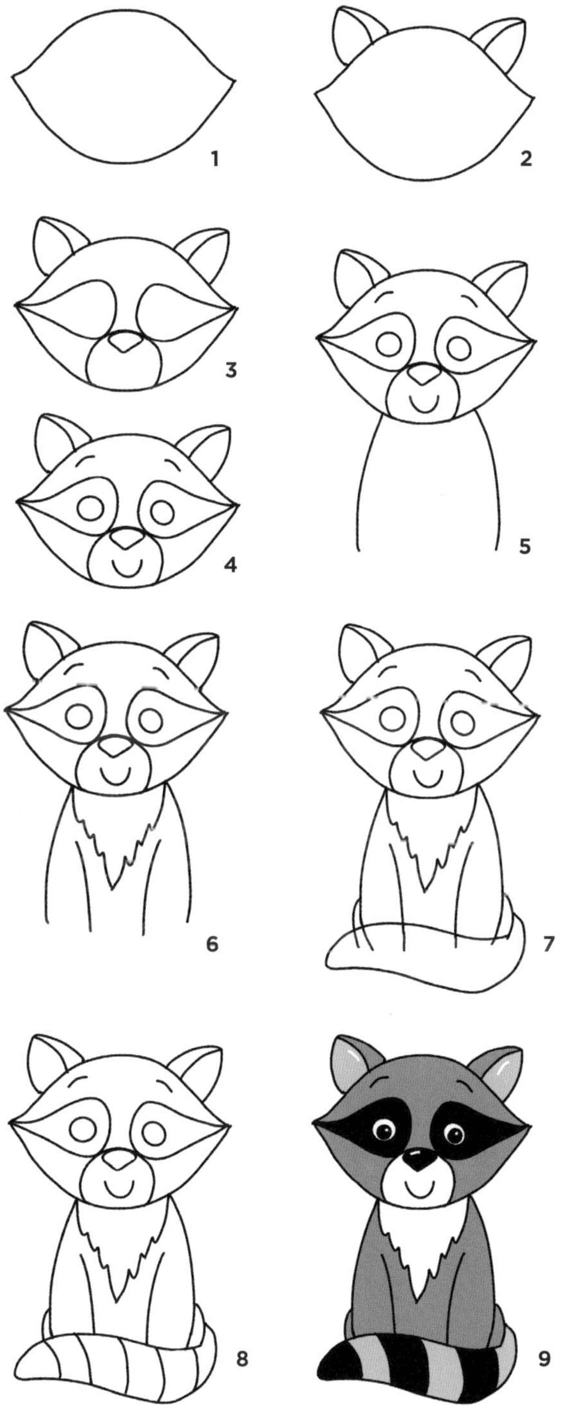

SKUNK

Before letting loose its infamous spray on a predator, a skunk will attempt to scare the predator off by doing a dance that involves stomping, slapping its tail and standing on its hind paws to display its backside as a warning. Once a skunk does spray, it needs to recharge for about ten days before it's able to spray again. Not only does skunk spray smell terrible, it's actually flammable too!

To draw a skunk, start with a side view of the head, which is somewhat like a sideways "v." Add a small, rounded ear on each side of the head and curving lines for the body shape. Draw the front and back legs, erasing the areas where the front legs overlap the body. Add a large, "s"-shaped tail with a pointed end, then sketch a stripe going down the skunk's head and back. Give it a nose and smile and add striped areas to the tail. Finish the face with an eye and an eyebrow, then color your skunk black and white with a pink or red nose.

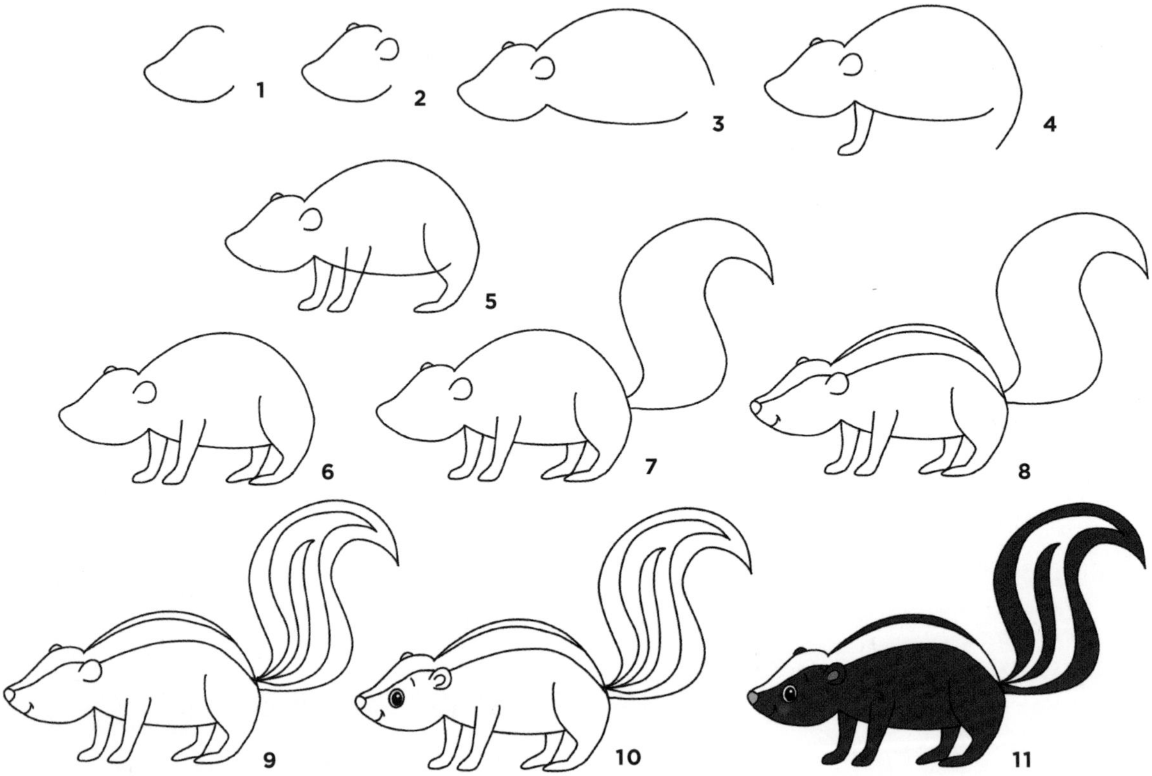

WOLF

Wolves are the ancestors of the domesticated dogs we keep as pets. They're pack animals, traveling and hunting in groups, and looking out for one another. Wolf saliva has antiseptic properties and can help heal wounds.

To draw a wolf, we'll start with a circle for the head and add a rounded rectangular shape for the muzzle, pointed up toward the sky. Sketch a pair of pointed ears on the head and erase the areas where these additional shapes overlap the original circle. Add a smaller triangle shape inside the front ear. Next, draw a "v" shape with zigzags on the sides in the chest area to show a patch of fur. Draw a curving back and a pair of front legs with rounded toes. Sketch a curving line for the back leg, along with a back foot. Connect the front and back legs to form the rest of the body. Draw a small nose, a closed eye and a small smile and make a zigzag line to separate the face from the rest of the head. Sketch a pointed tail that's separated into two parts. Finally, color your wolf. The gray wolf is the most common type, so I chose to color mine gray with white patches of fur on the face, chest and tip of the tail.

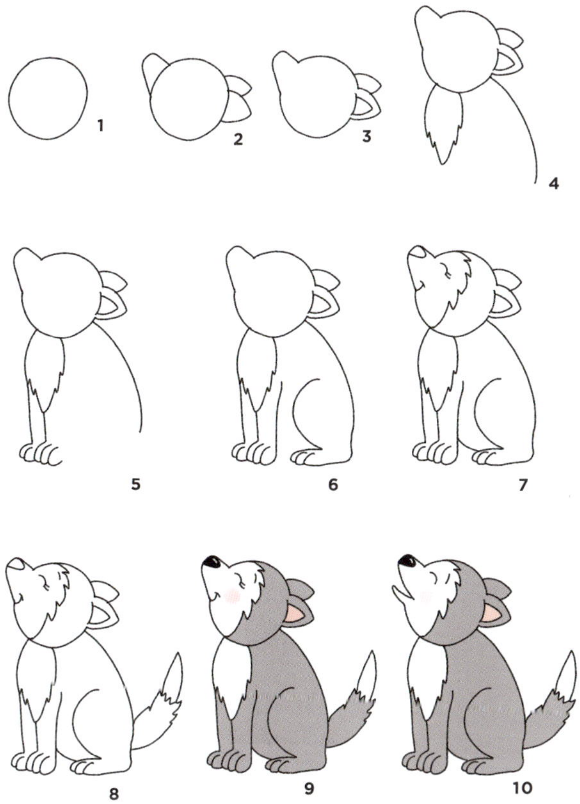

WOLF—HOWLING

Instead of a smiling wolf doodle, if you prefer to draw your wolf in a classic howling pose, all you have to do is make a quick adjustment to the mouth area. Just sketch a "v" shape below the nose and connect it to the base of the head to form the lower jaw.

Bonus: Now, try drawing both variations of the wolf to create a scene! Color a dark background, then use a white gel pen or paint to add a moon and stars for a fun night sky effect.

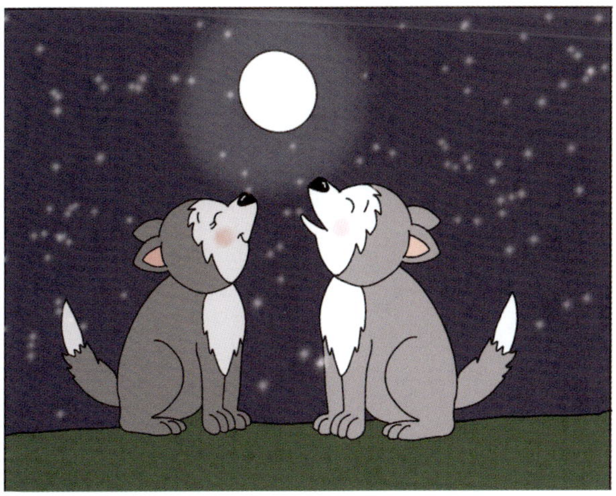

BOBCAT

Unlike most animals, bobcats have multiple homes. They have a main den, but they also have other auxiliary dens scattered all around their territory. They're able to live in the desert but prefer to make their homes in heavily wooded areas. A bobcat can run up to 30 miles per hour (48 kph) and its rabbit-like running gait (placing the hind feet in the same spot as the front feet) creates a bobbing appearance that lives up to its name.

The first step in drawing a bobcat is to sketch the face shape, adding zigzags to the cheek areas to show the animal's fur. Next, add ears on top of the head. Draw a long, curving line for the bobcat's back, as well as a short line curving down below the head for the chest. Sketch the front and back legs, adding a paw at the bottom of each leg. Add the legs and feet on the other side of the body and a short tail. Give your bobcat a face and, of course, its characteristic spots. All that's left to do is color your creation.

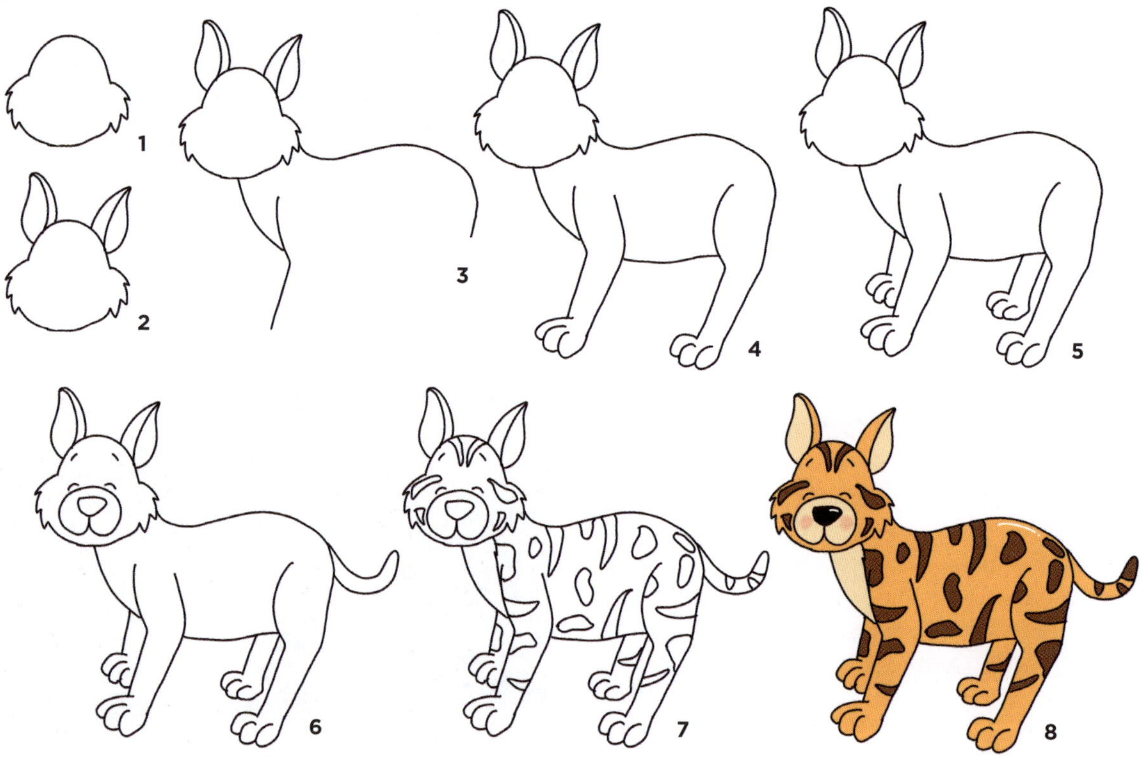

CHIPMUNK

Chipmunks are small, striped members of the squirrel family. Although they prefer solitude, they'll warn fellow chipmunks of danger with specific calls. High-pitched "chips" are an alert that a ground predator is near, while lower-pitched "chucks" warn of a predator in the air.

Start your chipmunk drawing with an arch for the top of the head. Add a "c" shape on either side for chubby cheeks and draw a pair of small, pointed ears. Divide the ears into two sections. Add a rounded "w" shape for the body and draw a pair of small feet peeking out from below it. Draw a pair of short arms and hands reaching up toward the head. Give your chipmunk a nose and divide the center of the body from the sides. Sketch a nut in between the hands. Give your chipmunk eyes, eyebrows and a smile. Draw lines to divide the eye areas from the rest of the face. Add a long tail, then divide the tail into striped areas. Finish your doodle by coloring your chipmunk.

Practice here

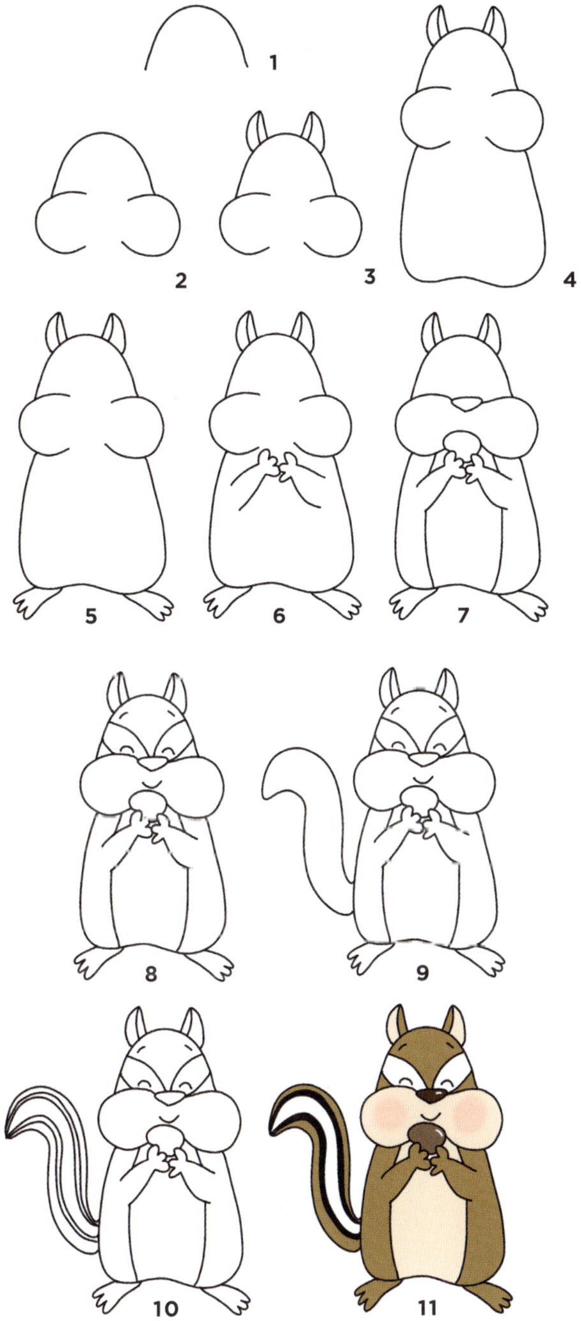

SQUIRREL

The name "squirrel" means "shadow tail" in Greek. Their tail helps with balance and acts as a parachute when jumping or falling. Squirrels can jump ten times the distance of their body length and their strong hind legs are actually double-jointed.

Let's start our squirrel doodle with a pear-shaped head and thin, pointed ears. Next, draw a curving line for the back and a backward "c" shape for the back leg. Add lines to indicate arms and the other back leg. Give your squirrel small hands with several fingers and feet with long, thin toes. Sketch a fluffy curving tail that ends with a point. To create the face, draw a nose in the center with a line on each side to separate the upper part of the head from the lower section. Add arch-shaped eyes, eyebrows and a smile with a pair of teeth showing. Draw a curving line to divide the bottom third of the tail from the rest of it. Finally, color your squirrel. Depending on the region, some squirrels are gray, while others have a reddish color.

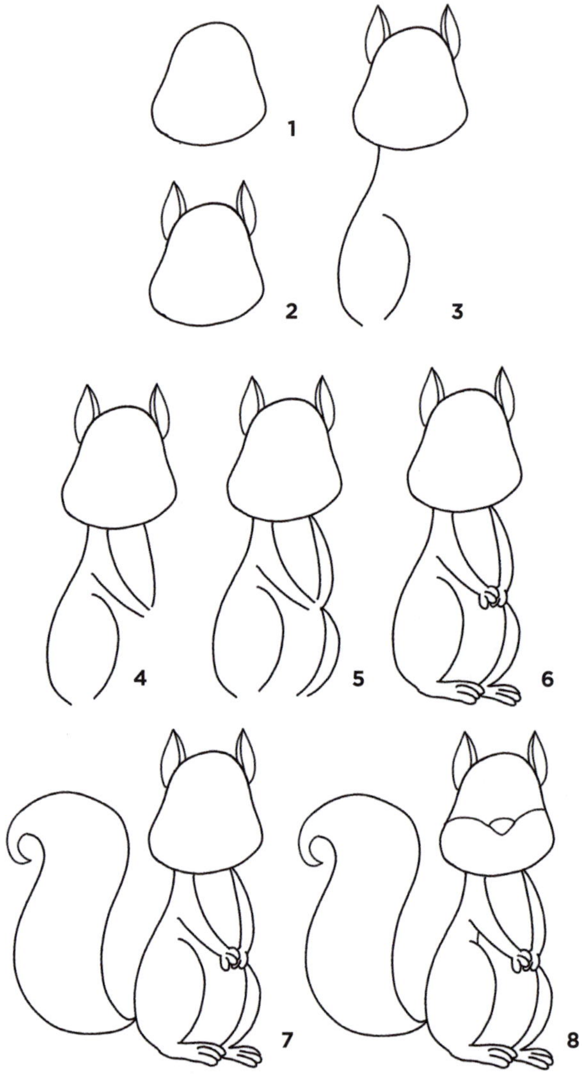

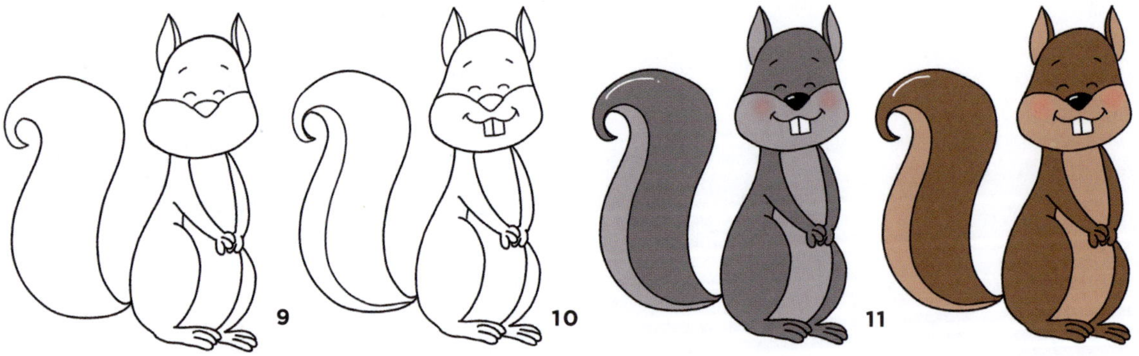

FLYING SQUIRREL

Despite their name, flying squirrels don't actually fly. Instead, these mammals glide from one tree to another using special parachute-like membranes called patagia between their front and back legs. Believe it or not, they can glide for distances up to 300 feet (91 m)! Flying squirrels are nocturnal, and not only do they have excellent night vision, some species actually glow, giving off a fluorescent effect under UV light!

Let's doodle this fun creature, starting with a "u" shape for the head. Add a pair of short, pointed ears and connect them to form the rest of the head shape. Draw a triangular nose, then sketch two curving lines to divide the top center section of the face from the rest. Then, add eyes and a smile. Sketch a curving horizontal line extending from each side of the head, with a small paw at each end. Next, draw two vertical curving lines with a paw at the bottom of each one. Connect the paws at the bottom with an arch. Then, draw curving lines between the front and back paws and the front paws and head to form the patagia. Draw a bushy tail and sketch detail lines inside the tail, as well as on the body. Finish your doodle by coloring your flying squirrel.

Practice here

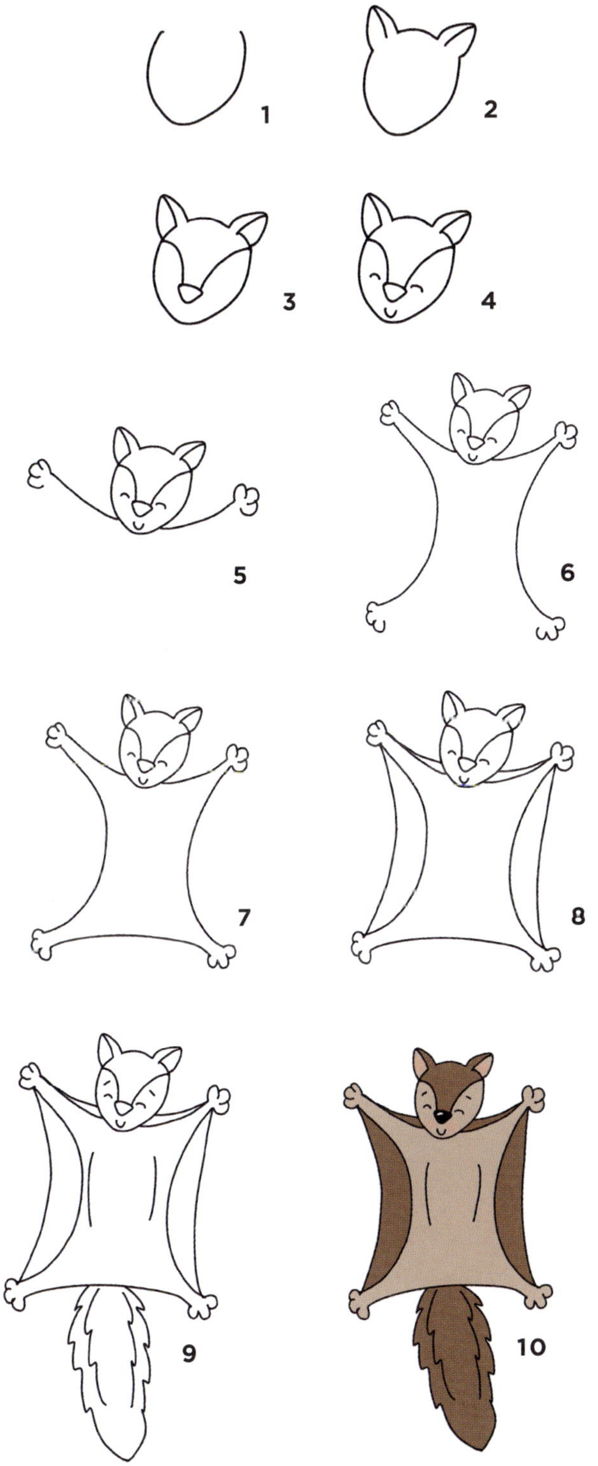

BROWN/BLACK BEAR

Did you know that bears have two layers of fur? A short under layer keeps the bear warm, while the outer, longer layer protects the skin and short fur from water. Bears can hear better than humans and their sense of smell is much stronger than ours, too. A bear may be able to track a scent from up to 20 miles (32 km) away!

Start your bear doodle with an oval-shaped head and a pair of rounded ears. Next, draw curving lines for the front and back of the body. Add a few more curving lines to become the front legs, as well as one for the back leg. Draw a paw at the bottom of each front leg, as well as the back leg. Give the bear a small, rounded tail. Next, make an oval inside the bottom part of the head, with a rounded triangle-shaped nose. Add eyes, eyebrows and a smile, then color your bear black or brown.

practice here

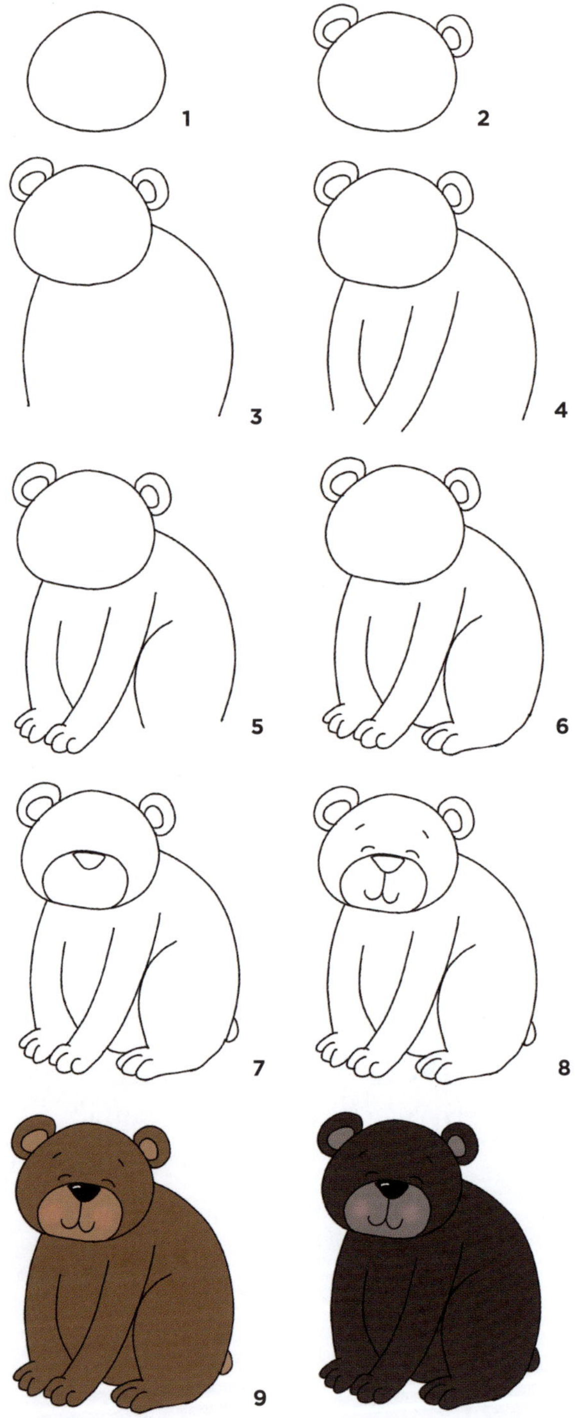

GIANT PANDA

Giant pandas spend 12 to 16 hours a day eating bamboo, which makes up 99 percent of their diet. Unlike most bears, pandas don't hibernate; they just move to lower spots on their mountain where it's warmer. Although they can weigh as much as 250 pounds (113 kg), they're surprisingly good at climbing trees.

Let's sketch a panda together, starting with an oval-shaped head and two rounded ears. Next, draw two large ovals inside the head, with a round eye in the center of each one. Add a nose and a smile to complete the face. Sketch an oval-shaped body below the head and add an arm on each side. Erase the areas where the arms overlap the body. Draw two oval-shaped feet, erasing the overlap areas, and add an oval and three small circles in each one to form the paws. Finally, color your panda with black ears, black arms and feet, a black nose and black patches around the eyes.

practice here

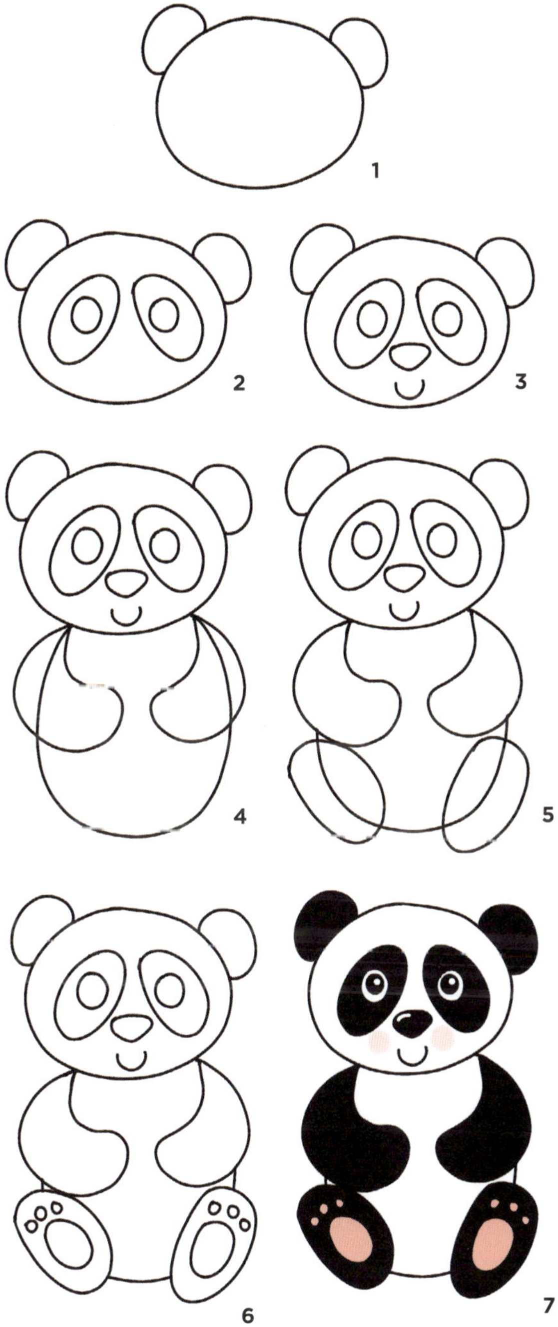

RED PANDA

Red pandas are incredible acrobats! They spend most of their time in the treetops and use their long, bushy tails to help them balance. Those tails are also useful for keeping red pandas warm when wrapped around their bodies. The average red panda eats about 20,000 bamboo leaves every day.

To draw this adorable endangered animal, start with a wide arch for the top of the head and two large, pointed ears. Draw a few zigzags on each side of the arch to show the furry texture of the face and make a wide "u" shape to connect them. Inside the head shape, draw the distinctive white patches: two that look like eyebrows, a curving one on each cheek and one in the mouth and nose area. Add a smile, a nose and eyes to complete the face. Draw an arch for the back and a long tail shape wrapping around the front of the body. Sketch short curving lines to indicate the presence of legs and add smaller pointed shapes inside the ears. Finally, divide the tail into striped sections. Color your panda reddish brown, leaving the facial patches white and making the tail stripes and inner ears darker brown.

practice here

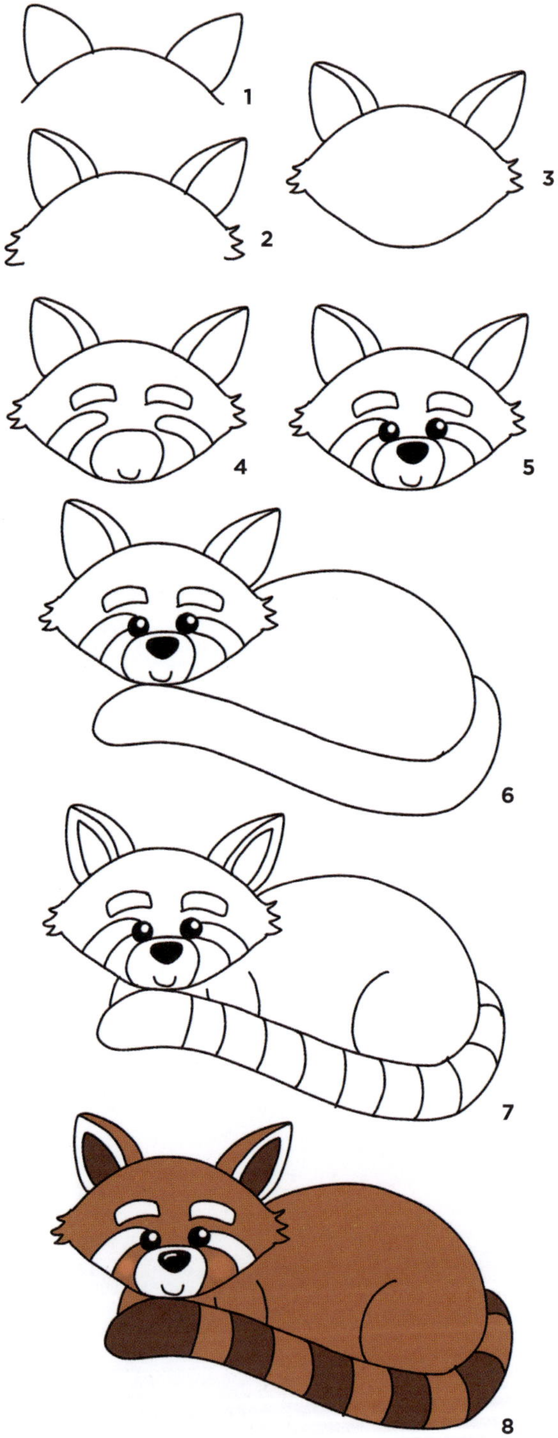

HEDGEHOG

Hedgehogs got their name from the fact that they enjoy living in hedges and they make grunts that sound like pigs. Each hedgehog has between 5,000 and 7,000 quills on its back, which it can raise in self-defense when it's threatened. Fortunately for humans, though, these spikes aren't barbed or poisonous.

To doodle your own hedgehog, start by sketching the shape of the face and belly. Then, create the rest of the outline by drawing a curve with lots of zigzags to represent the quills. Add a small, rounded ear and draw a series of short lines to separate the front of the body from the back. Give your hedgehog tiny hands and feet, as well as a face, then fill in the quill area with lots of short lines for texture. Add color to finish your doodle.

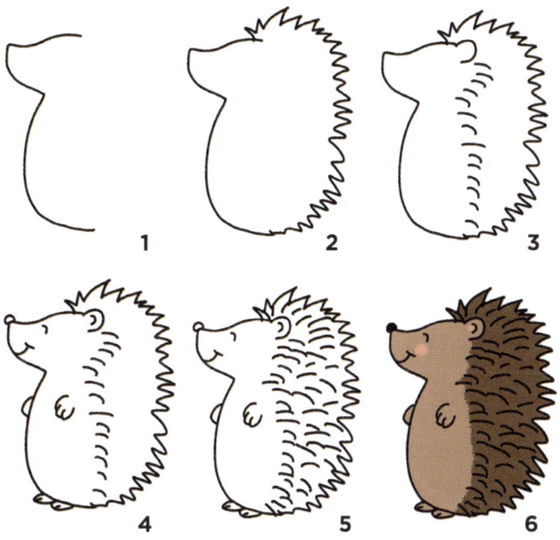

BEE

Although a bee's brain is the size of a grain of sugar, it's surprisingly sophisticated. Honeybees can be trained to detect human illness and have also been used to detect hidden land mines and bombs! When a worker bee locates a good food source, it heads back to the hive and communicates with the other bees by doing a "waggle dance," moving its body in the direction of the food!

To doodle a cute bee, start by forming an oval for the body. Add a short line on one end for a stinger, then divide the body into sections with curved lines for the stripes. Add two teardrop-shaped wings on top of the body, then give your bee a face with eyes, a smile and eyebrows. Color the body yellow and black, leaving the wings white.

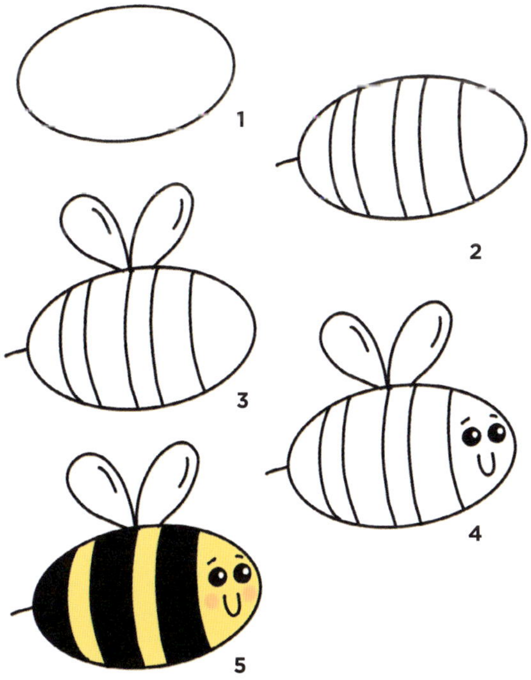

WOODPECKER

Despite the way they repeatedly smash their heads into trees, woodpeckers don't get headaches! This is thanks to a bone called the hyoid, which wraps around the entire skull and offers shock protection.

To draw a woodpecker, start with a backward "c" shape for the head and a curving line for the front of the head and body. Give the bird a wing with a few zigzags to show texture and a long tail divided into three feathers. Add a long, pointed beak that points upward on a diagonal. Draw a triangular shape on the top of the head and erase where it overlaps your original lines. Add a band around the eye area with concentric circles for the eyes. Draw two pointed sections in the lower head and upper chest area and add a pair of legs and feet that extend out from the body to the left. Finally, give your woodpecker a tree to stand on by drawing vertical lines with a series of long and short texture lines inside. For a realistic woodpecker, color the body black or dark gray, with a white head and a black band around the eye. The feathers on top of the head and the area at the bottom of the head are red. Or, color your bird in any way you like.

practice here

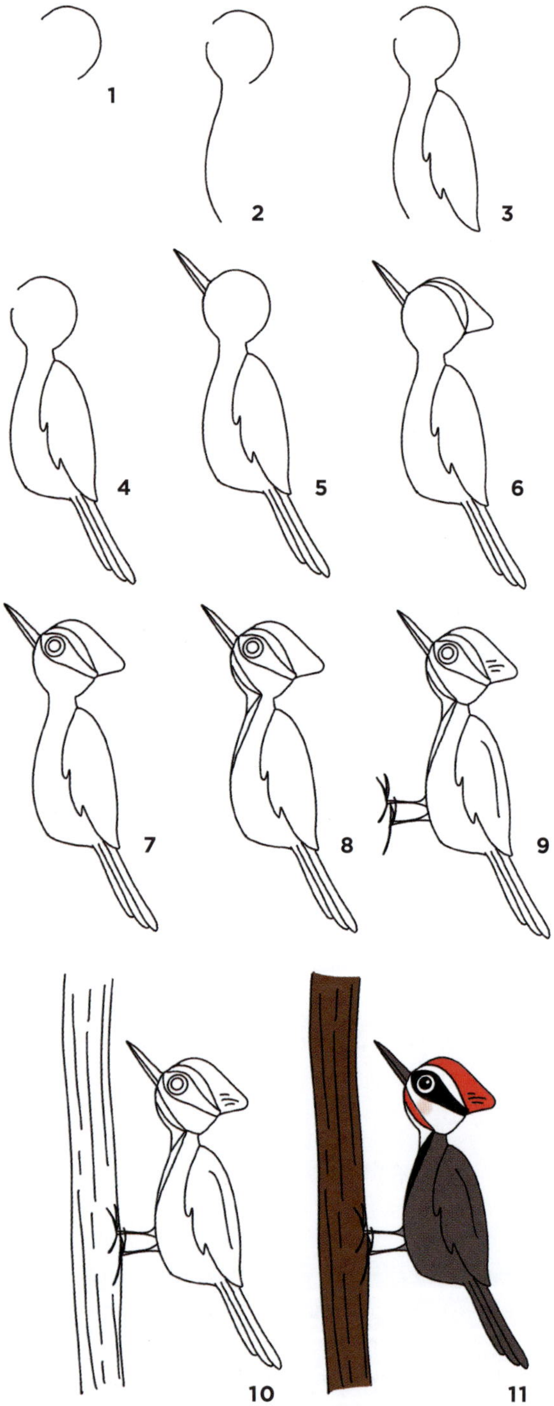

BARN OWL

Instead of chewing their food, barn owls swallow it whole, bones and all! The "leftover" parts are broken down and formed into pellets, which the owl coughs up, then uses to build its nest. Barn owls' ears are uneven, at a different level on each side of the head, which helps them to locate sounds without turning their heads.

To draw a barn owl, sketch an oval-like shape where the top part is narrower than the bottom, creating a head. Next, draw two large circles in the head section for eyes and create a sideways "8" shape around them. Sketch a long, thin, pointed beak and erase the line where it overlaps the eye section. Add a long, thin wing on each side of the owl's body and divide a section of the body for its chest. Draw a series of zigzag lines on the chest to give the appearance of a feathered texture. Add feet by drawing three ovals together for each foot, then sketch a pair of horizontal lines under the feet to create a tree branch. Draw a few leaves on the branch, then finish your doodle by adding color. Barn owls are usually light brown with darker brown stripes or spots.

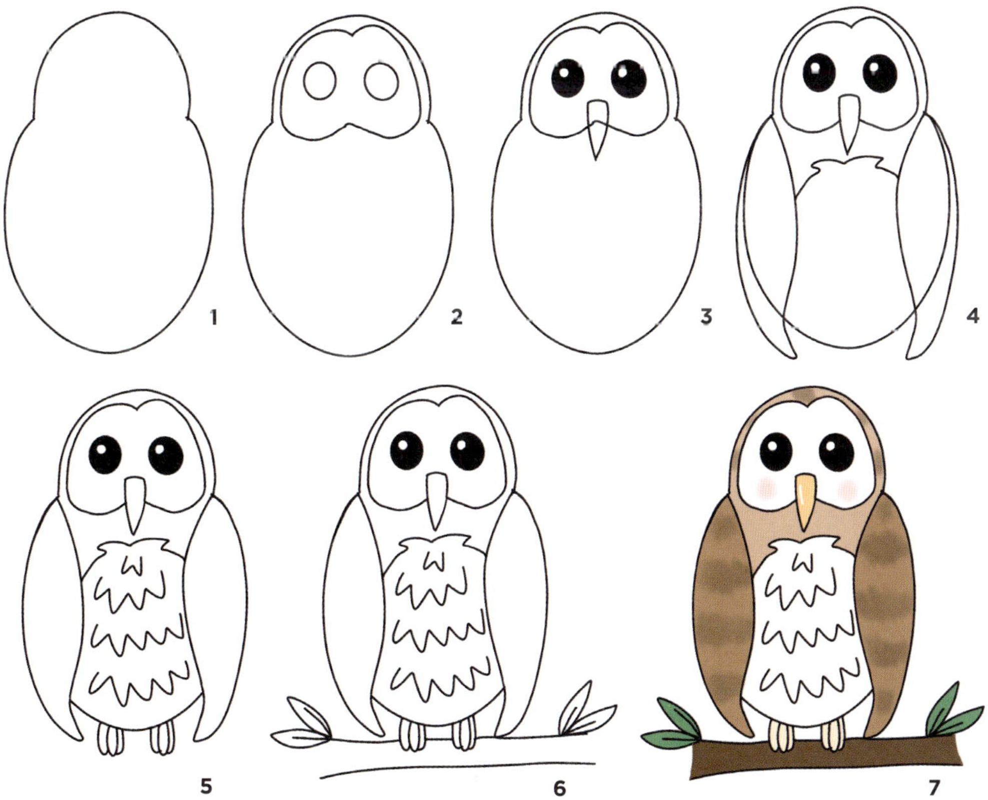

GREAT HORNED OWL

The great horned owl gets its name from the large tufts called plumicorns on its head, which resemble horns although they're made of feathers. It's the most common type of owl found in North America, as well as one of the largest, measuring more than 2 feet (1 m) tall with a 7-foot (2-m) wingspan. The shape of their wings and feathers allows great horned owls to fly silently, taking their prey by total surprise.

Let's draw our own version of this magnificent creature, starting with the plumicorns. Sketch a slightly rounded "v" shape and connect it at the top. Add a little tuft on each side. Draw a pair of eyes below the "v" with two concentric circles and trace the eye section with a rounded "w" shape. Add a long, pointed beak and create the head shape. Next, draw the rounded body and a long, thin wing on each side. Erase any lines that overlap. Draw three small ovals for each foot, then add texture markings by drawing scalloped lines on the wings and body. Finally, color your owl.

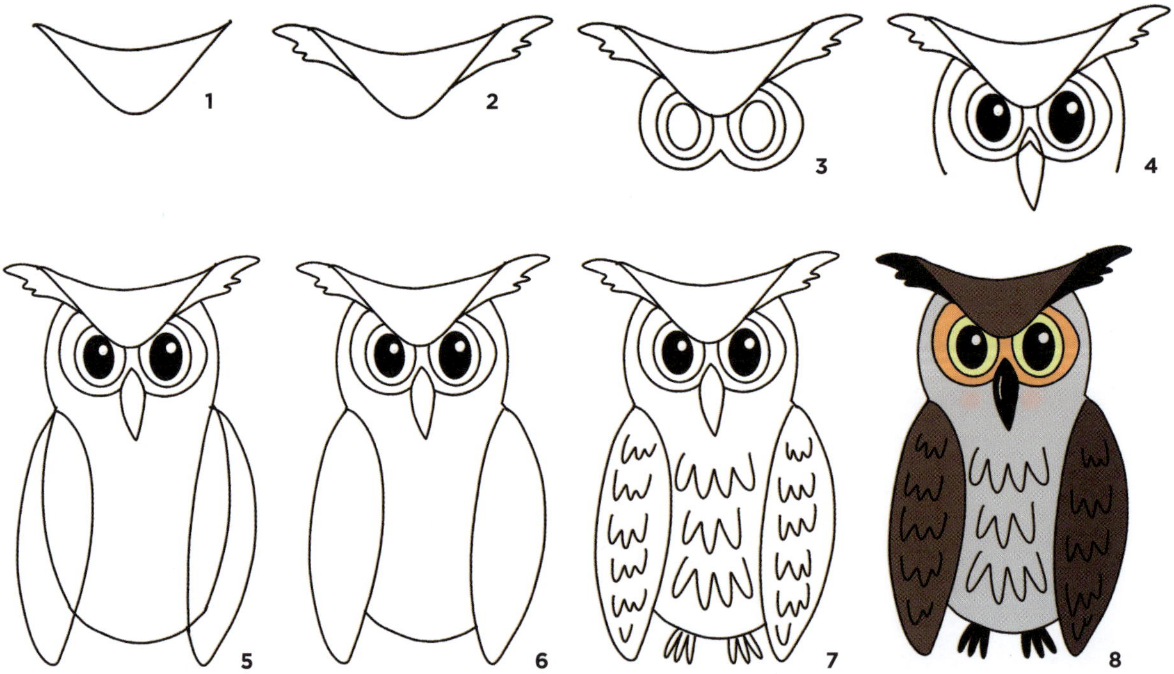

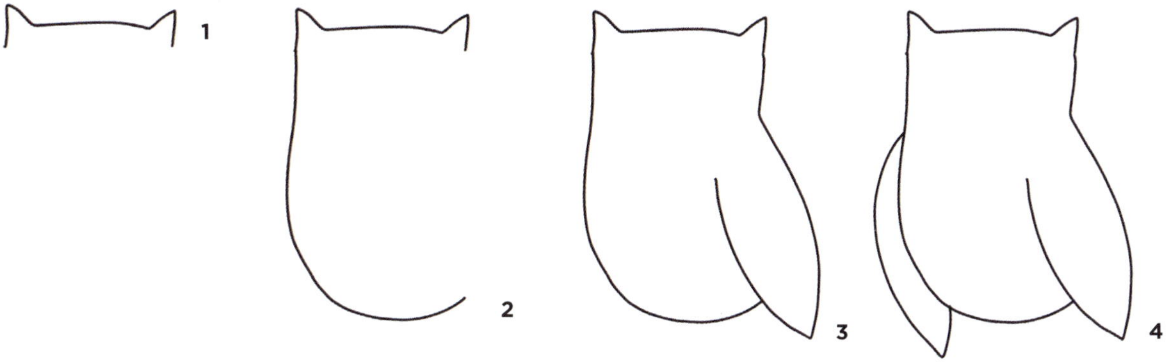

SCREECH OWL

Screech owls are typically between 7 and 10 inches (18 and 25 cm) in height with a wingspan of 18 to 24 inches (46 to 61 cm). One of the distinguishing characteristics of this type of owl is the prominent tufts of feathers on top of their heads. When a screech owl is frightened, it does its best impression of a tree branch, flattening its feathers, pointing its tufts and standing as tall as possible in the hopes that it will blend right into the tree.

To draw your owl, start with two points connected by a slightly curved line. Create the body shape and add a wing. Draw a second wing on the other side of the body and add a pair of large, round eyes. Draw a triangle beak and divide off the wing and top of the head from the rest of the body with a curving line. Add a pair of feet and draw a few scalloped lines on the chest area for a feathered texture. Finally, color your owl in any way you like.

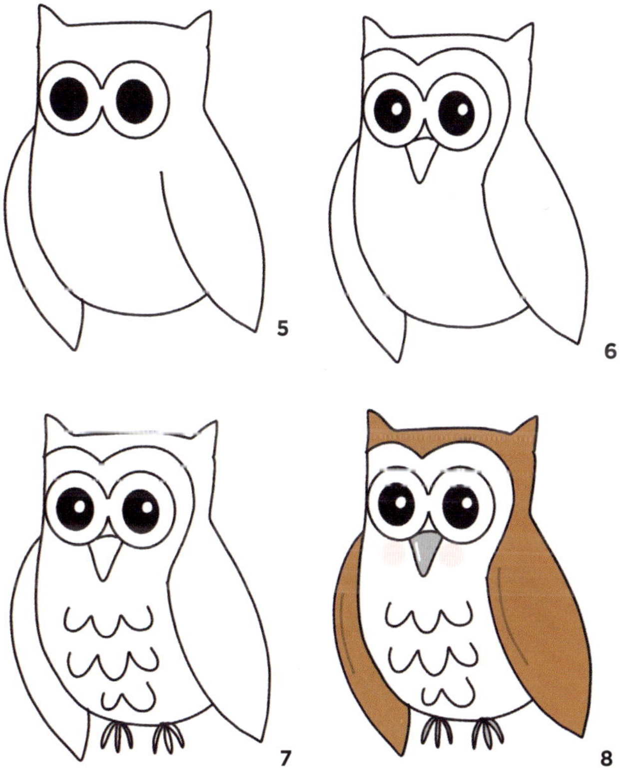

EAGLE

Not only are eagles among the largest birds on the planet, they're also one of the fastest, flying at 75 to 100 miles per hour (121 to 161 kph)! This flight can take place at altitudes as high as 15,000 feet (4,572 m) above the earth. An eagle's eyesight is about five times better than that of the average human, due to the fact that their eyes have 1,000,000 cones per square millimeter.

To draw an eagle, sketch a curving line for the head and add a smiling beak. Finish drawing the head and add zigzags in the neck area to create a feathered texture. Next, sketch a large wing and a curving line for the front of the body. Add a "u" shape below the body and a long three-ridged tail. Draw a leg and foot extending down from the "u" shape. Then, add another "u" shape, leg and foot next to the first one. Finally, add bumpy lines inside the wing for texture and divide the tail into three long sections. Give the eagle an eye and color your drawing, making the body brown, the legs, feet and beak yellow-orange and the head and tail white.

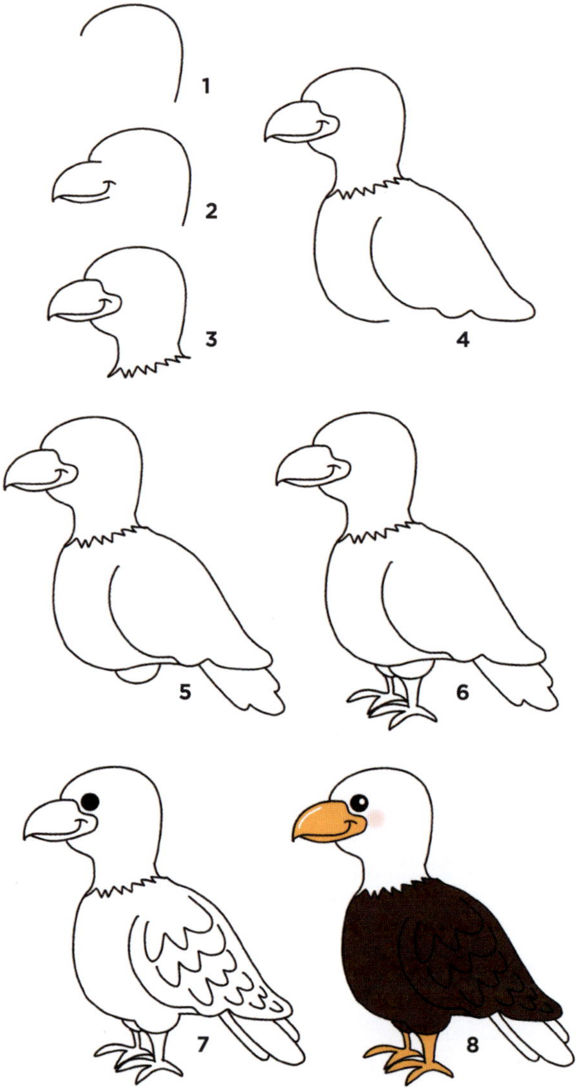

practice here

CARDINAL

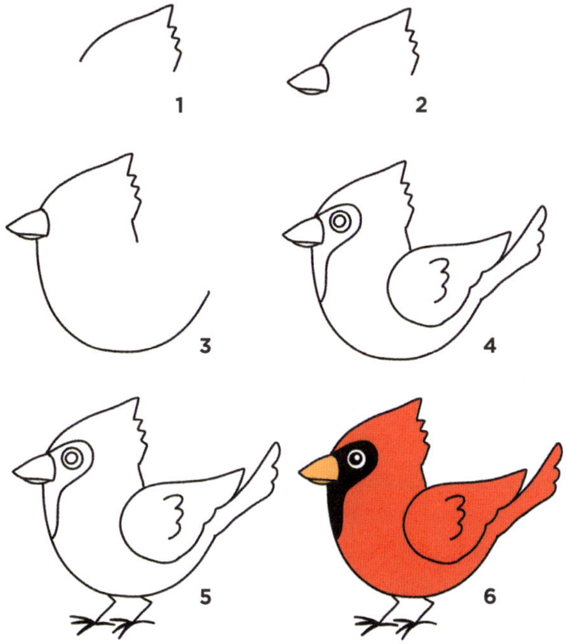

Both male and female cardinals sing, but only the males have the bright red bodies we associate with this type of bird. The females are actually a light brown color with red accents. The vivid red color comes from the carotenoid pigments in red berries and fruits a male cardinal eats. This bird gets its name from a reference to the bright red robes worn by clergy called cardinals in the Catholic church.

To draw your own cardinal, start by sketching the top of the head, which rises to a point, then add some zigzags to show the texture. Add a beak, then draw a semicircle for the lower body. Next, draw a wing. Sketch a long tail that extends upward. Give your bird an eye and divide the front of the head from the rest of the body. Draw some scallops in the wing for texture and add a pair of legs and feet. Finish your doodle by coloring your cardinal.

IN THE HABITAT

ACORN

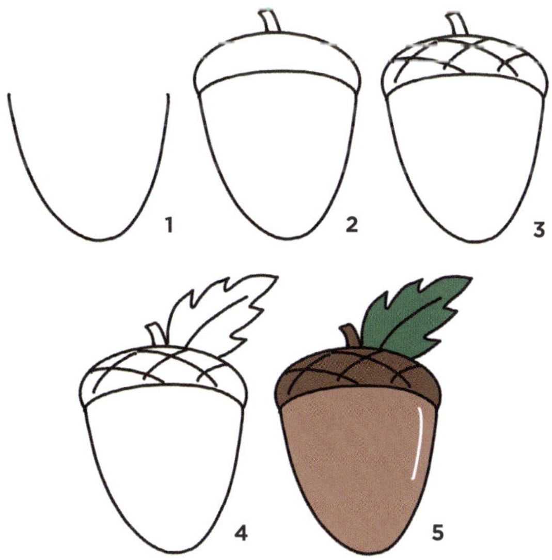

An acorn may seem small, but it can grow into a mighty oak tree. We often think of them as a squirrel's favorite snack, but many other animals feed on acorns as well, including birds, mice, pigs, bears and deer.

To draw an acorn, start with a "u" shape, then sketch a curving line to connect the ends. Draw another curving line to form the cap of the acorn and add a small stem on top. Add texture to the cap by sketching a crisscross pattern. If you like, draw a leaf next to the stem, then color your doodle.

PINE TREE

Many species of pine trees can live for hundreds of years. These evergreens have no flowers and no fruit; instead, they have pollen-filled pinecones, which produce seeds after pollination. Pine trees provide an ideal habitat for many species of birds and animals.

Start your pine tree doodle with an upside-down "v" shape. Add a wavy line on each side below the "v." Draw a set of diagonal lines underneath for the next layer, with wavy lines at the ends. Repeat two more times until your tree has four layers. The wavy line at the bottom should go all the way across, connecting your lines for the base of the tree. Add a small rectangle for the trunk, then color your tree.

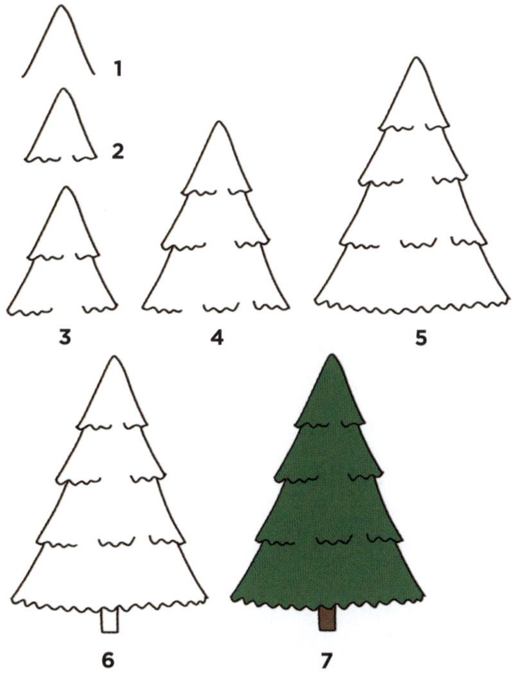

TREE STUMP

In the forest, not only will you find plenty of trees, you'll also come across stumps where all kinds of trees have fallen or been cut down. Since stumps are difficult and/or costly to remove, they're usually just left in place.

To doodle a tree stump, start with short lines that curve in opposite directions for the base. Sketch an oval shape on top, then add detail lines inside to represent the tree's rings. Next, draw a few roots below the stump. Add detail lines, then color your drawing.

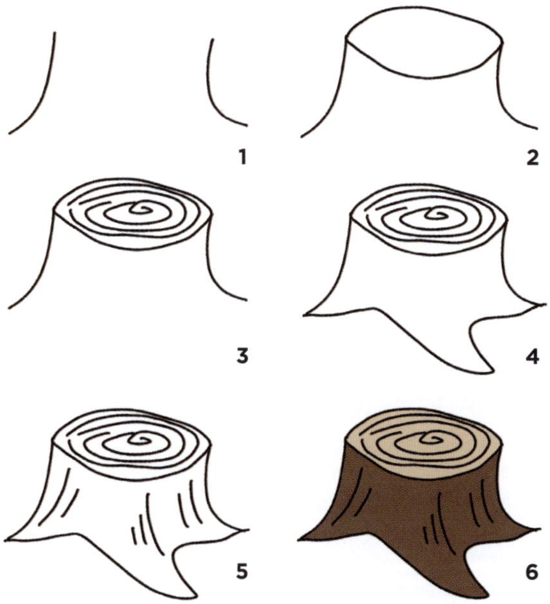

BAMBOO

Bamboo is the fastest-growing plant on Earth! It can actually grow 1½ inches (4 cm) in an hour, or more than 2 feet (1 m) per day! It's an eco-friendly wood alternative that's great for building structures, flooring, furniture, fencing, paneling and more. It's also a healthy snack that contains fiber, potassium, vitamins and other nutrients for both people and pandas.

To doodle bamboo, start with two vertical lines connected at the bottom by a very thin oval. Below it, draw another set of lines and an oval, repeating this pattern until your bamboo is as long as you'd like it to be. Next, connect the bottom set of lines and the top set. Finally, add several sets of thin, pointed leaves and color your drawing.

practice here

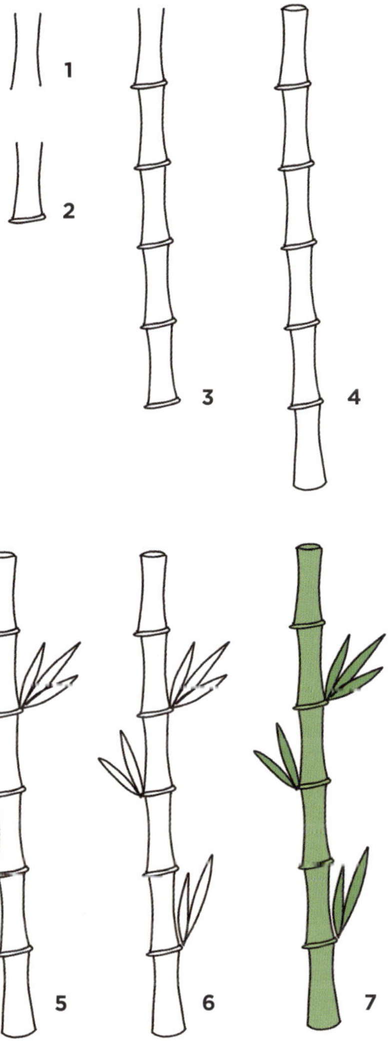

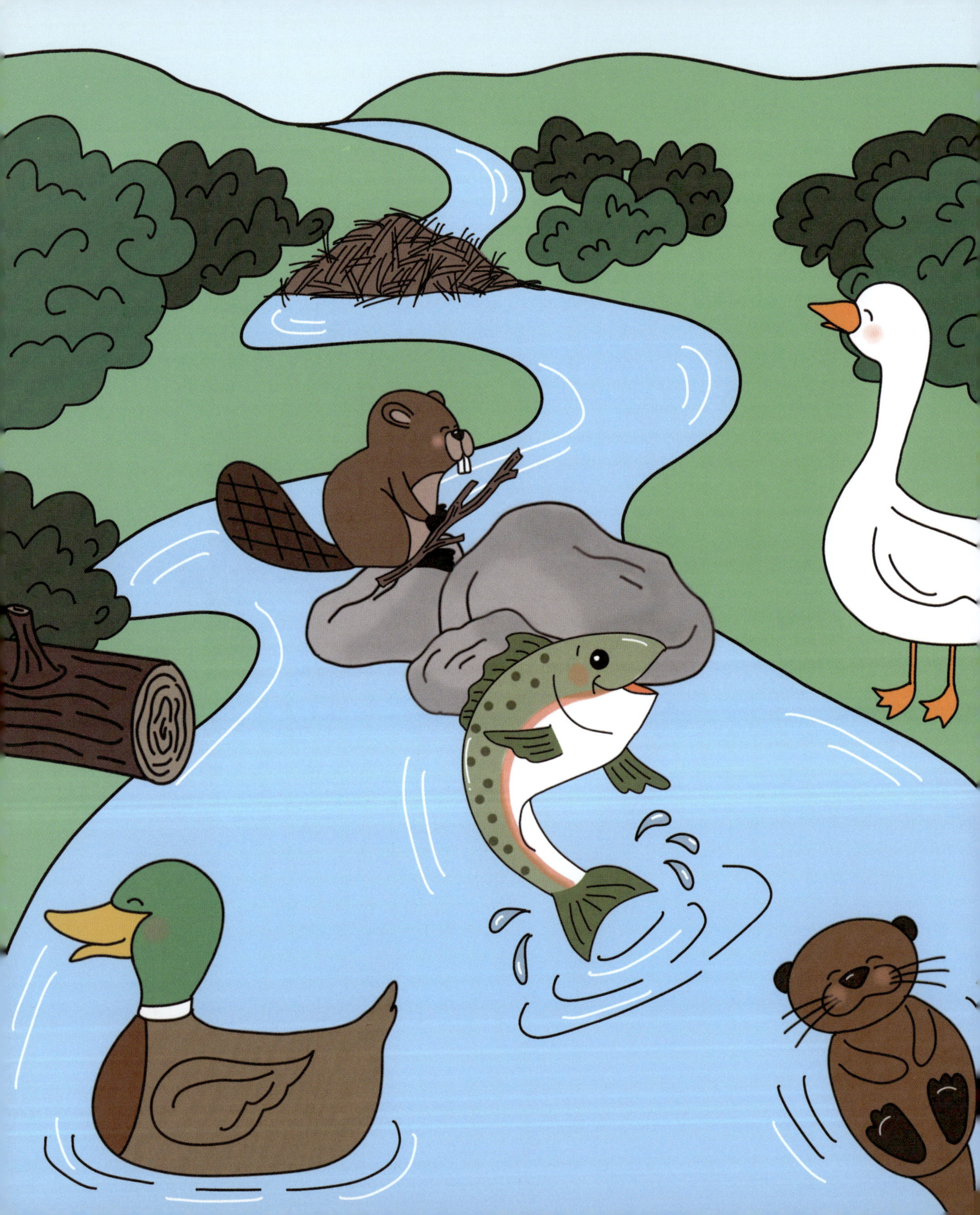

IN THE River & Lake

Water is necessary for the survival of humans and animals alike, but for some species, it's also home. Rivers and lakes are perfect habitats for many freshwater animals. Of course, you'll find fish in these waters, but there are also hundreds of species of mammals, amphibians and insects living in freshwater habitats. As we learn to draw some of them, we'll also doodle important facets of their ecosystems so that you can combine them with the animals to create your own unique scenes.

FROG

Frogs are cold-blooded amphibians that breathe through their skin. They require a habitat with freshwater and plenty of food for their carnivorous diet. Believe it or not, frogs do have teeth and they're also physically unable to swallow with their eyes open.

To draw a frog, start with an oval head that has two circles overlapping it on the top. Next, add a round body and curving lines on each side of the body to form legs. Draw a webbed foot at the base of each leg, with small circles for toes. Add short lines to show the bend in each leg, then add two more curving lines inside the body to form arms. Draw webbed hands with circles for fingers. Erase the spots where the arms and eyes overlap the frog's head and body. Add an upside-down "u" shape for the belly and smaller circles inside the eyes. Finally, draw a mouth shape with a semicircle tongue. Color your frog to make it pop off the page. I chose green and yellow for mine, but frogs can come in other colors too!

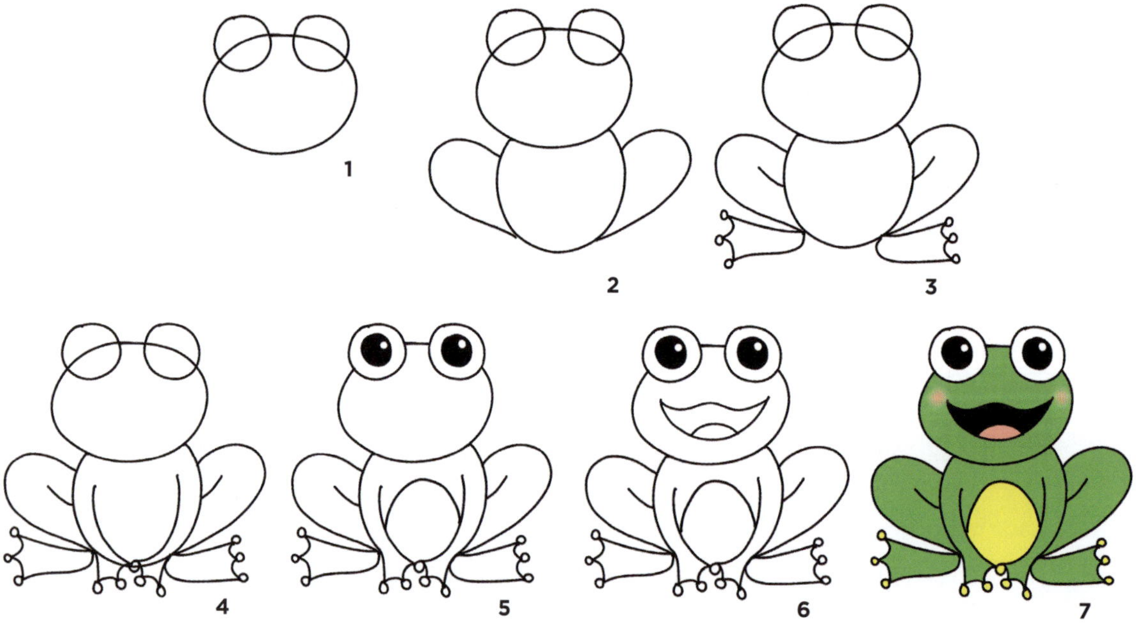

DRAGONFLY

Dragonflies are beautiful insects that can move each of their four wings independently, making them incredibly masterful flyers. They also have remarkable vision, thanks to two enormous eyes that have 28,000 lenses each. Dragonflies can see a broader color spectrum than humans and have nearly 360 degrees of vision. In fact, it takes about 80 percent of their brainpower to process everything they can see.

To draw a dragonfly, we'll start with a small, rounded head with a little semicircle and an oval body below it. Next, sketch a long, thin tail-like section, divided by a series of short horizontal lines, and sketch a pair of antennae. Draw four slightly rounded wings, two on each side of the body, then add angular lines for the dragonfly's legs. Finally, draw those giant eyes. Color your dragonfly in any way you like, and don't be afraid to blend several colors to make the wings really stand out.

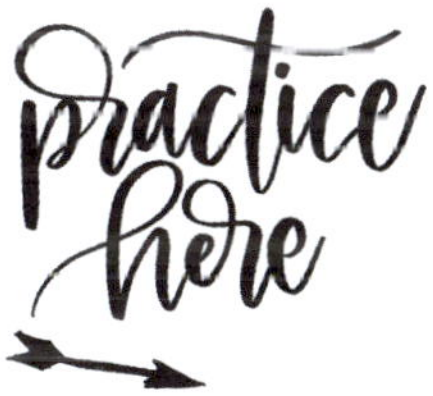

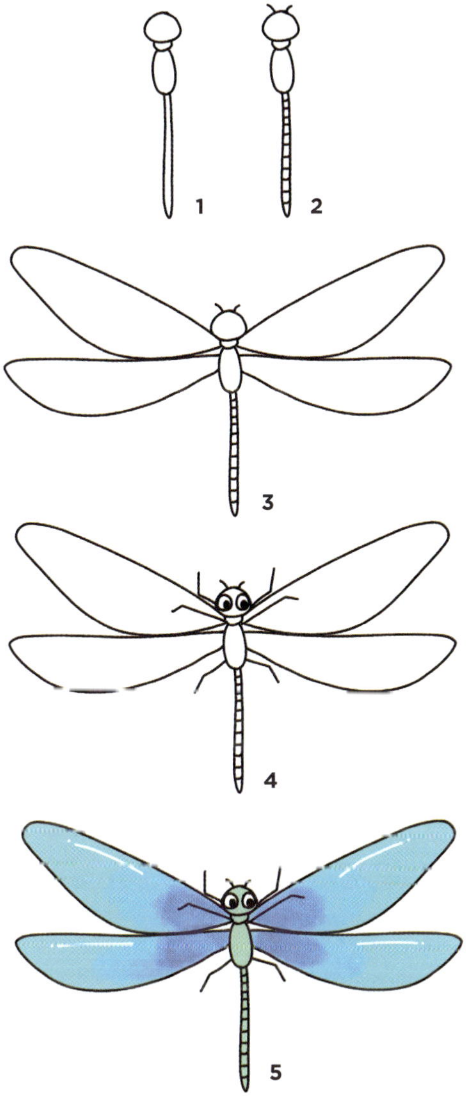

DUCK

Ducks are a type of waterfowl found in every region of the world except Antarctica. They rely on their waterproof feathers to keep them warm and dry. As ducks swim, their webbed feet work like paddles, propelling them through the water. We're going to doodle a mallard, but you can easily change the colors to represent one of the other 130-plus types of ducks in the world if you like.

To start this sketch, first make a curved line for the top and back of the duck's head. Next, add a long, sideways "v" shape for the top of the bill and a curving "v" shape to separate it from the head. Draw the lower part of the bill, then extend the head down and sketch a band around the neck. Form the duck's body and tail, then add a wing, wing detail lines, an eye and a curving line toward the front of the body. Color your duck using the mallard's signature look or any other colors you like.

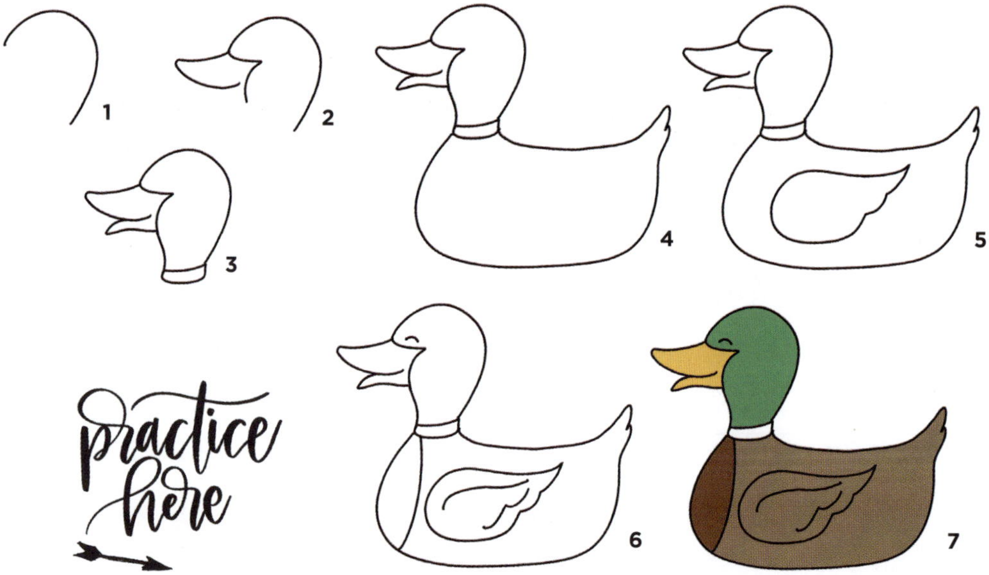

DUCKLING

During the first 12 to 36 hours of a duckling's life, it "imprints," which means it chooses one guardian (almost always its mother) to follow closely as it grows. The duckling will stick with its mother constantly, often walking in a straight line with its siblings as it learns where to find food, shelter and safety. Ducklings spend up to 70 percent of their early life eating, which is important, because they grow to their full adult size in just 90 days.

Start sketching your adorable duckling by making a small, "c"-shaped cheek with a semicircle around it for the head. Add a rounded triangle for the beak, then draw a curved line below the head for the base of the body. Then, sketch the top of the body and a small, rounded tail. Add a paisley-shaped wing and an eye to finish your doodle. Finally, color your little duckling.

Bonus: To help it swim, you can sketch a wavy oval shape around the base of the body with some detail lines to form a puddle or a lake.

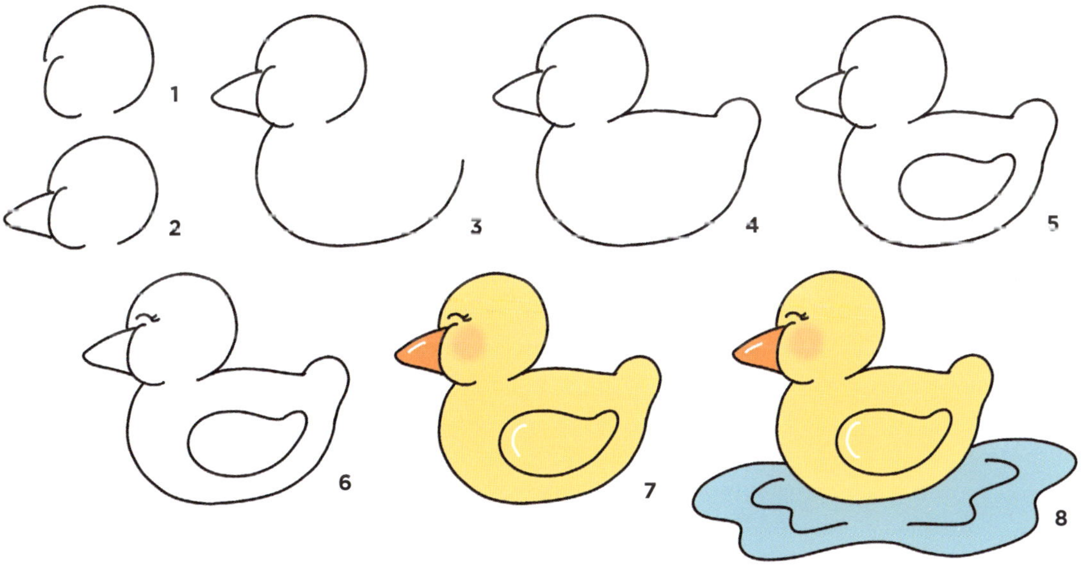

GOOSE

Geese are extremely social waterfowl that care for those in their family or group. When flying in their well-known "V" formation, if a goose gets sick or hurt, others will drop out of formation to protect it. Many geese mate for life and are very protective of their mates and children. There are different types of geese, so their appearance can range from the all-white snow goose to the distinctive black and gray pattern of the Canada goose. We will sketch the basic bird, then you can color it in whatever way you like best.

First, draw an upside-down "J" shape for the back of the head and neck, then draw a curving line to the right of it to form the rest of the neck, along with the bottom of the head and front of the body. Finish sketching the body shape with a tail that points downward. Add "v" shapes for the bill and draw a feathered wing inside the body. Draw two skinny legs with webbed feet and add accent lines to the body and wing. Finally, color your goose in any combination of white, brown, gray and black.

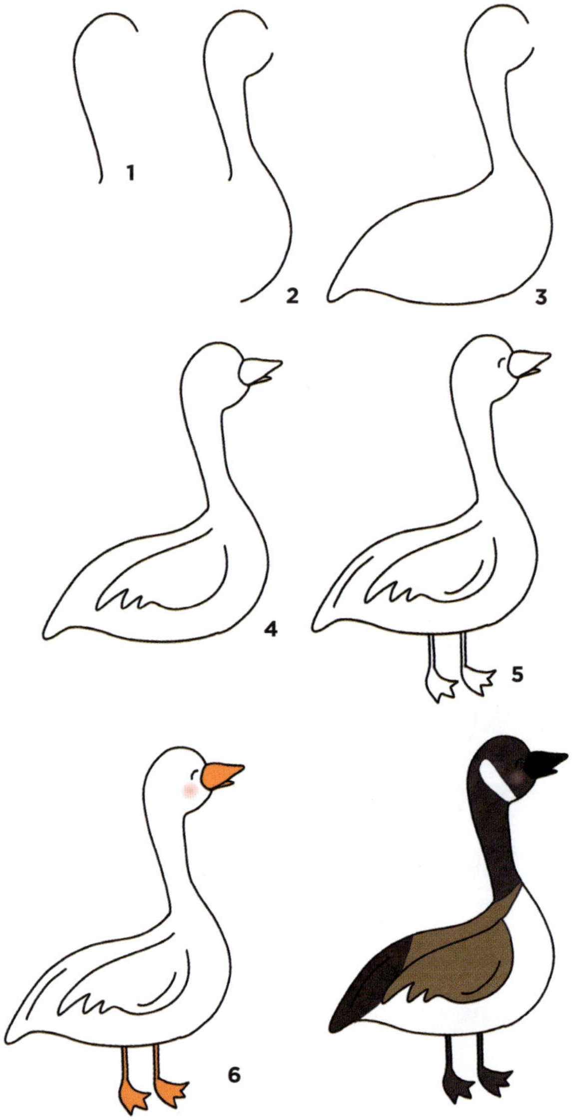

practice here

SWAN

Swans are known for their grace and beauty, as well as the fact that they mate for life. They're also highly intelligent and can fly as fast as 35 miles per hour (56 kph).

The first step in drawing a swan is to create an arc for its long, curved neck. Next, draw a backward "s" shape to finish the neck and form the front of the body. Add a "v"-shaped bill, along with a smaller "v" to divide it from the head. Next, sketch a wing with bumps to represent the feathers. Finish sketching the body shape, including a feathery tail. Finally, add an eye, the black area touching the beak and detail lines to show more feathers. Since swans are mostly white, you only need to color a few areas to complete your doodle.

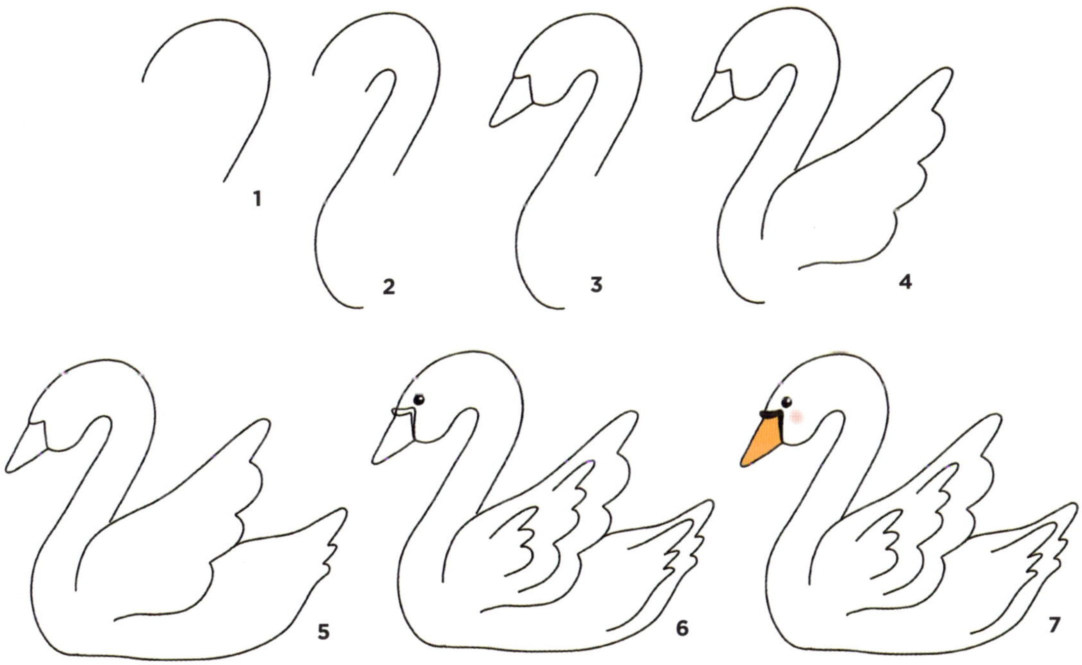

BEAVER

Beavers are famous for being very busy animals and for the dams they build, but did you know they also help give us the flavor of vanilla? Beavers secrete a compound called castoreum from sacs under their tails, which is a Food and Drug Administration-approved natural flavoring for food, as well as an ingredient in some perfumes.

Drawing this interesting mammal isn't as hard as it might seem. First, create a "3" shape for the head and back, then add a nose and snout. Next, draw a curving line for the neck and stomach and connect it to the back. Sketch a curving line for the leg, then add feet. Draw an arm and two little hands, followed by those well-known beaver teeth. Make a curving line to separate the stomach area from the rest of the body, then add eyes and small, rounded ears. Finally, draw the wide, flat tail with a checkerboard pattern. Color your beaver using different shades of brown, black and gray.

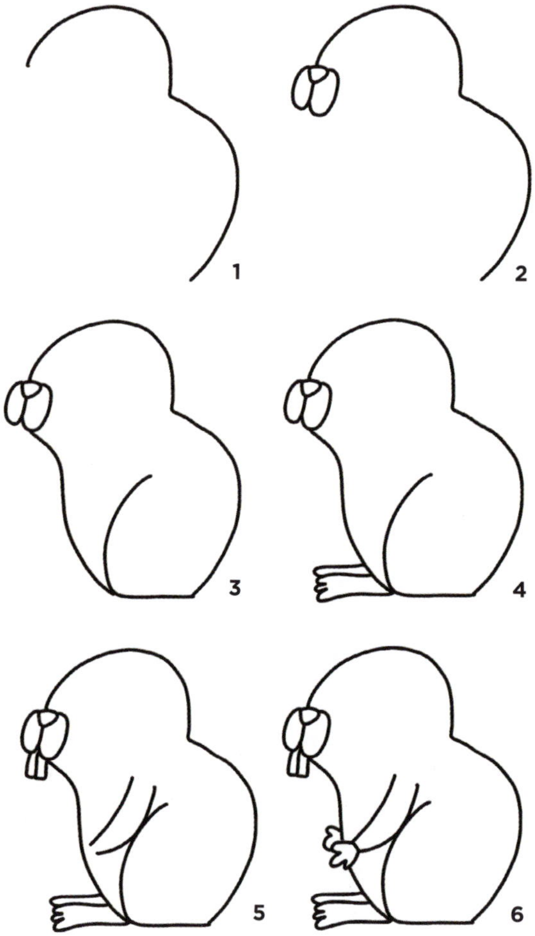

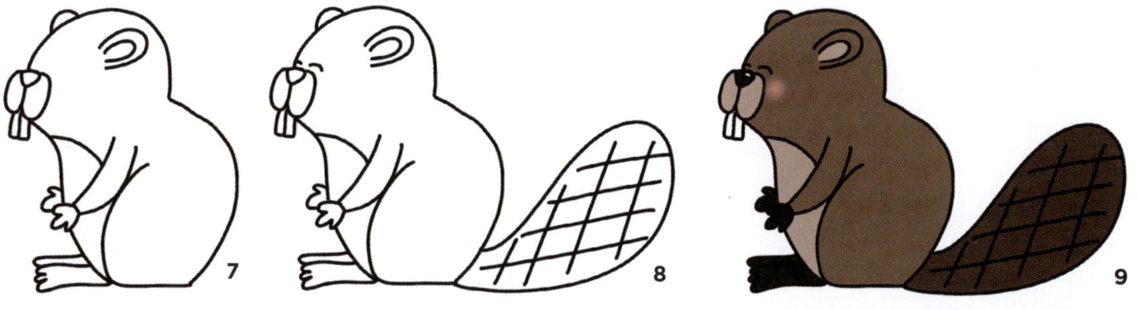

OTTER

While otters actually live in burrows close to a river's edge, these semiaquatic mammals spend the majority of their time in the water playing, searching for food and snoozing on their backs. Not only are they playful, otters are resourceful too. They're one of the few mammals that use tools; for example, they'll use rocks like hammers to break open hard-shelled prey. Did you know that an otter can dive up to 250 feet (76 m) and hold its breath for as long as eight minutes?

To draw this adorable river dweller, start by creating an oval-shaped head attached to another oval for the body. Add two little semicircles for ears, then sketch a pair of arms and feet inside the body oval. Next, add some personality with a cheerful face, including a rounded "w" for the snout, a pointed nose, eyes and whiskers and finally sketch the rounded, triangle-shaped tail. The last step is to bring your otter to life by adding color.

practice here

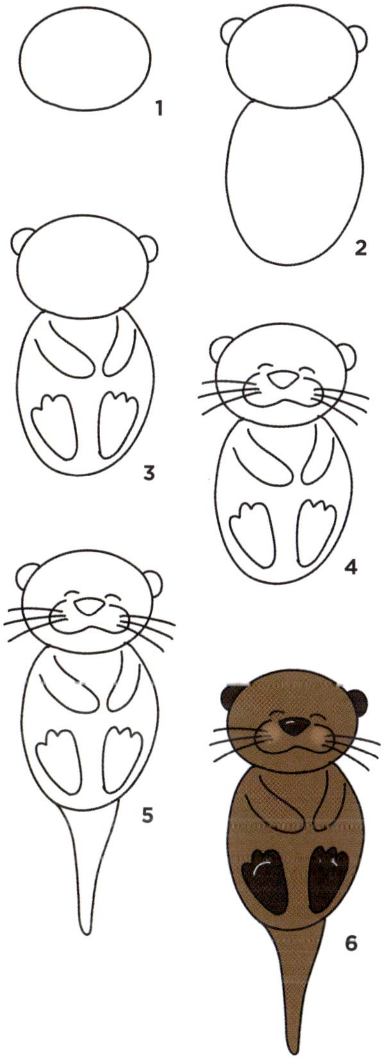

MUSKRAT

Muskrats are semiaquatic rodents that are named for their musky smell and their rat-like looks. They make homes by burrowing into the banks of bodies of water or pushing mud up from marshes. Muskrats are an invasive species in Europe, where they were introduced in the 20th century.

To doodle a muskrat, start with a rounded head and a curving line for the back of the body. Next, sketch a curving line for the leg and another for the front of the body. Add a foot at the base of the leg and a short arm with three fingers. Draw a second foot and arm, then add two small, rounded ears. Next, sketch a long, thick tail with a rounded point at the end. Finally, add an eye, a nose and whiskers. Color your muskrat brown with a lighter brown tail.

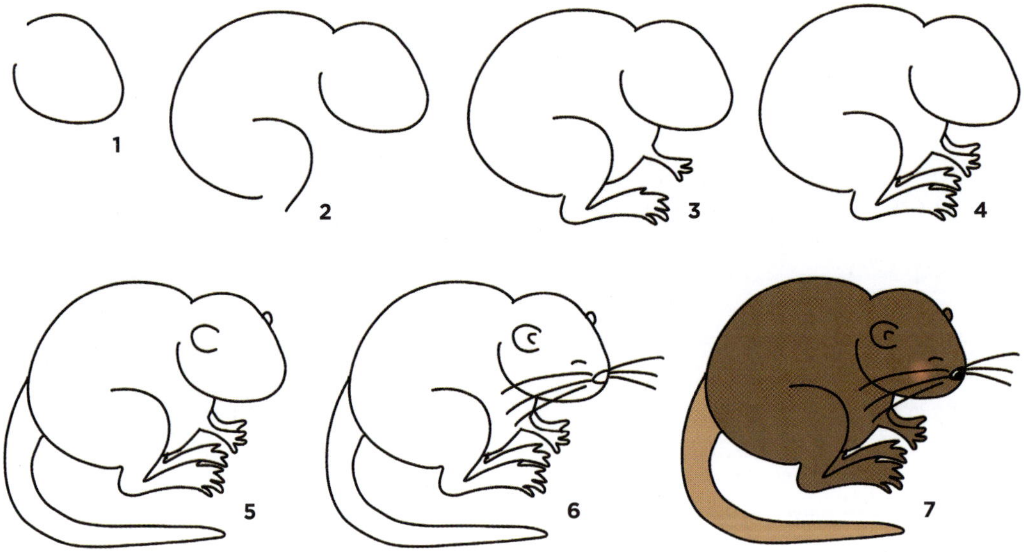

practice here

TROUT

One type of fish commonly found in rivers and lakes is trout. Depending on what environment trout live in, they take on very different colors and patterns because their appearance acts as camouflage to protect them from predators. We'll start by drawing a basic trout doodle, then color it in different ways.

First, sketch a backward "c" shape for the fish's body, then add two curving lines underneath for the base of the body and tail. Next, add fins on the top and sides of the body. Draw a "u"-shaped tail and add a smile. Finally, finish the mouth with a "v" shape and add details like an eye, an eyebrow and a gill. Now comes the fun part: using color to make your fish one of a kind. I used green, pink and white to simulate a rainbow trout. Another option to color your fish is using shades of blue, gray and brown for a lake trout. I also used my colors to add spots all over the trout's body. Feel free to experiment, blending colors and trying out different combinations.

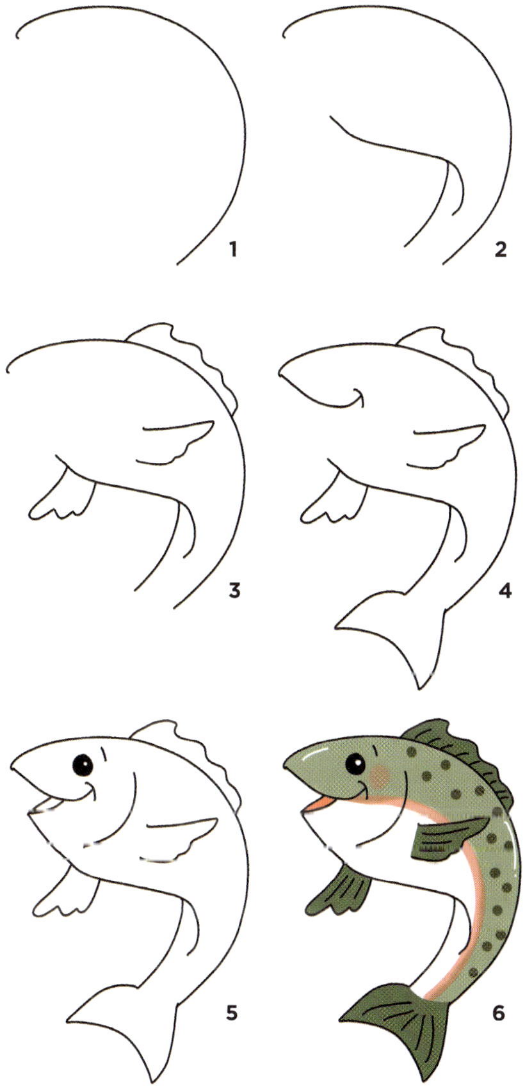

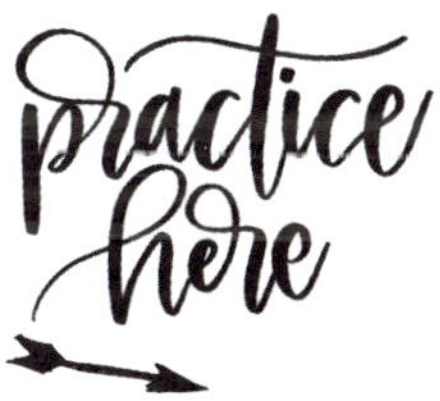

BLUEGILL

Another type of fish commonly found in freshwater is the bluegill. Also known as bream or copper nose, this species is known for its blue-colored gills and yellow-orange belly. Bluegills prefer shallow water and like hiding in aquatic plants and underwater logs.

To doodle this fish, start by sketching the main body shape, which is like a pair of parentheses turned sideways. Add a smile on one end and two lines to form the tail section on the other end. Sketch a zigzag line that ends with a rounded bump for the dorsal fin on top of the body, along with two little fins on the underside. Add another fin inside the body, along with a curving line for the gill. Draw the rest of the tail, add an eye and fill in the fins with detail lines. The final step is to color your fish using shades of blue, green, orange and yellow.

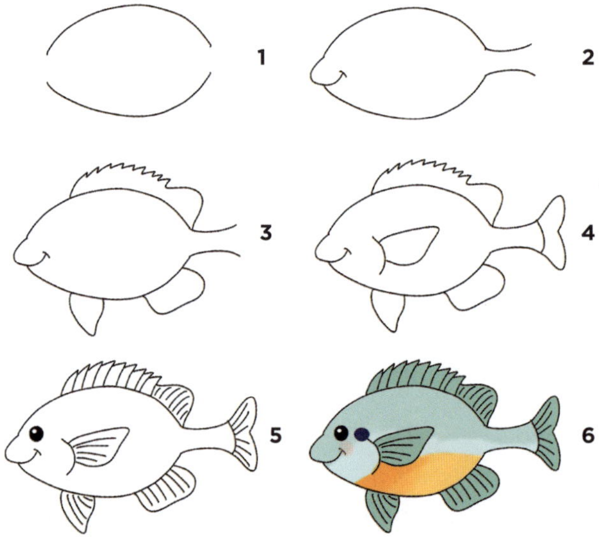

AXOLOTL

One of the most fascinating aquatic creatures is the axolotl, which is now only found in the wild in Lake Xochimilco, an ancient lake in southern Mexico City. Unlike other amphibians, the axolotl never undergoes metamorphosis, keeping juvenile characteristics all of its life. Axolotls are of great interest for scientific study, because they can actually regenerate parts of their bodies, regrowing a limb without even a scar!

To draw this amazing animal, start with a rounded head that has three elongated gills on either side. Add an oval body and a long, wavy tail with a pointed end. Sketch basic shapes of arms and legs inside the body area. Finally, draw a face with large eyes and an open mouth and sketch a curving "v" shape inside the tail. Color your axolotl to bring it to life.

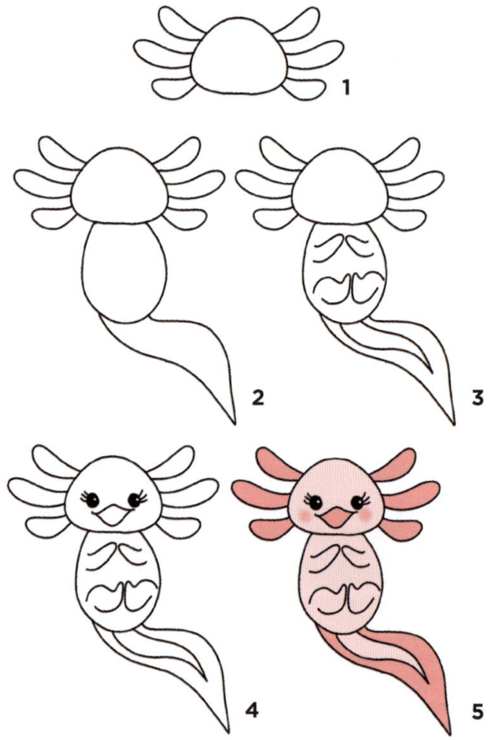

IN THE HABITAT

BRANCH/STICK

Fallen branches are essential for many river animals to construct their shelters. These branches might be found on the banks, in the water or even in the hands of a busy beaver.

Start by drawing two slightly wavy lines with a bit of space in between them. This forms the main part of the branch. Next, sketch a few rectangular shapes coming off either side and erase the marks where the smaller sections join the center one. Close off the top and bottom of the branch with short lines, then add texture by drawing short detail lines and dots. Finally, color your branch in a shade of brown. To create larger or smaller branches, just change the amount of space in between your original lines. More space creates a bigger branch, while lines that are very close together will give you a twig.

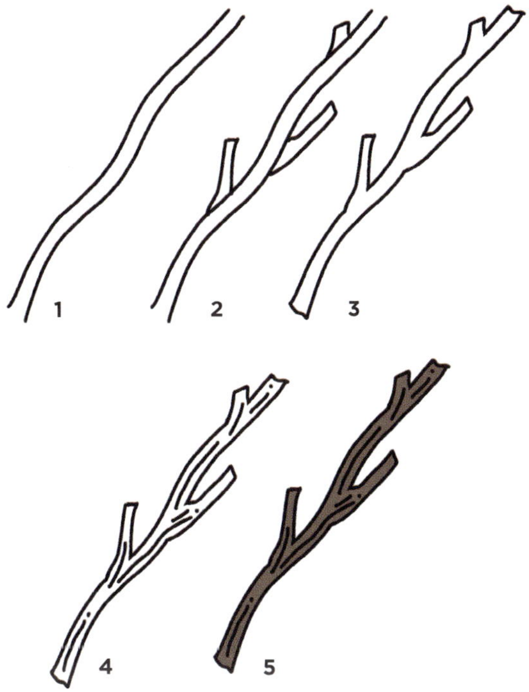

BUSH

Bushes are a great addition to a river or lake scene, as they add color and texture to the area around the water.

Sketching a bush is very easy. All you have to do is make a round or an oval-like shape with bumps all around the outside. Just as there are all sizes and shapes of bushes in nature, you can do the same with your doodles. Once you have the outline drawn, add some small, bumpy lines on the inside of the shape to represent leaves and show texture. Finally, color your bushes in any way you like.

Bonus: Draw and overlap several bushes to give your scene some extra depth.

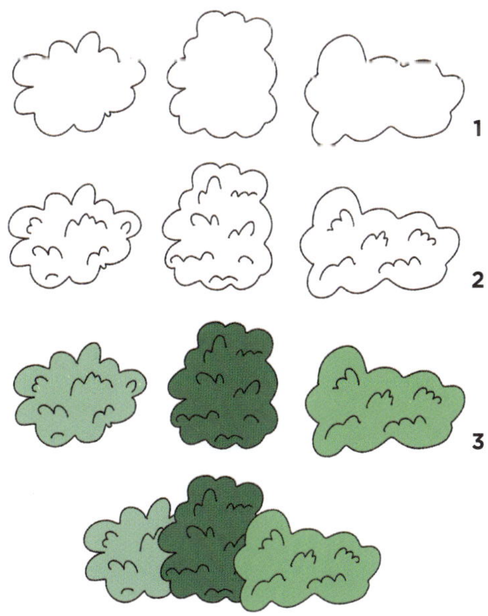

DAM

Fortunately for us, it takes a lot less time to doodle a dam than it takes beavers to build one.

Start by drawing a slightly wavy hill shape with a line underneath for the base. Next, draw pairs of lines going in all directions inside the shape to create the illusion that the dam is created by a pile of sticks. Keep adding more lines until your shape is full. Finally, color it brown. To add it to a river scene, you'll want to choose a spot and draw the dam across the entire expanse of the water at that point. And, of course, don't forget to doodle a busy beaver nearby!

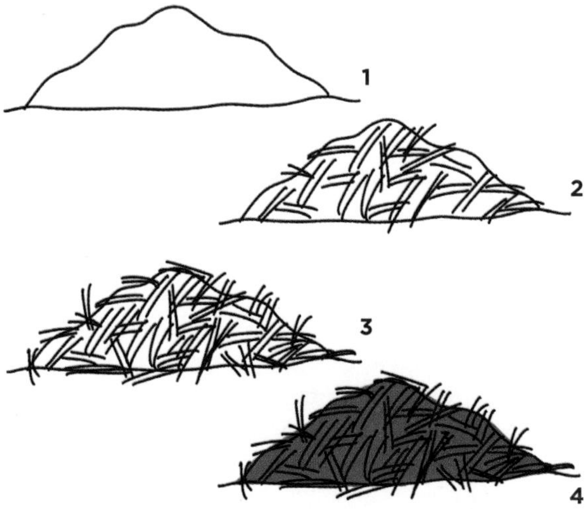

LOG

Like branches, logs are commonly found in areas where there's freshwater.

To draw one, start by sketching two horizontal lines with space in between them. Next, draw an oval on one end and a curved line on the other to connect the lines. Make two short lines that curve in opposite directions about halfway down the log to indicate a cut branch. Erase the overlapping line, then draw a "c" shape where this branch meets the rest of the log. Finally, add texture by doodling wavy lines all over the surface of the wood, including rounded ones inside the oval. Color your log brown, making the cut surface a lighter shade.

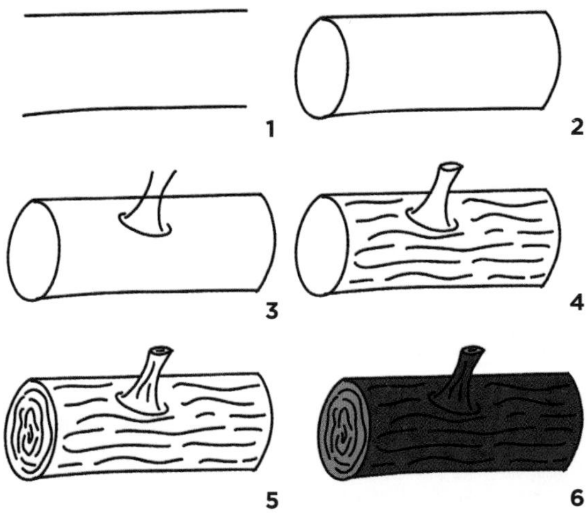

RIVER

If you want to draw your animals in their habitat, you'll need to start by creating a river.

First, sketch a wavy line to represent a hilly area in the distance. Then, draw a curving line coming down from the center of the hills. You can make the line curve as much or as little as you like, depending on how straight you want your river's path to be. Then, draw a second curving line that starts in the same spot but gradually gets farther apart from the first line as you go. This gives the perspective that the river starts far away, then gets closer to you at the bottom. Color your grass and river areas, then add curving highlight lines in the water with a white gel pen to show its movement.

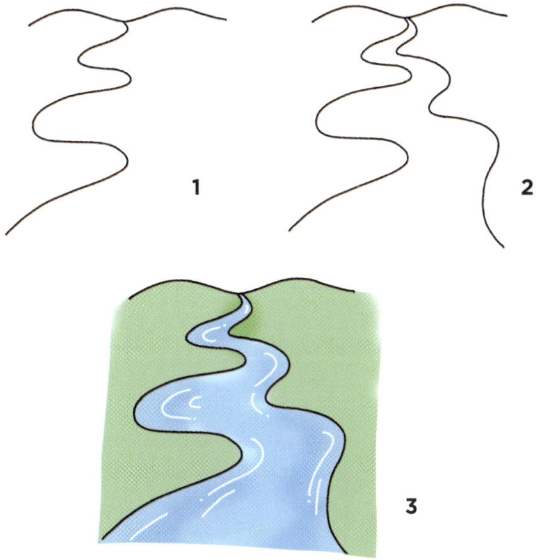

ROCK

Rocks of all sizes are commonly found in and around the water.

Drawing a rock may be the easiest doodle there is, because all you have to do is create a very imperfect shape. In nature, every rock is totally unique, so yours can be the same way. Start by sketching any shape you like, playing around with making some areas higher or lower than others for variety. Then, add a few detail lines on the inside to show texture. Finally, color your rock in shades of gray or brown. For extra detail, you can shade certain areas darker than others. Just like with the bushes, layering a few rocks in front of each other will give your drawing some dimension.

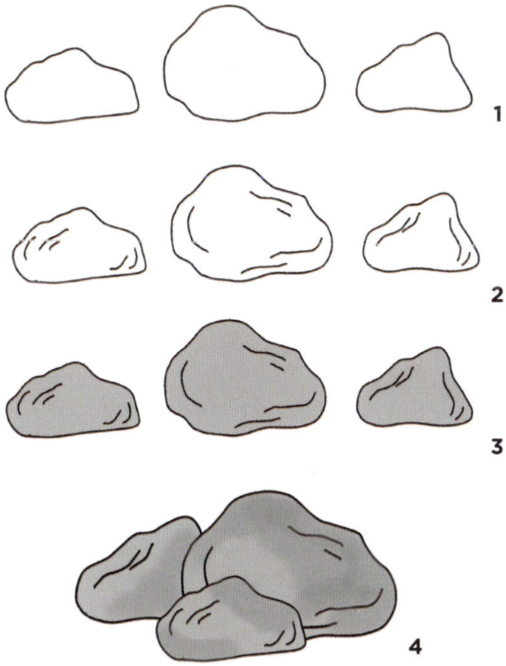

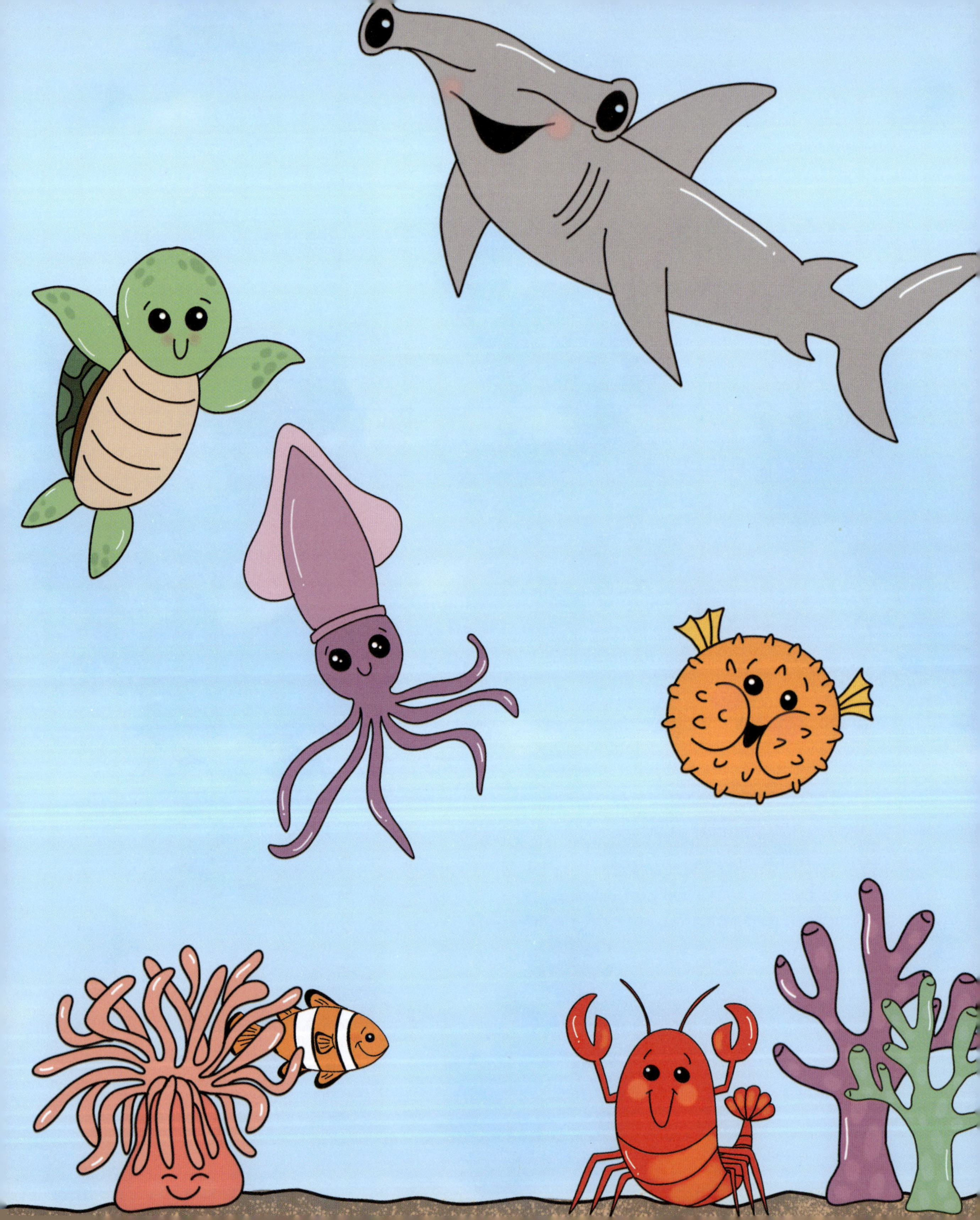

IN THE Ocean

A whopping 70 percent of the Earth's surface is covered by the ocean, which contains more than 96 percent of the planet's water. Although we divide it into distinct regions—the Atlantic, Pacific, Indian, Arctic and Southern—the ocean is really one continuous body of salt water. The ocean plays an essential role in the planet's weather and climate, and it also produces about 70 percent of the oxygen on Earth. Many types of animals make their homes in the ocean, including the world's largest living structure, the Great Barrier Reef. Let's take a closer look at some of these animals and learn to draw them in their habitat.

ANGELFISH

Did you know that angelfish get their name from their shape? If you turn this fish sideways, the shape resembles the head, wings and dress of an angel! Marine angelfish can be found in warm saltwater habitats like coral reefs. There are also freshwater species of angelfish that live in the Amazon River Basin. Angelfish can be a variety of colors and patterns, but all have thin, flat bodies that allow them to easily navigate through small spaces.

The first step in drawing an angelfish is to sketch two curving lines for the top and bottom of the body. Next, connect the lines at one end to form a smiling mouth. On the other end, draw a "U"-shaped tail with a scalloped edge. Add a large fin to the top of the body, with a wavy edge. Draw another large, wavy fin on the bottom of the body. Add two long, very thin fins below the mouth. Erase the lines where the large fins meet the body, then draw an eye. Sketch new lines to define the back area of the body from the back of the fins. Draw a series of stripes on the main part of the body and the area connecting the body to the tail. Add an eyebrow and detail lines on the edges of the fins. Color your angelfish in any way you like to complete your doodle.

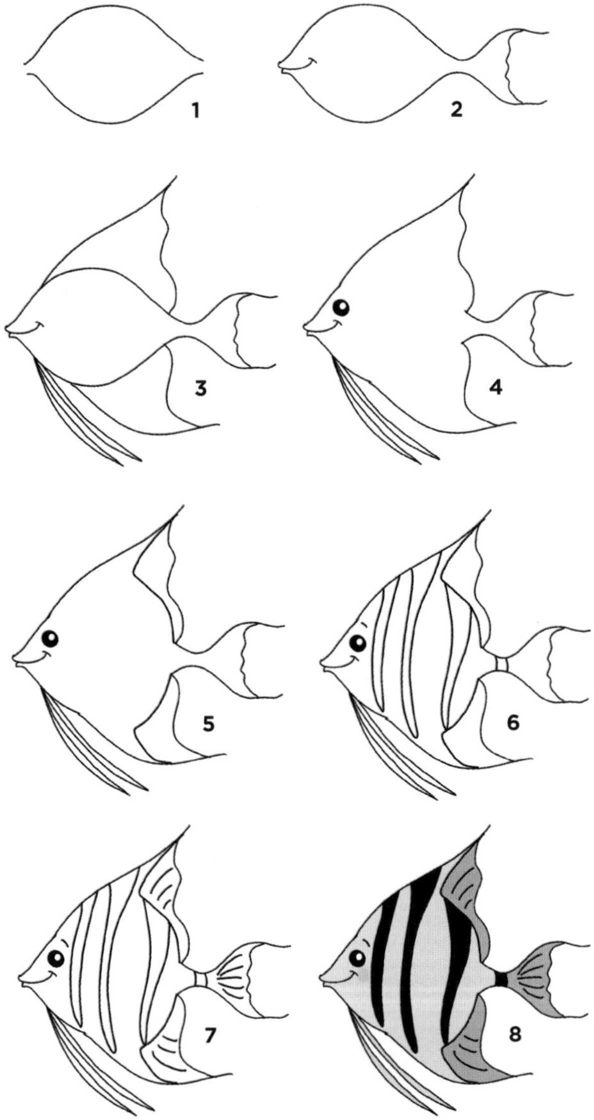

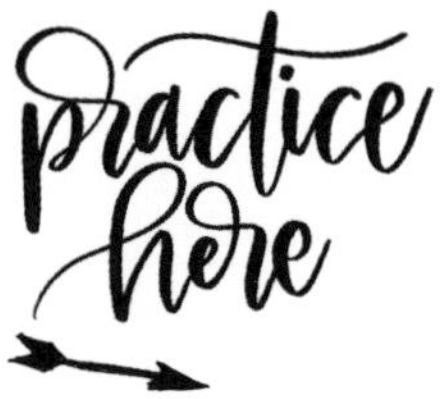

CLOWNFISH

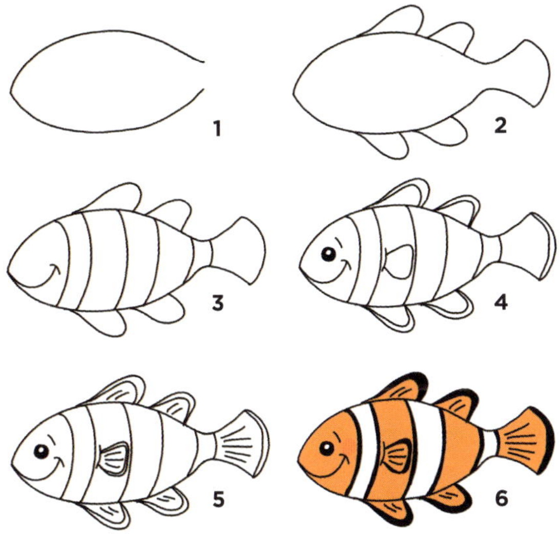

Clownfish are also known as anemonefish, because they have a symbiotic relationship with sea anemones. They aren't strong swimmers, so they stay close to the anemone for protection. In return, the clownfish clean the anemones, get rid of parasites and attract prey with their bright colors.

To draw this fish, start with the basic body shape, then add a short, rounded tail and four fins. Next, give your fish a smile and add curving lines to form three stripes on the body. Add an eye and an eyebrow, a tiny fin on the side of the body and detail lines on the fins. Finally, color your clownfish orange, leaving the stripes white.

BUTTERFLY FISH

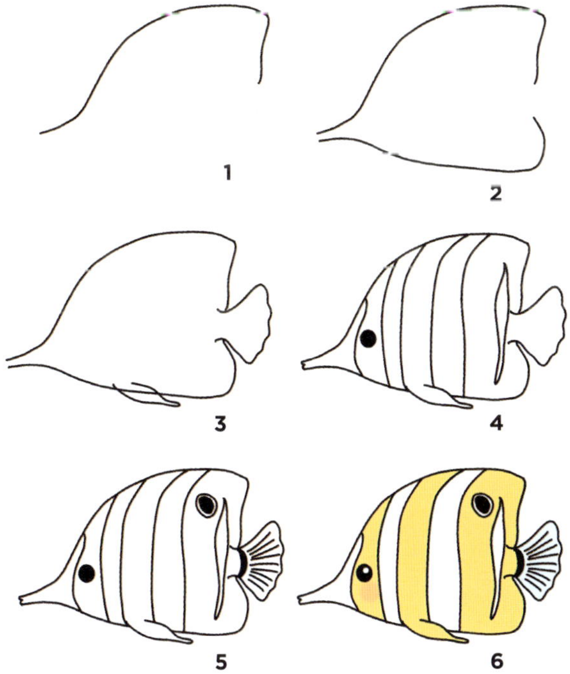

Butterfly fish are small, brightly colored and patterned fish with thin, disk-shaped bodies. They also have extended snouts that allow them to feed inside cracks and holes. There are more than 110 species of this tropical fish, which are found on coral reefs. Many butterfly fish have large spots called ocelli on their bodies that can be mistaken for eyes to confuse predators.

The first step in sketching a butterfly fish is to draw a line for the top of the snout that extends up, creating the dorsal fin. Next, draw the bottom of the snout, along with the bottom of the basic body shape. Add a scalloped tail, as well as a small lower fin. Create a pattern of stripes on the body and draw an eye, as well as a large black ocellus spot. Add detail lines to the tail, then use bright hues to color your fish drawing.

BLUE TANG

Did you know that young blue tang fish are actually yellow? It's only after they reach adulthood that these fish take on the distinctive color pattern with a bright blue body, dark accents and a yellow tail. An adult blue tang can change its color slightly depending on its mood; for example, when it's stressed, it will become a darker, more violet hue. Blue tangs are social fish that play an important role in the coral reef. They eat algae and plankton off of the coral, keeping the coral from suffocating.

Draw the body shape of your fish first, with two arches to form the top and bottom. Add a smiling mouth in between the arches. Next, draw a triangular-shaped tail with a smaller triangle inside. Sketch two lower fins and an eye. Add hook-shaped detailing from the eye to the tail and back around. Draw a small fin on the side of the body and divide the end section from the rest of the fin. Add short detail lines on the top and bottom fins, then color your drawing. The body should be a bright shade of blue, with dark blue or black accents and yellow inside the tail and side fin.

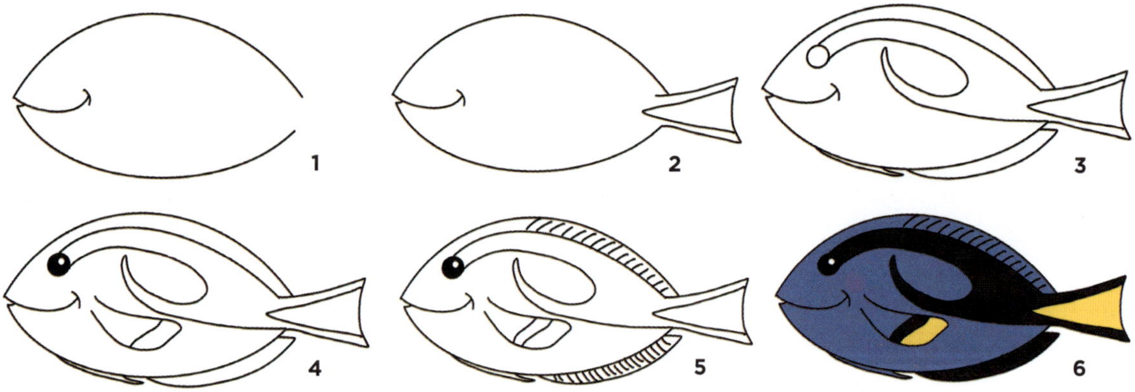

practice here

PUFFER FISH

When a puffer fish feels threatened, it can expand to twice its original size by quickly gulping water into its elastic stomach. Puffing up also makes its spines stand on end, which hopefully deters the predator, because it's impossible for a pufferfish to swim while inflated. Most puffer fish also contain TTX, a lethal neurotoxin, making them some of the most toxic vertebrates in the world to humans.

To draw a puffer fish, start with a circle, then add two "c" shapes inside for puffy cheeks. Add two small fins near the top of the circle, then draw a face. Finally, sketch lots of small "u" shapes all over the circle. Erase any areas where these overlap other lines. Then, color in your fish. There are 193 species of puffer fish that are a huge variety of colors, so feel free to choose your favorite

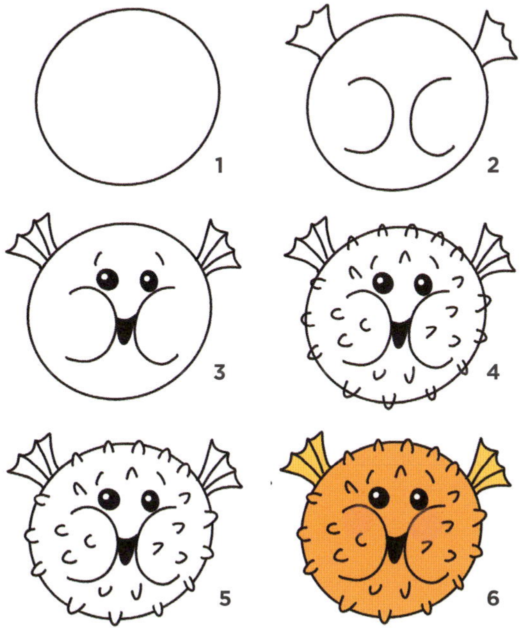

BLOBFISH

Unfortunately for the blobfish, it's commonly referred to as the ugliest animal in the world. While underwater, this deep-sea creature looks like a normal fish, but on dry land, the decompression causes it to become deformed and resemble a gelatinous blob, particularly since it has soft bones and few muscles.

Drawing a blobfish is simple, because you start with an imperfect shape that's rounded on the top and flat on the bottom. Draw a frown, then outline it with a shape that looks like a hot dog. Make a large, round nose that overlaps the center of the mouth. Add an eye on either side of the nose and a small set of fins, one on each side of the body. Color your blobfish in shades of pink or gray.

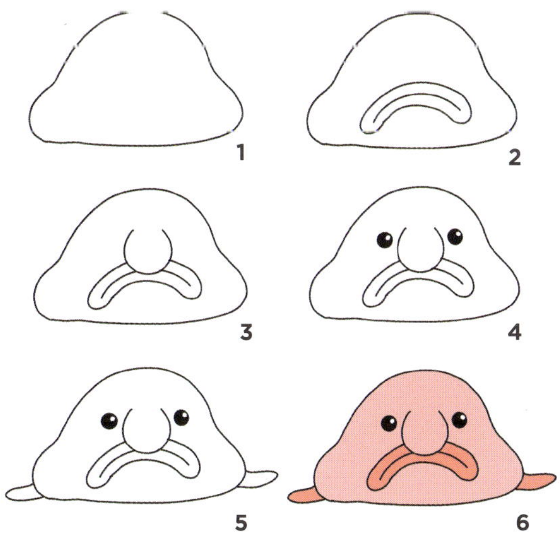

WHALE

Whales are the largest of all animals on earth. They're warm-blooded marine mammals that breathe air and even grow hair on their bodies. Rather than laying eggs, they give birth to live young and produce milk to feed their babies.

To doodle a basic whale, start with an arc that curves upward on one side. Sketch a large smile, then add a line for the whale's lower body. Give your whale a tail that divides into two pointed ends. Add a small fin and a pair of eyes. If you like, you can add details like water droplets over the top of the head and spots on the head or body. Color your whale blue, gray or any other color you prefer.

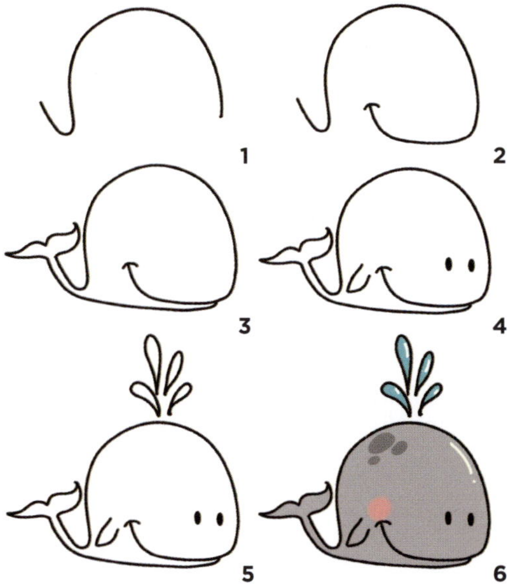

SHARK

A shark's body is made of cartilage, like our ears and the tips of our noses; they actually have no bones! Their skin feels like sandpaper because it's made up of tiny scales that help reduce friction in the water so they can swim as smoothly as possible. If sudden, intense pressure is applied on a shark, it will go into a state called tonic immobility, which is like a trance, allowing scientists and doctors to safely touch and interact with it.

To draw a shark, start with the basic body shape, which is similar to a football, with a curving line on the left side. Add the dorsal fin and a tail. Next, add two more fins and a line to divide the upper and lower parts of the body. Finally, add gills and a face, then color your shark.

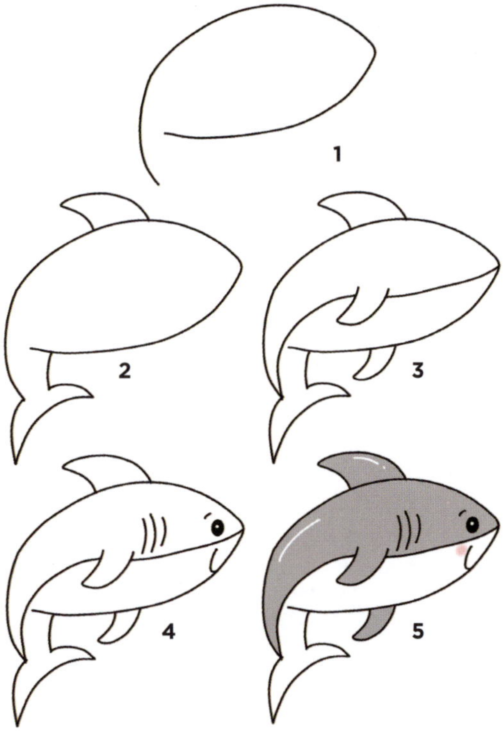

BOTTLENOSE DOLPHIN

Bottlenose dolphins are incredibly intelligent and social creatures, and they're also awesome acrobats. They communicate with each other with squeaks and whistles, as well as body language, and they use a special process of clicking and listening for an echo (echolocation) to find food. We're going to draw our dolphin in the middle of a trick, balancing a ball on its nose.

First, sketch the nose and underside of the body. Then, make a curved line for the head and back. Add three fins and a tail. Give your dolphin an eye and draw a line separating the underside of the body from the rest. Finally, add a ball on top. Color your dolphin and the ball in any way you like.

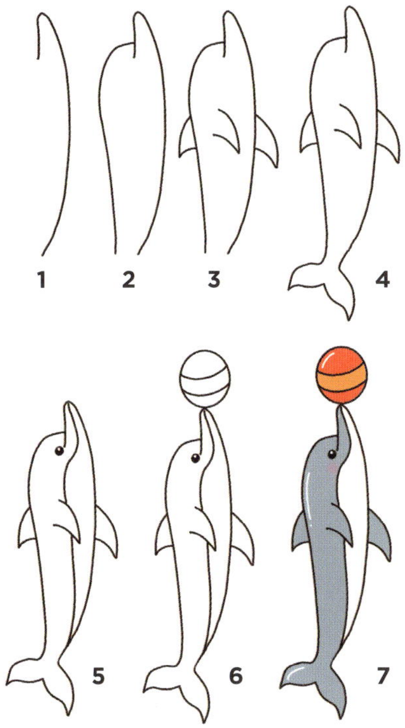

MANATEE

Manatees weigh about 1,000 pounds (454 kg) and eat between 7 to 15 percent of their body weight every day. That means the average manatee spends seven hours a day eating about 150 pounds (68 kg) of food! Mama manatees and their calves stay together for two to four years and form a strong bond.

To draw a manatee, we'll start with the head, which is an upside-down "u" shape and a backward "3" shape put together. Next, we'll sketch the back and lower portion of the large body and add a tail. Draw a flipper on each side of the body (erasing the overlapping line), then add a cheerful face. Finally, add a few detail lines and color your manatee gray.

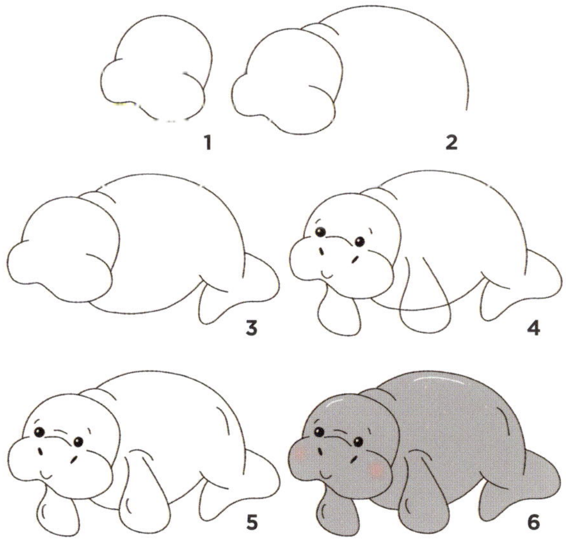

HAMMERHEAD SHARK

Hammerhead sharks use the hammer parts of their heads, called the cephalofoil, for hunting down their prey. Although they have no natural predators, these sharks are actually rather shy and can become frightened by sudden movements, lights and sounds. Almost all species of hammerhead sharks are critically endangered due to human activity.

The first step in drawing one is to make a slightly wavy horizontal line with a "c" shape on each side for the hammer. Then, sketch the main part of the body. Add the dorsal fin on top, along with two other fins and a tail. Then, draw two more fins and add curved lines for the shark's gills. Erase the overlapping line, then draw an eye on each side of the "hammer" and a smile (or whatever type of mouth you choose). Finally, color your shark and add a few highlight lines with a white gel pen.

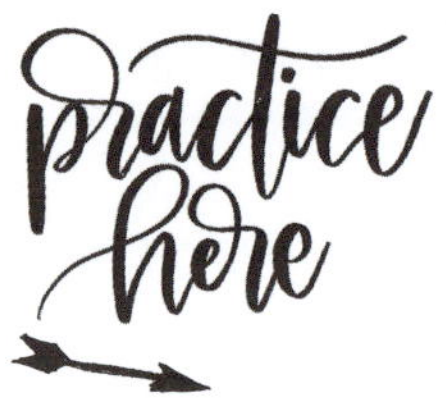

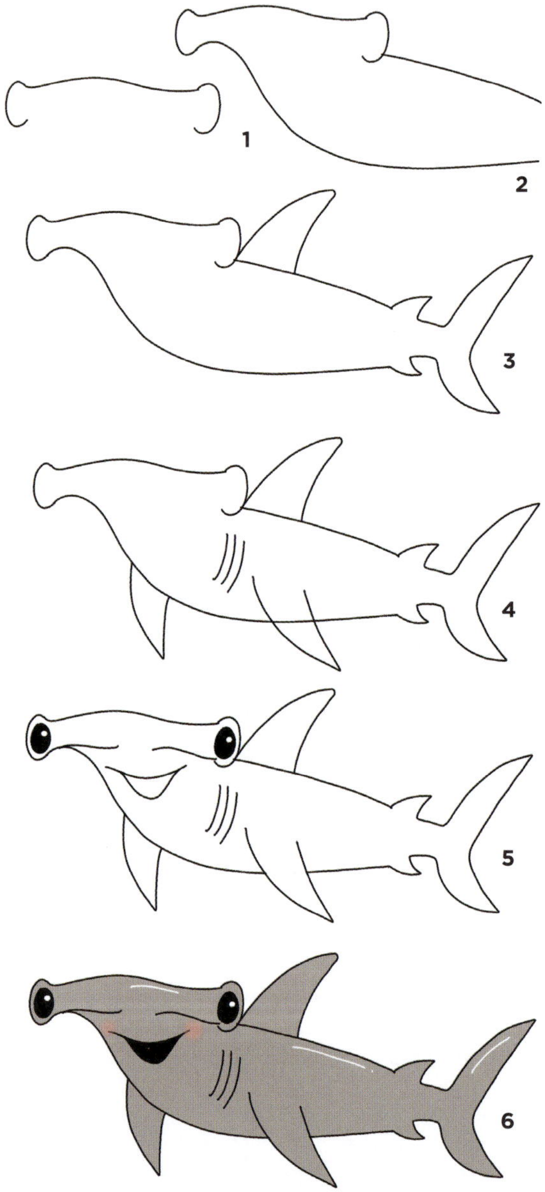

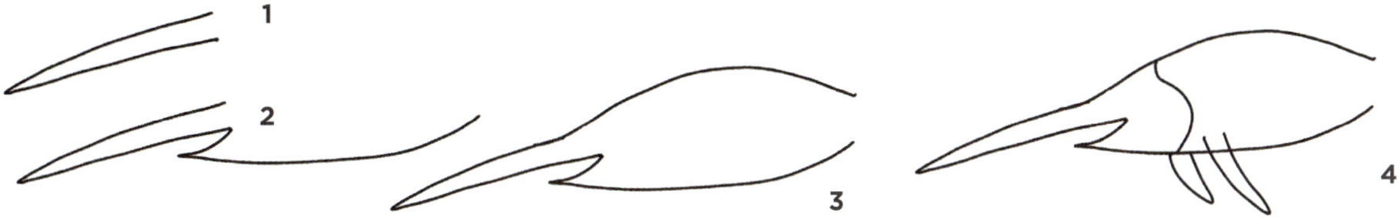

SWORDFISH

Swordfish are among the fastest fish on the planet. Although they have no teeth, they're fierce predators thanks to their long, pointed bill called a rostrum. Swordfish are cold-blooded, but they have a special muscle behind their eyes that allows them to heat their own eyes and brains so they can see and think in cold water.

To draw a swordfish, start by sketching a long "v" shape for the rostrum. Add curving lines to form the basic body shape. Give your fish long, thin front fins and divide the front of the body from the rest. Add a back fin and a crescent-shaped tail. Then, draw a large, ruffled fin on top of the body and divide it with many detail lines. Draw a horizontal line to separate the upper and lower body, then give your fish an eye and color it in.

practice here

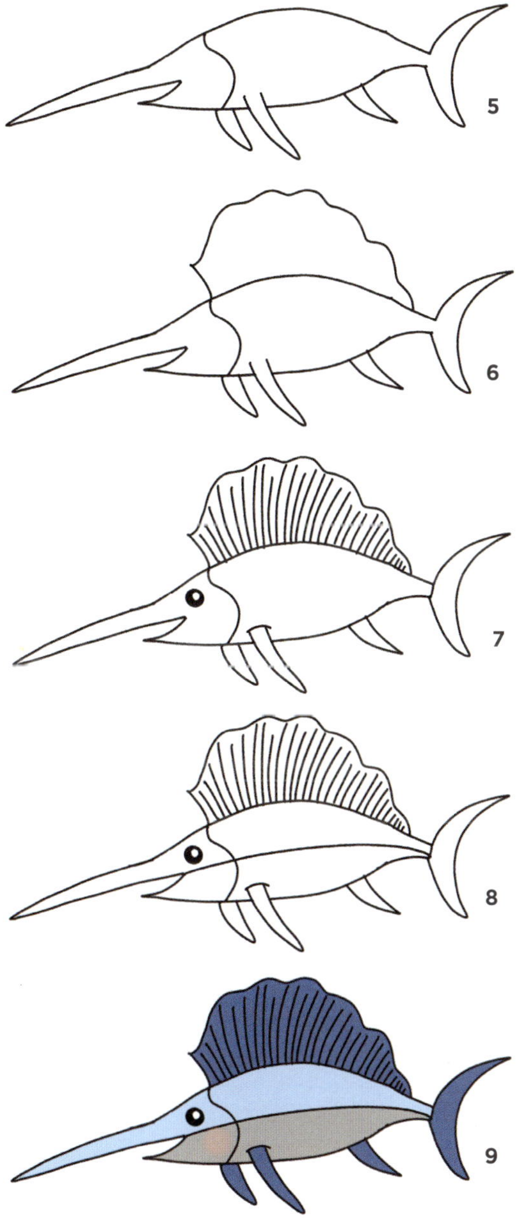

OCTOPUS

The octopus is known for its eight limbs, but did you know it also has three hearts? It's also sometimes said that an octopus has nine brains because its brain is decentralized. That means the majority of the brain's neurons are located in the arms, making each arm able to independently touch, taste and move. An octopus can change colors in an instant and can regrow a limb if necessary.

To draw this fascinating creature, we'll start by forming an oval-shaped head with an arm on each side. Continue sketching arms until you have a total of eight. They can wave and curve in all directions. Add small semicircles to each arm, then draw a face. Color your octopus however you like, since they have the ability to become thousands of different colors.

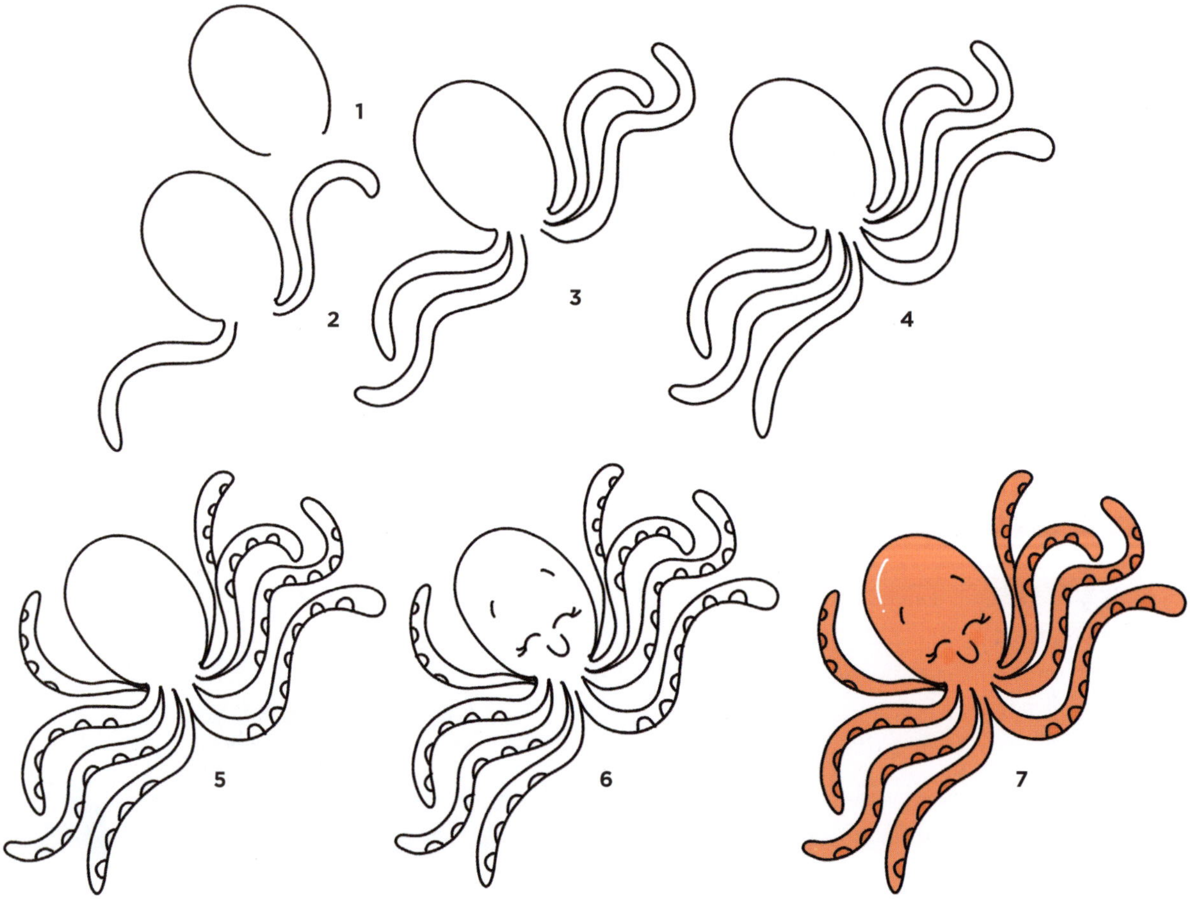

SQUID

Some squid have the ability to fly short distances, using their water jets to jump from the water. This is one method they use to escape from predators. Another is squirting ink, which is mostly made up of melanin and makes the water cloudy and hides the squid from the predator's view as it swims away.

For our squid doodle, we'll start with a rounded cone shape that has a thin band at the bottom. Next, add the head underneath and a curving "v" shape around the cone. Now, it's time to add six tentacles, which can wave in any direction. Finally, draw a face, then color your cheerful creature, adding highlights with a white gel pen.

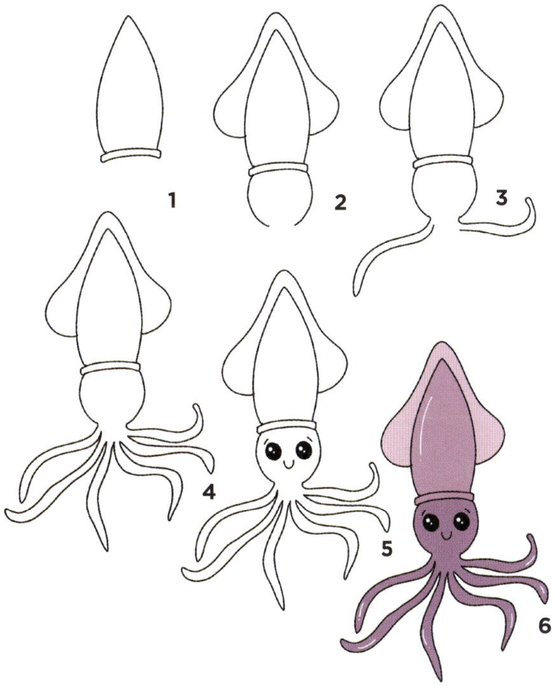

MANTA RAY

Manta rays have the largest brain to body weight ratio of any fish. They're extremely intelligent and have long-term memory. They can even recognize themselves when seen in a mirror.

To start our drawing, sketch a long, wavy horizontal line with two bumps in the center. Under that line, draw the body, which is like a pair of parentheses with a small shape protruding from each side. Connect your top line to the body, forming the wings. Then, add a long, thin tail. Finally, add details like a face, gills for breathing and a long line to divide the top of the ray from its underside. Color your doodle in any way you like.

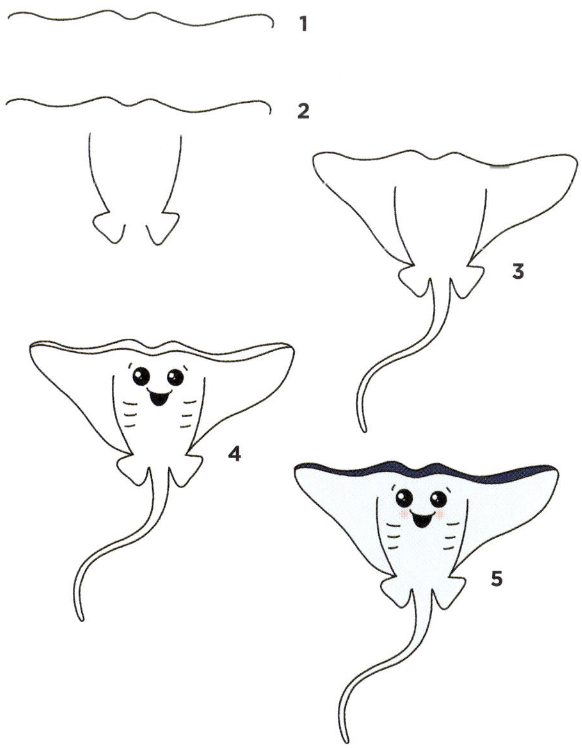

CLAM

Clams are shellfish that can survive in both freshwater and salt water, and spend most of their time buried in either sand or the riverbed. They have two equal-size shells that are connected by a muscle that allows them to open and close. Throughout history, clamshells have been used as currency as well as in jewelry making. The life expectancy of a clam varies from 1 year to 500 years!

To draw a clam, start by sketching the rounded shape of the upper shell, then draw a line below it to represent the presence of the lower shell. Add detail lines to show the texture, and although real clams don't have faces, feel free to give yours eyes and a smile. Clams can be different shades of white, brown or gray, so you can choose how you'd like to color your drawing.

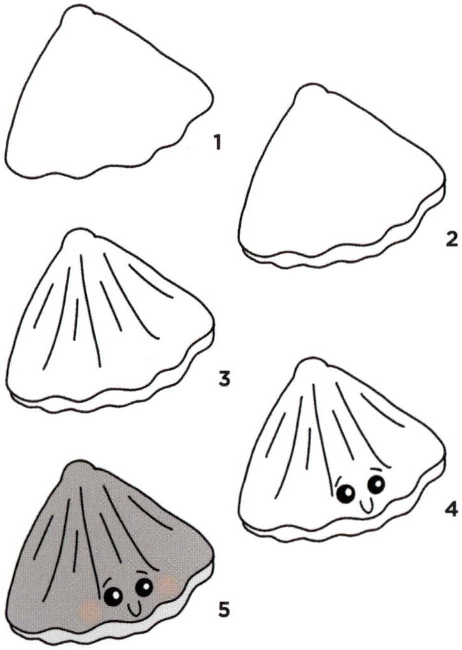

CRAB

Did you know that a crab's shell is actually a skeleton on the outside of its body? There are more than 4,500 species of crabs in the world, all of which walk and swim sideways.

To doodle our crab, we'll start with the body, which is composed of two curving lines that connect on the sides to form points. Then, we'll draw a wavy line from one point to the other. Next, add the front pair of legs, which starts with two oval shapes and has claws on the end. Draw three more legs on each side of the body, which can be simple half-moon shapes. Finally, give your crab a cheerful face and color it. I chose to make my crab red, but you could also make it blue, gray or even white.

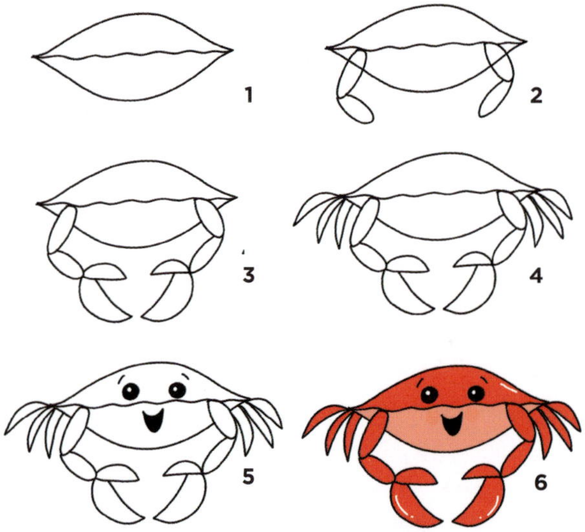

JELLYFISH

The body of a jellyfish is made up of 98 percent water. It has no heart and no brain, just a "nerve net." It also has only one opening that serves for both eating and pooping! Aren't you glad to be a human? All jellyfish are able to sting, but the box jellyfish is the most venomous, able to kill an adult human within minutes after a single sting.

To draw this fascinating creature, start with a semicircle and draw an oval at the bottom. Next, make several wavy tubes extending out from the oval for the tentacles. Continue making more tentacles—it's up to you how many! Give your jellyfish eyes and a smile, as well as a few detail lines. Add a bumpy border around the oval, erasing the spots where it overlaps the tentacles. Color your jellyfish in any way you like.

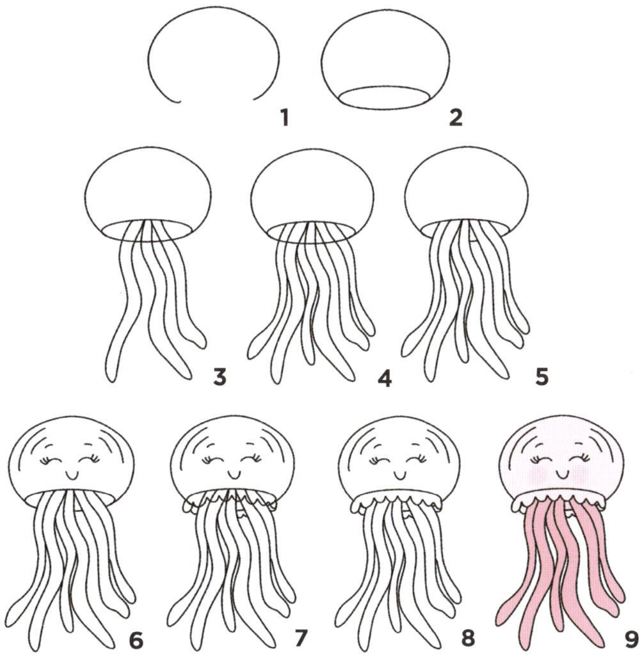

LOBSTER

Lobsters never stop growing throughout their lives, which can be up to 100 years, but they don't have centralized brains like humans. Believe it or not, they chew their food with their stomachs, which is where their teeth are located.

To doodle a lobster, we'll start by making a large teardrop shape for the head and body. Next, add a curving triangle for the rest of the body and a wide, bumpy tail. Sketch six lower legs and two that are higher on the body. Add claws and divide the tail into sections. Finally, add antennae, a face and lines to represent the sections of the abdomen. Then, color your lobster. I used shades of red and orange, but lobsters can also be green, yellow and blue.

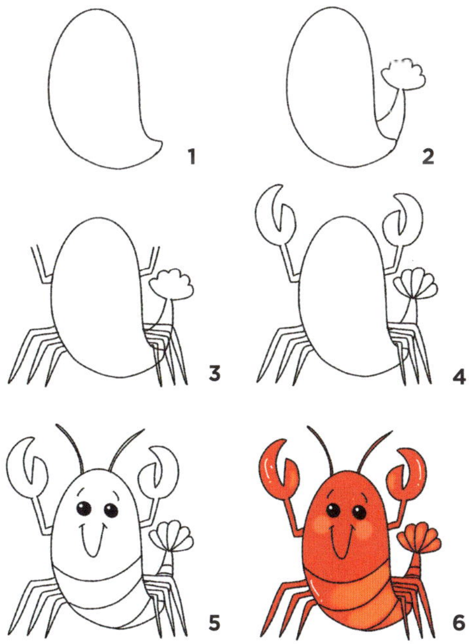

SEA TURTLE

Unlike land turtles, sea turtles can't retract into their shells. These turtles are agile swimmers and amazing divers that can stay underwater for several hours at a time, even sleeping underwater. Sea turtles create their nests in the sand, and it's the temperature of the sand that determines whether the hatchlings will be males or females.

Let's start drawing our swimming sea turtle by sketching a round head and an oval body. Add two large front flippers and two smaller back flippers. Sketch a rounded shell, then add details like a face, lines on the belly and a pattern of spots on the shell. Finally, color your sea turtle. Of course, there are green sea turtles, but some are black, brown or gray too.

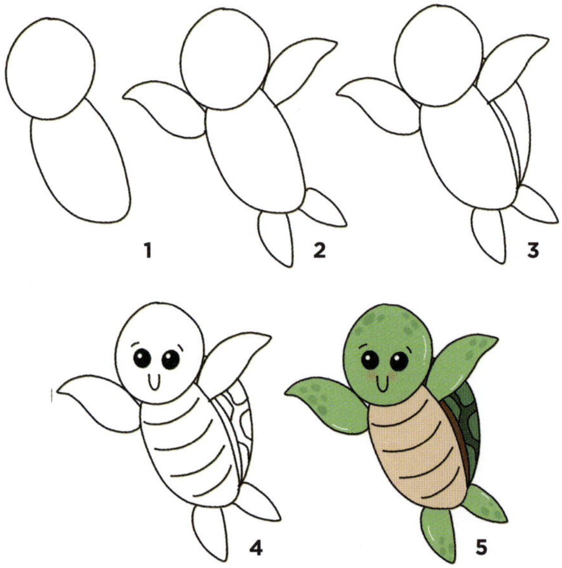

SEAHORSE

Male seahorses are one of the few animals that carry their young. The female lays thousands of eggs in a pouch on the male's abdomen, where they remain until hatching. Seahorses are the only type of fish with tails capable of grabbing and holding on to objects (like monkey tails!).

Ready to draw your own seahorse? Start with an outline similar to the number "3" that ends with a spiral. Sketch a curving line for the stomach and continue it around to finish the tail. Draw a scalloped line connected to the head and back with short lines to form the coronet. Give your seahorse a fin and a long, thin beak with an oval at the end. Erase the line where the fin overlaps the body and add detail lines inside the fin and belly. Sketch an eye and a cheek, then color your seahorse. Add a few bubbles for fun!

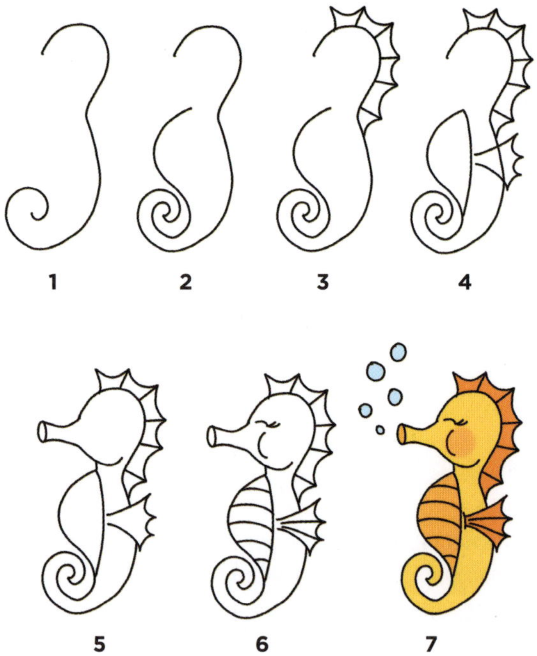

STARFISH

Although starfish are able to walk and move, they have no brain or nervous system. They also have no blood. When a starfish catches food, its stomach actually comes outside of its body to take it in and digest it, then recedes back inside. What a fascinating creature!

Let's start your starfish doodle by drawing an imperfect star shape for the body. Add a face in the center, then a series of ovals on each of the arms that get smaller as they approach the points. Color your starfish yellow, brown or pink for a natural look or any other colors you like.

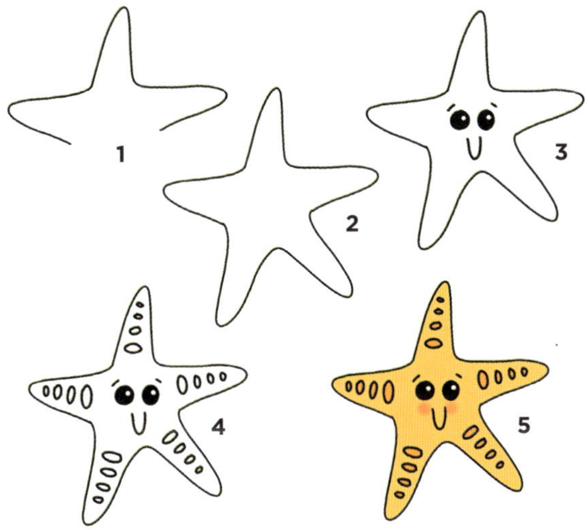

SEAGULL

If you've ever worried about a seagull stealing your french fries at the beach, you've got good reason—a gull can smell food from 3 miles (5 km) away! Seagulls also eat up to 20 percent of their body weight each day. If you feed a seagull, it'll remember your face and recognize you the next time it's looking for a treat.

To draw your own seagull, start with a curving line for its head and back, then add a long, thin tail. Use horizontal lines to split the tail into three feathers. Next, add a curving beak and draw the front part of the body. Give your gull a wing, an eye and a pair of legs and feet. Finally, add color to your doodle. Most seagulls are white with black and gray accents.

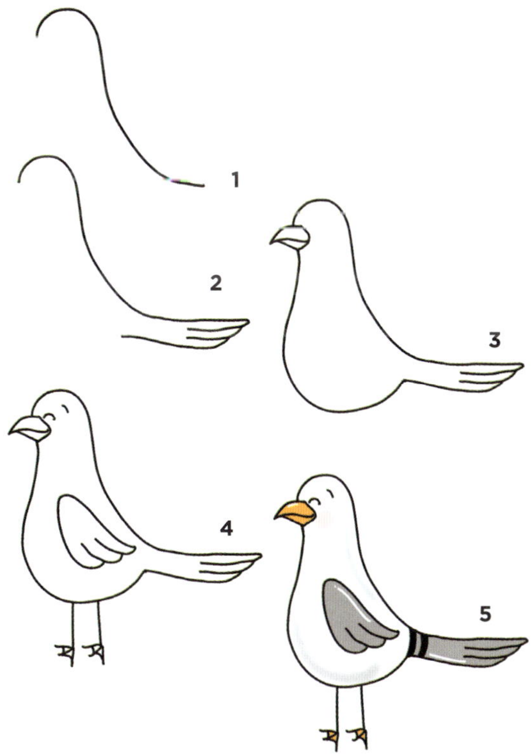

CORAL

Although they look like plants, did you know that corals are actually living creatures that are related to jellyfish and anemones? They're incredibly diverse in color and size, and have proven very beneficial to humans. Many antiviral drugs and other medicines have been created based on discoveries from coral reefs.

To draw a small part of a coral reef, all you have to do is create a wavy shape with various branches. These should be unique, not the same size or shape. Finish off the bottom of the shape like a tree trunk and add curving lines at the top of each branch. Color your coral any shade you like and feel free to add spots or any other texture you like to add even more visual interest. For a fun effect, draw lots of these in various shapes and sizes, grouped together on your ocean floor.

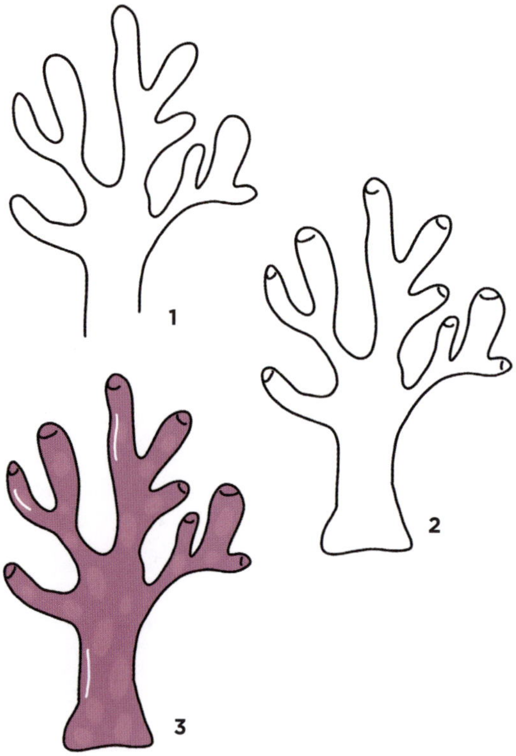

SEAWEED

One additional part of the environment you may want to draw is seaweed. While it's technically alive, seaweed is a plant, rather than an animal like anemone and coral.

To draw your own, start with a bumpy line, then draw a second one on the other side, joining your first line at the top and bottom to form points. Repeat this until you have as many pieces of seaweed as you want. Draw lines through the center of each leaf and add a few rock shapes around the bottom. Color your seaweed and rocks and place them on the ocean floor.

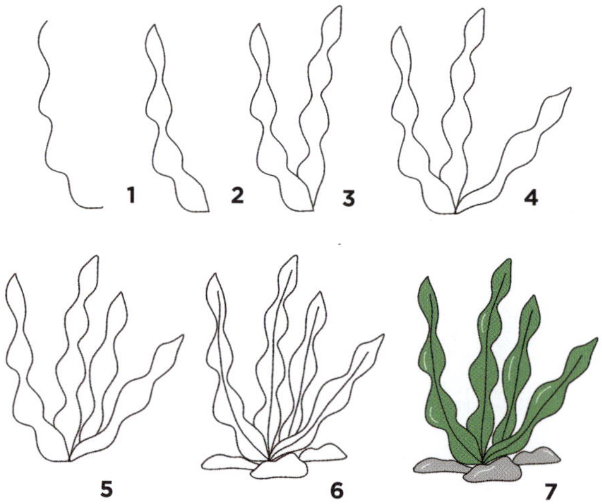

ANEMONE

Sea anemones may look like plants, but similar to coral, they're actually living creatures that provide important symbiotic relationships for many other forms of marine life. Anemones come in a huge variety of colors and are known for paralyzing prey by stinging it as it passes by.

To make a doodle of this sea creature, we'll start by sketching a base that's flat on the bottom and imperfectly rounded on the sides. Then, add a series of tentacles reaching out from it in all directions. Keep adding more and more tentacles until your anemone looks full. Finally, you can add a face if you like. Color your anemone in any shade of the rainbow. You can even make several of these and group them together along the bottom of the ocean to add some bright color to your drawing.

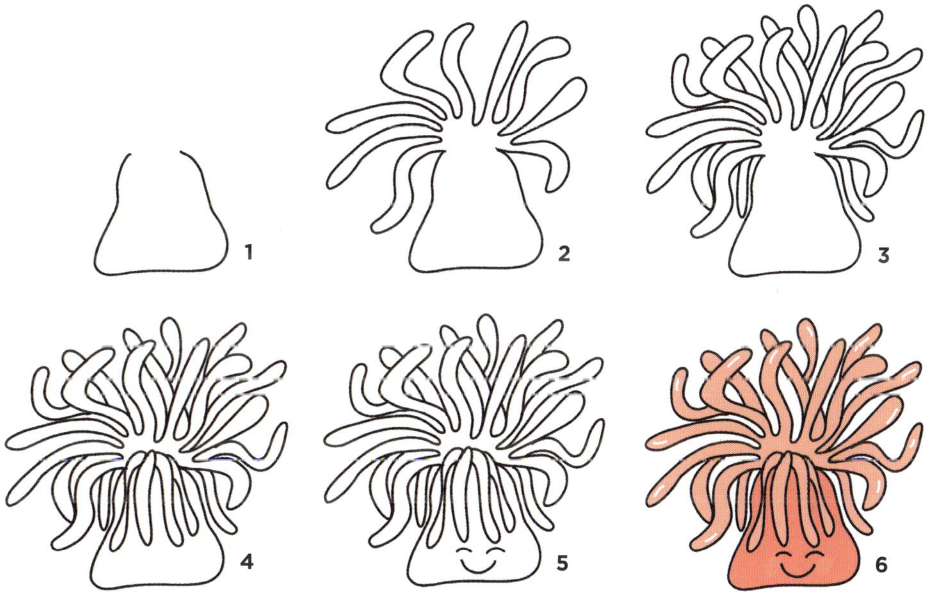

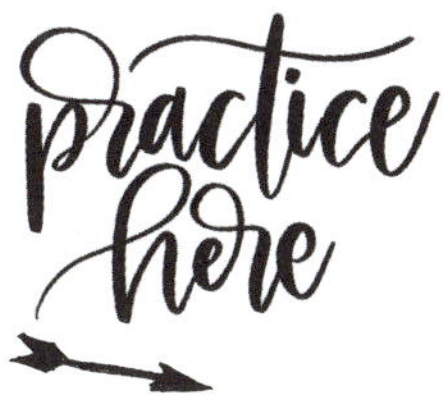

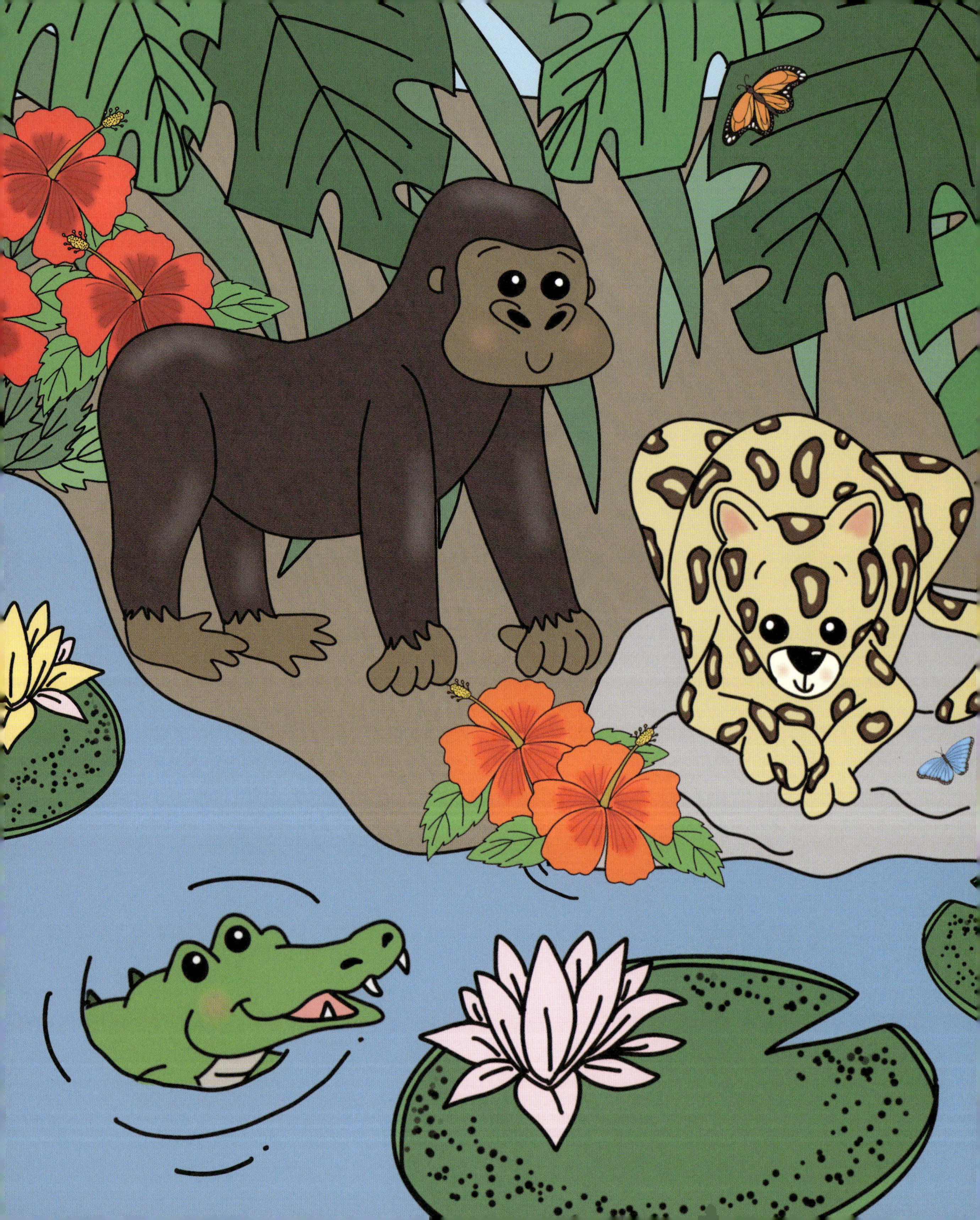

IN THE Jungle

Although tropical rain forests cover only about 6 percent of the Earth's land surface, they're home to more than half of the planet's terrestrial species! They also absorb greenhouse gases from the atmosphere and play a huge role in maintaining the Earth's supply of freshwater. The plants found in the rain forest have helped to create important—and even life-saving—medicines to treat a number of medical conditions. The world's largest rain forest is the Amazon, which is located throughout eight countries in South America. Let's take some time to learn how to doodle some of the animals (and plant life) found in this fascinating habitat.

MONKEY

There are more than 330 species of monkeys, most of which are primarily found in rain forests. These fascinating creatures show affection by grooming each other, picking dirt and bugs from their companions' bodies. Monkeys are highly intelligent and have been observed using stones as tools in the wild.

To doodle a monkey, start by drawing an arch with an oval at the bottom. Add a pair of large, rounded ears that are divided into inner and outer sections. Divide the oval in half and add nostrils to the top section. Draw a rounded "m" shape inside the top of the head, then give your monkey eyes. Sketch a pair of arms and add large hands with fingers. Draw a leg on each side of the body, as well as a foot with toes. Connect the legs to the body and divide the center of the body from the sides with zigzag lines to indicate fur. Finally, add a long, curving tail. Finish your sketch by coloring your monkey.

practice here

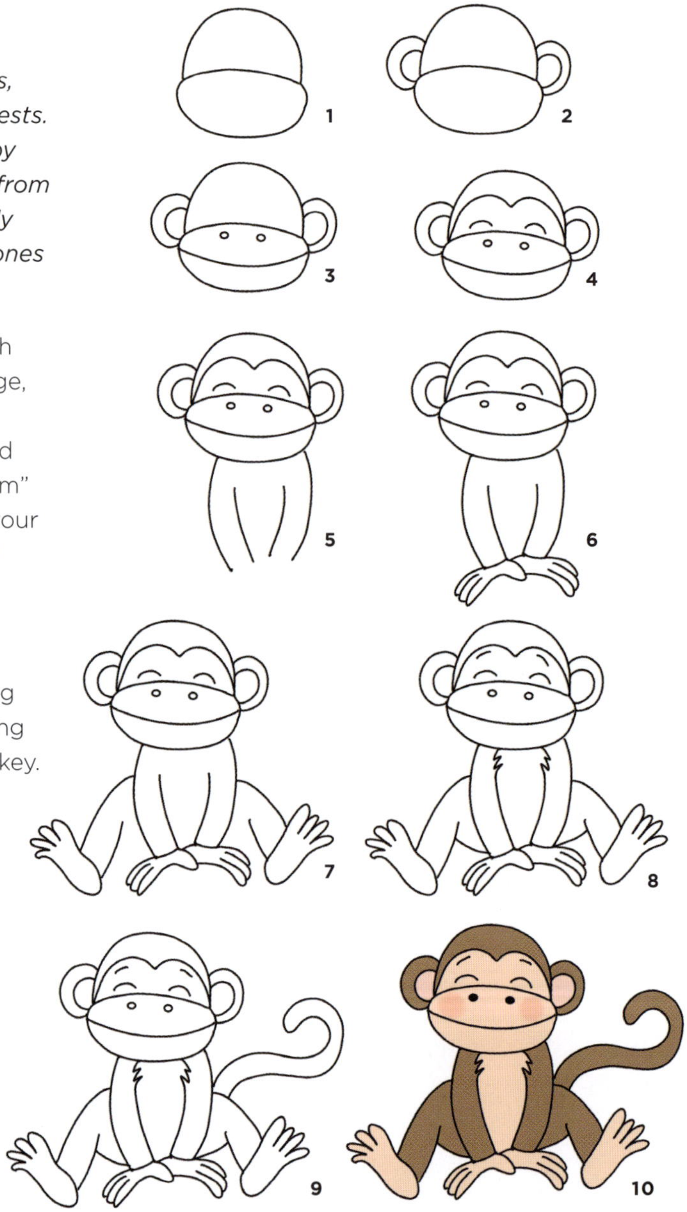

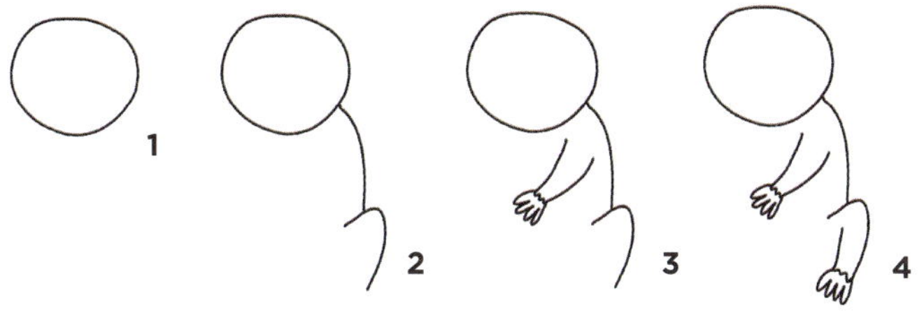

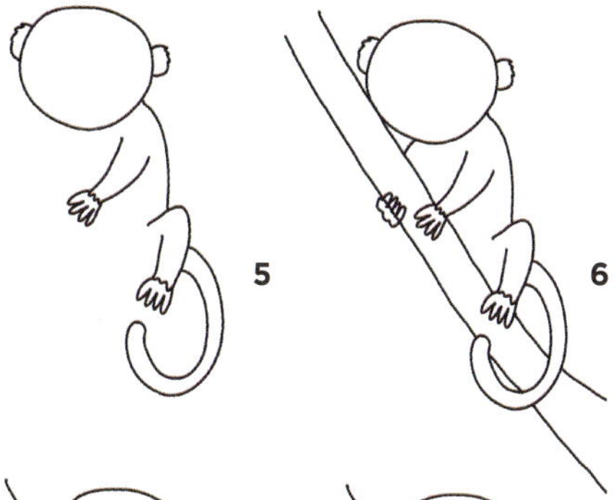

FINGER MONKEY (PYGMY MARMOSET)

Finger monkeys are the smallest known monkeys in the world, with bodies measuring only 5 to 6 inches (13 to 15 cm) (not including their tails) and weighing less than a stick of butter. The tail of a pygmy marmoset is longer than its body, with a pattern of black rings. Their diet consists of plants, insects and fruit.

To draw this tiny monkey, start with a round head and two curving lines for the side of the body and leg. Add an arm with a small hand and finish the leg with a small foot. Draw a long, curling tail extending down below the body and small, rounded ears with some short zigzags to show a furry texture. Sketch a set of parallel diagonal lines to the left of the body for a branch and draw a small hand holding onto the bottom of the branch. Add a curving line to the left of the branch for the other leg and draw a foot below it. Erase the lines where the branch overlaps the monkey's legs, hands and feet.

Sketch a heart-shaped face with two large eyes, along with other facial features like a nose and a smile. Draw a series of short lines to separate the tail into sections. Add leaves to the branch and replace the smooth line at the top of the head with zigzags to show the texture of the fur. Finally, color your finger monkey in shades of gray, pink and/or brown, with darker rings on the tail.

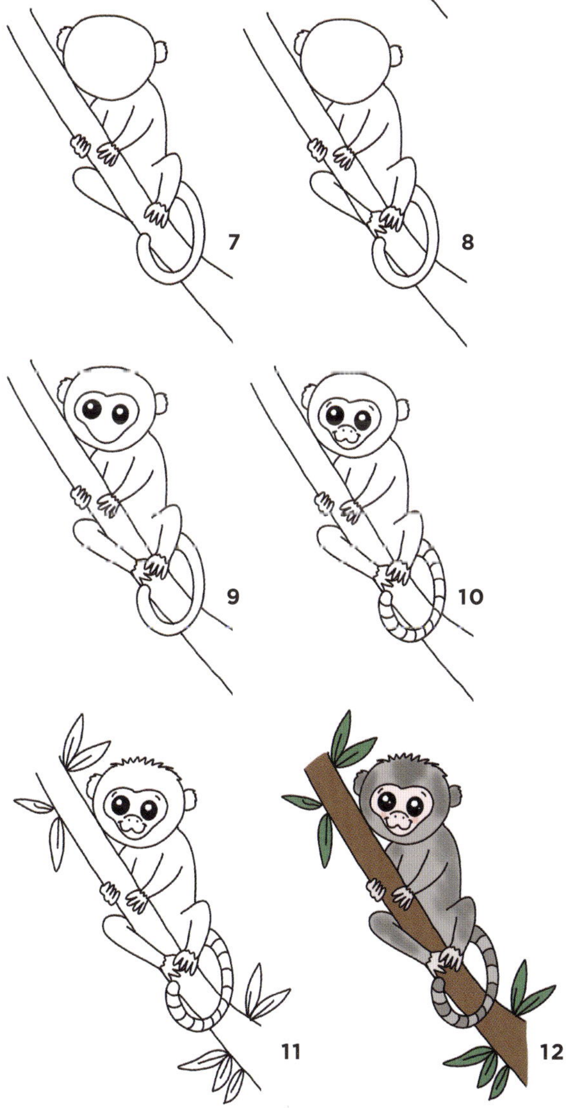

GORILLA

Gorillas are very social animals, living and traveling together in family groups called troops. They're incredibly intelligent; in fact, some gorillas have even learned to communicate with humans using sign language! The nose print of a gorilla is as unique as a human fingerprint and can be used to identify an individual animal.

Start drawing your gorilla with a curving line for the head and neck. Extend that line down to form the back end and leg. Add the shape of the face and a line for the front leg. Draw a curving line to finish the back leg and connect it to the face with a wide "c" shape for the lower body. Finish drawing the front leg and add another front leg to the right of the face. Sketch the final leg, then add zigzags at the bottom of each leg to show where the fur stops. Add face details like eyes, nostrils and a smile, as well as tiny rounded ears. Draw two front hands that are shaped like fists and two flat back feet. Finally, color your gorilla using shades of brown, black or gray.

Practice here

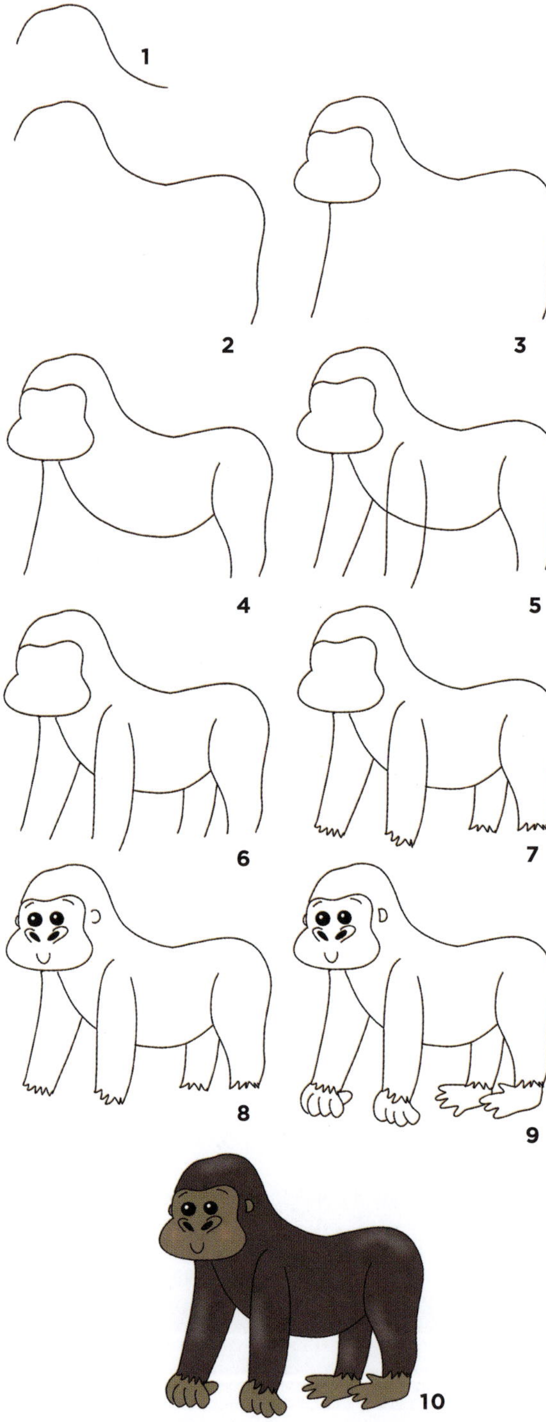

TIGER

Tigers are the largest species of wildcats in the world, weighing up to an impressive 800 pounds (363 kg). Every tiger has its own completely unique stripe pattern. That's good news, since it means you literally can't draw it wrong!

To begin your tiger drawing, draw a head shape with a slightly defined chin. Then, add curving lines for the chest and back. Draw lines extending down from the body for the two front legs, then add a curving line for the back hip and leg. Draw a tail wrapping around from the back of the body. Add front paws and the suggestion of back ones. Next, draw stripes all over the body using curving triangle shapes and divide the tail into striped sections. Sketch a nose, mouth, and cheeks and add eyes. Add a few more stripes on the head and face and zigzag lines inside the ears and on top of the head for a furry texture. Finally, add color to make your tiger orange with black stripes and a white chest.

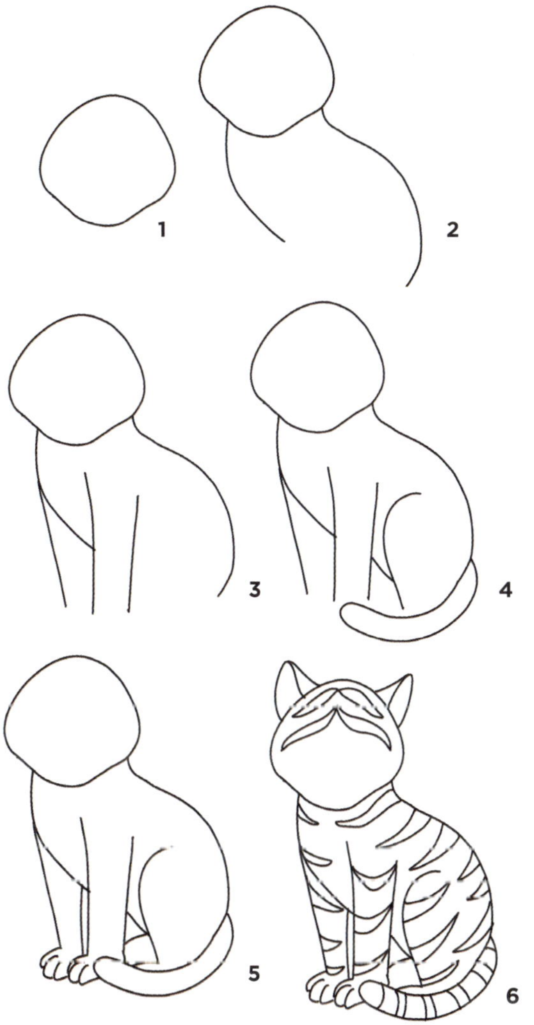

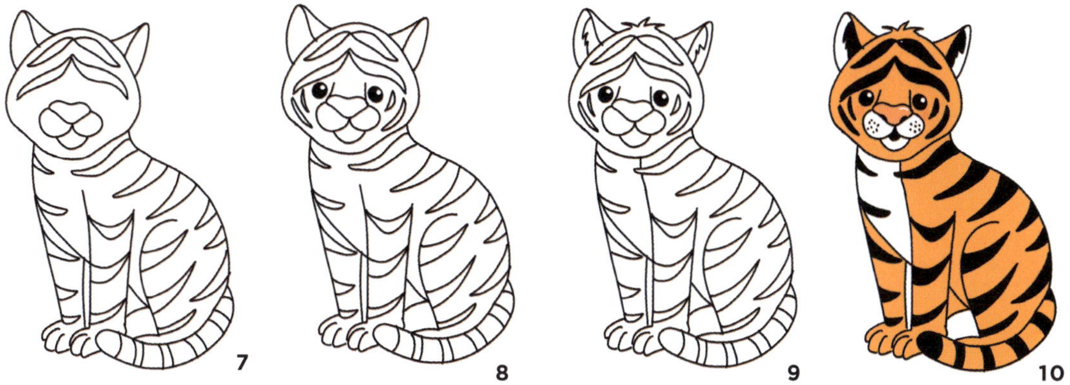

JAGUAR

An adult jaguar can weigh up to 300 pounds (136 kg) and has the strongest bite force of all the felines. The jaguar is a symbol of power in many indigenous Latin American cultures. While jaguars are found in 18 countries from Mexico to Argentina, about half of the world's wild jaguars live in Brazil.

The first step in doodling a jaguar is to draw the face shape with two small, rounded ears. Next, draw an arch around the head for the back and two smaller arches for the back legs. Add front legs and paws. Draw a curving tail coming around the side of the body, then start adding spots to the body. Add eyes, a nose and other face details, then fill in the face and tail with spots. Color your jaguar, making sure to keep the insides of the spots light-colored like the rest of the body.

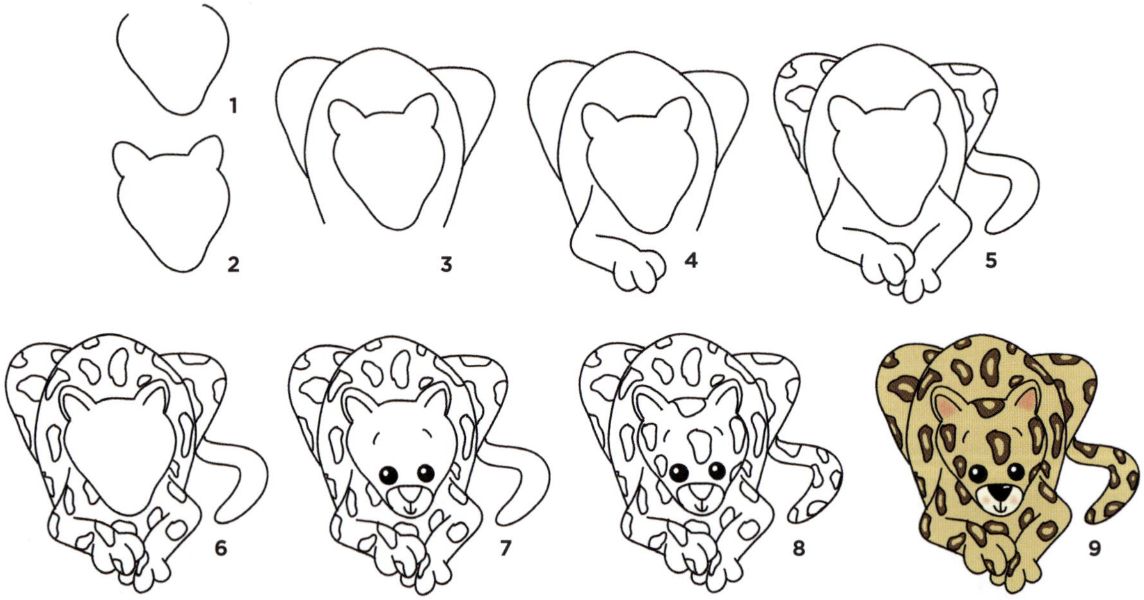

ALLIGATOR

Did you know that alligators are more closely related to dinosaurs than they are to other modern reptiles? They closely resemble crocodiles (which you can learn to draw on page 176), but have their own distinct features. Alligators are the loudest reptiles in the world, able to reach 90 decibels with their mating calls, which is about equal to the volume of a lawn mower.

To doodle an alligator, start by drawing two bumps for the tops of the eyes and a short, curved line for the back of the head. Next, add a long, curving line for the back and tail. Draw the alligator's snout and smile, then add a lower jaw. Sketch the lower body and the rest of the tail. Add a front leg and foot, as well as a second front foot. Draw a back leg and foot, then separate the stomach from the rest of the body. Erase where the body and legs overlap. Sketch texture lines on the stomach. Doodle eyes, nostrils, teeth and a mouth and add a series of spikes down the back and tail. Finally, color your alligator.

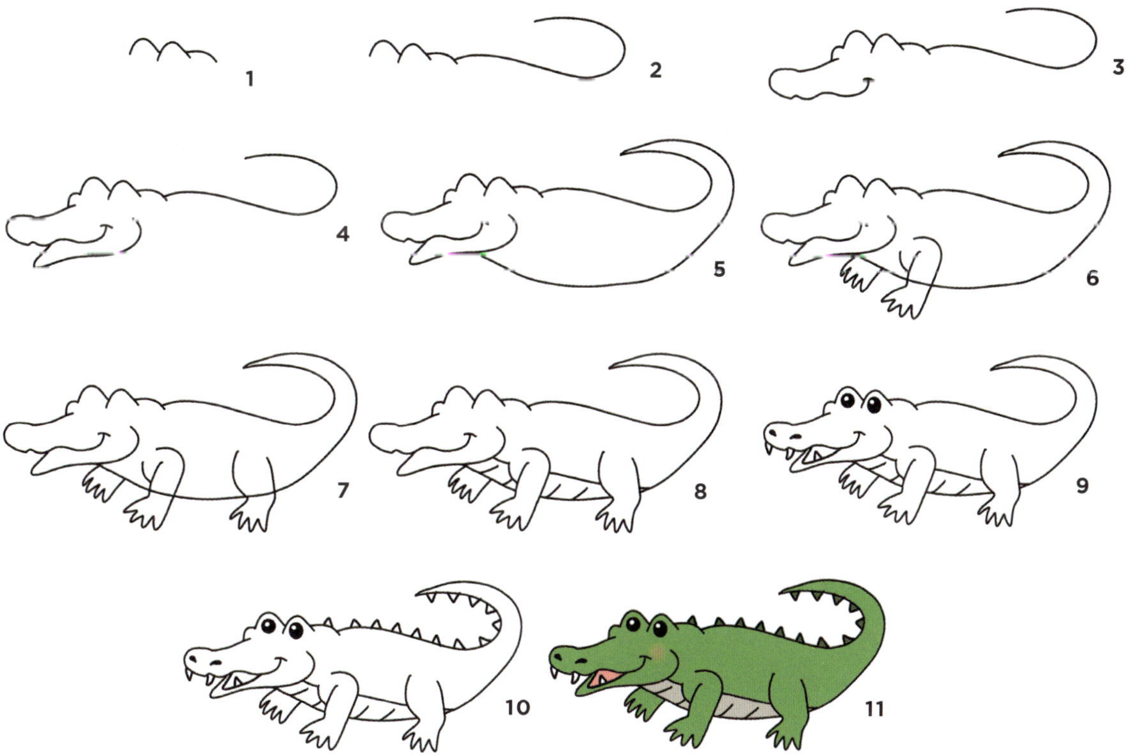

TOUCAN

The bright colors of the toucan are designed to help camouflage it among the vibrant plants in the rain forest. These exotic birds find shelter in trees that have been hollowed out by woodpeckers. Toucans' long beaks have bone on the inside and keratin on the outside, which means the beak is actually rather soft. In fact, toucans are unable to use their beaks for fighting or digging due to this texture.

To doodle a toucan, start with a curving, pointed beak that's divided into a top and bottom. Curve the dividing line up into a smile and add a backward "c" shape around it. Sketch an oval body shape and add lines to divide the body into three parts. Draw an eye and two feet. Add a pointed wing on each side of the body. Erase the area where the left wing overlaps the body. Draw a horizontal branch under the feet and sketch a few leaves on it. Add a curving line to separate the tip of the beak from the rest, and fill in the eye. Finally, color your doodle. The tip of the beak and the outer body should be black or dark gray. The beak is typically shades of orange or yellow and the inner body is yellow and red, with blue feet.

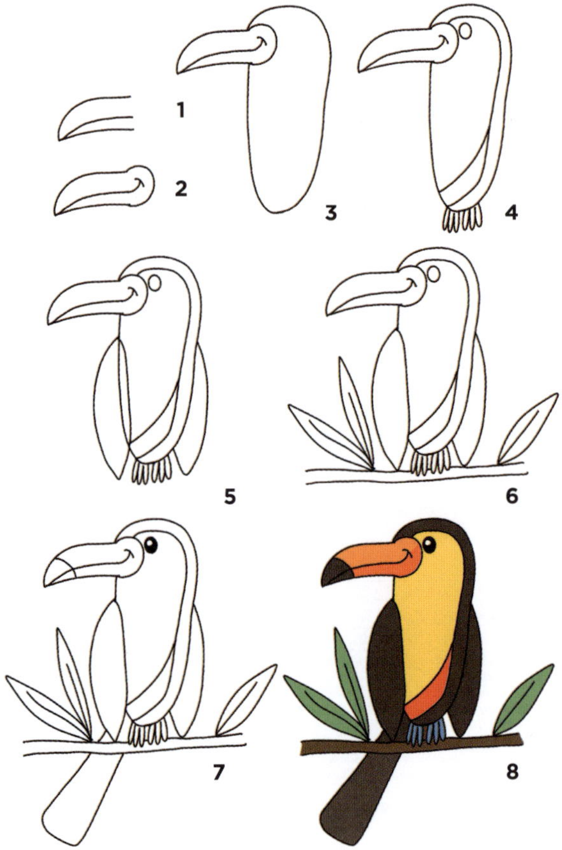

practice here

SCARLET MACAW

The scarlet macaw is an intelligent, social parrot found in tropical climates. Be careful what you say around this bird, because it's able to mimic sounds, including human speech. The average macaw's life span is between 50 and 60 years.

To draw this gorgeous parrot, start with an upside-down "u" shape for the head and close it off with a scalloped line across the bottom. Draw an oval-shaped body below the head and a wing on each side of the body. Next, add a long tail with five thin sections. Draw a beak in the center of the head, with an eye on either side. Fill in the eye and then add detail lines on the wings and tufted feathers on top of the head. Draw scalloped lines across the front of the body for feathery texture. Create a tree branch by sketching horizontal lines below the bird, then add feet to connect the bird's body to the branch. Erase any overlapping lines. Finally, draw details like leaves on the branch and curving lines around each eye. Color your macaw, making the body and head red, the feet and part of the wings blue and part of the wings yellow.

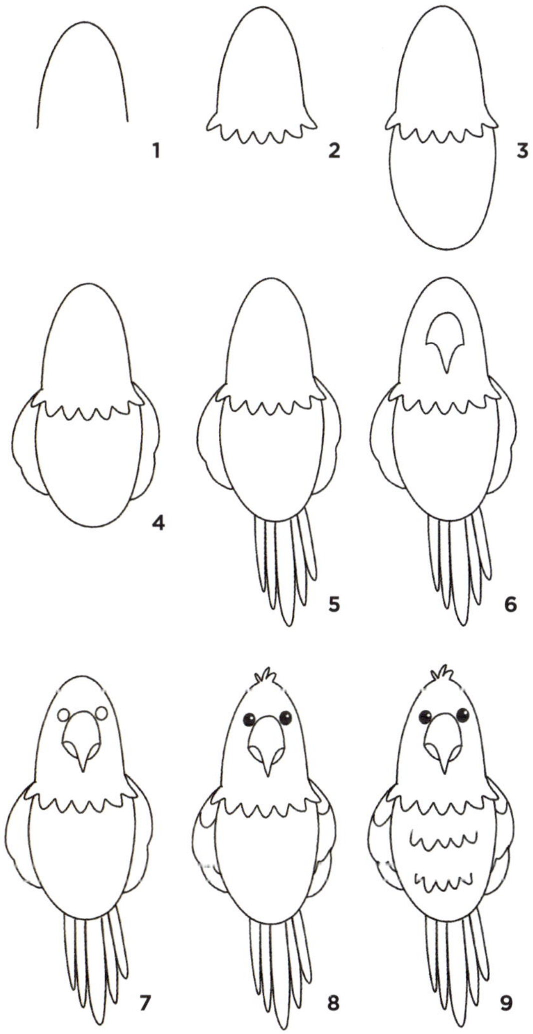

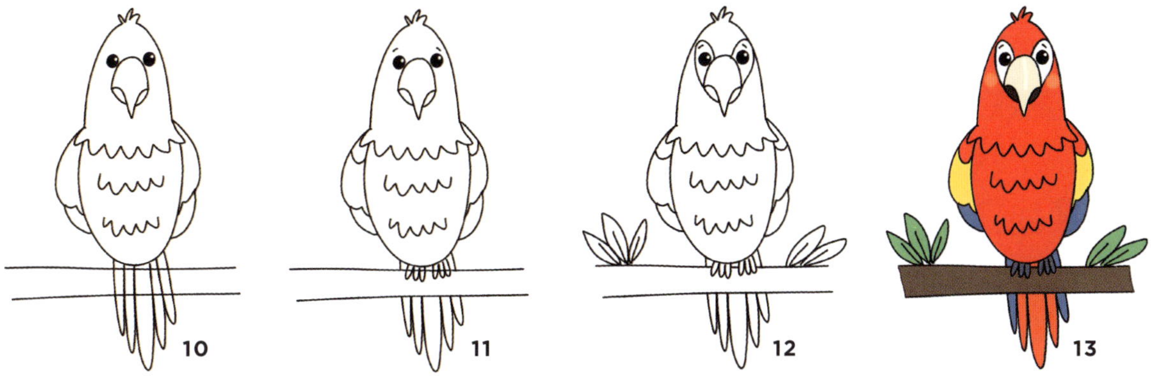

COCKATOO

Cockatoos are extroverted birds that enjoy social interaction and making lots of noise. Unlike many species, they co-parent their young, with the male and female taking turns sitting on the eggs and nurturing their hatchlings until they're ready to leave the nest. Cockatoos are extremely intelligent and resourceful birds that experience a range of emotions. They use their raised crests to express things like curiosity, fear, frustration and alarm.

Let's start our cockatoo sketch by drawing a curving "v" shape for the top of the beak. Continue the line around to form the bottom of the beak and add a small smile line. Next, sketch the top of the head, with a few bumps for feathers. Draw a line below the beak that curves around to form the front of the body, then add a line for the bird's back. Sketch a wing on the side of the body, along with a long tail divided into several sections. Give your bird a pair of feet and draw parallel lines to create a tree branch for it to sit on. Add a few leaves to the branch. Give your bird an eye, then draw a series of curving triangle shapes on top of the head to form the famous crest. Sketch a few bumpy detail lines inside the wing, then add color to finish your doodle.

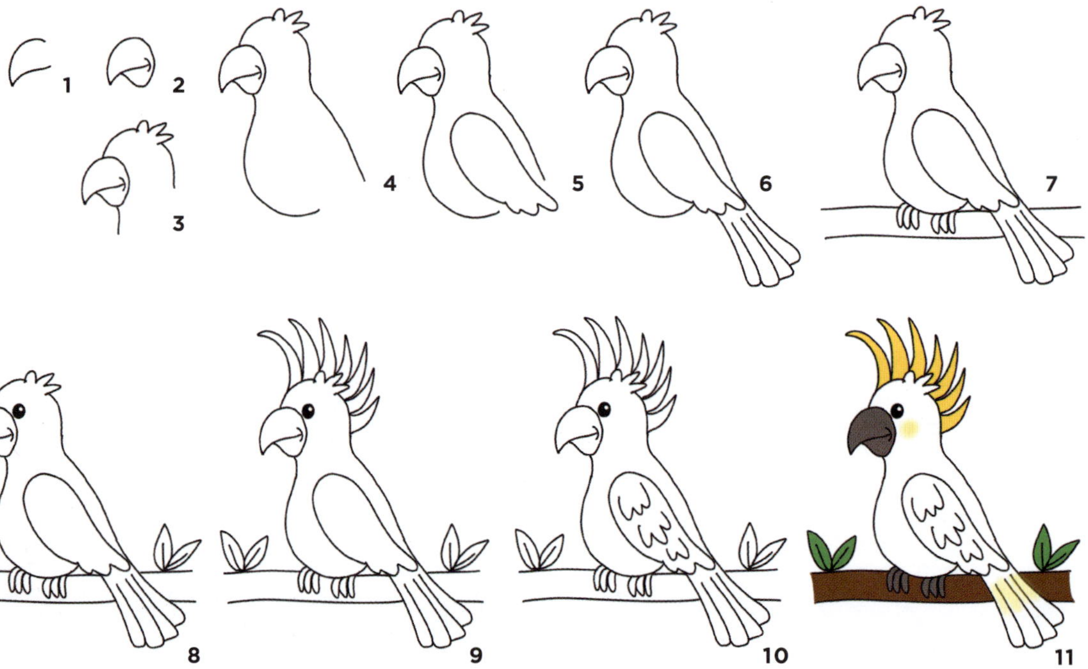

BLUE-FOOTED BOOBY

The color of a blue-footed booby's feet actually comes from a substance called carotenoid, which is an antioxidant found in the fish the booby eats. The brighter the bird's feet are, the healthier it is, and the more attractive to the opposite sex. When blue-footed boobies mate, the males do a special dance, stomping around and putting their colorful feet on display to attract a female.

The first step in drawing this unique bird is to sketch the body shape, which resembles a peanut with two small rectangular areas on the bottom where the legs attach. Add a "c"-shaped wing on each side of the body, along with legs and large webbed feet. Draw a beak in the center of the head with a line that curves up into a smile on each side. Add eyes and an outline around the face. Draw eyebrows and short lines on the body to indicate the feathery texture. Finally, color the bird, making sure the beak and feet are a brilliant blue!

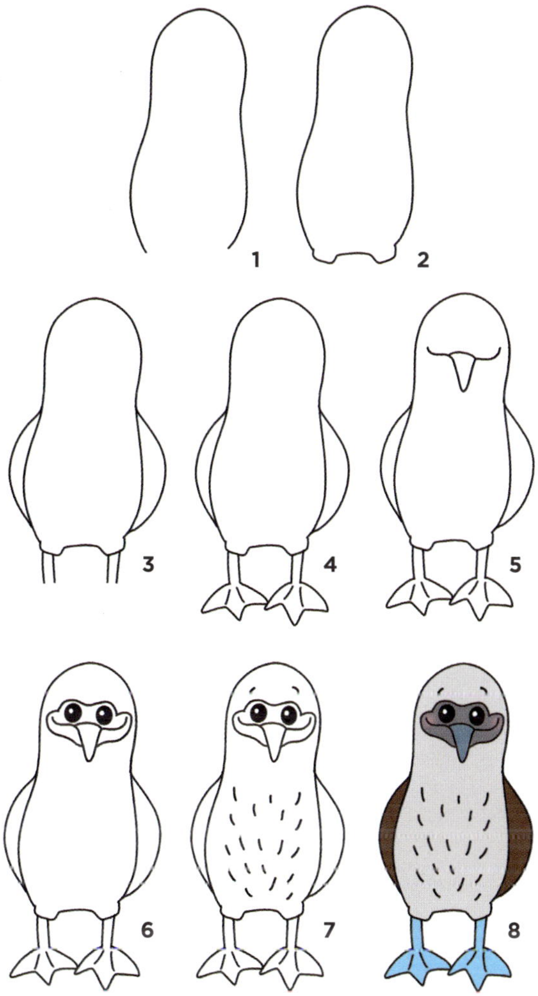

practice here

FLAMINGO

Flamingos get their name from the Spanish word "flamenco," which means "fire," as a description of their brightly colored feathers. Their feathers actually become colored due to the beta-carotene in their food. They stand on one leg and tuck the other under their feathers to help preserve body heat, alternating legs to regulate their body temperature.

Start your flamingo doodle with a wavy line for the head, long neck and back. Add a second curving line for the lower part of the head, neck, and body and join it to the first line to form a short, pointed tail. Sketch a curving beak and divide it into two sections. Draw a wing, then add a pair of very long, thin legs with webbed feet, crossing one leg over the other to form a backward "4." Give your flamingo an eye, then color it using your favorite shades of pink.

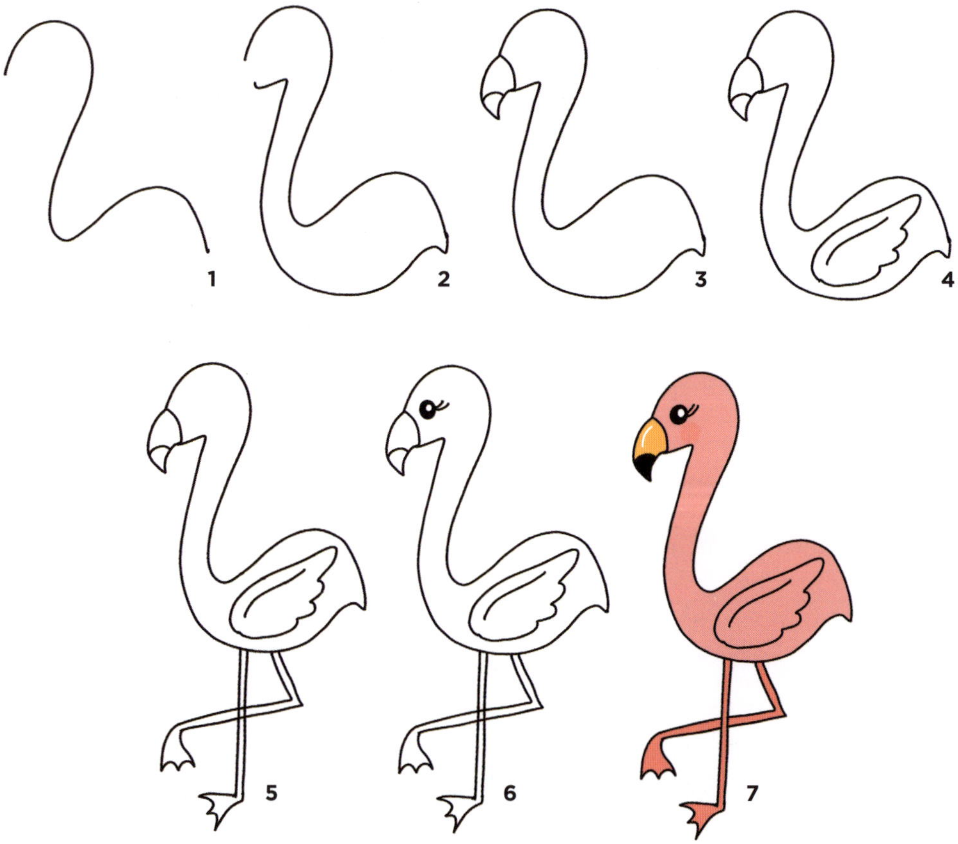

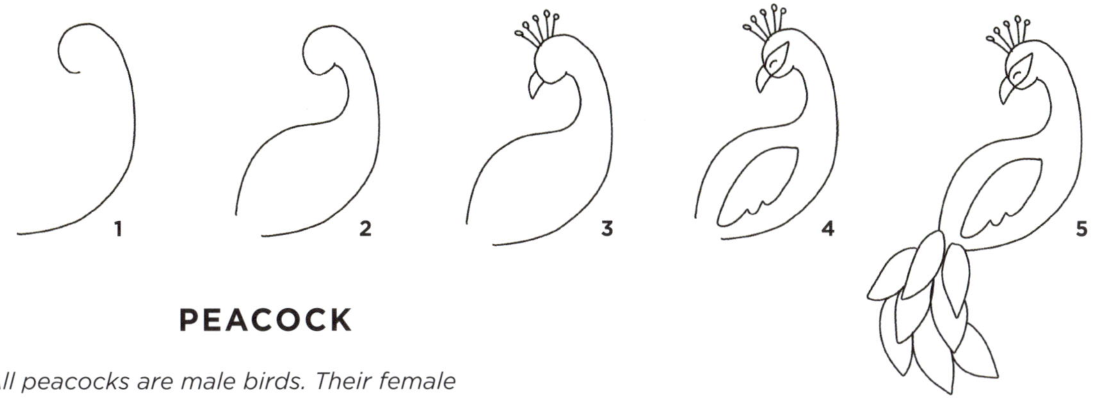

PEACOCK

All peacocks are male birds. Their female counterparts are called peahens and babies are called peachicks. The long, colorful tail feathers of a peacock are called its train. This train is used for attracting females, who choose mates based on the size, color and quality of the feathers. At the end of every mating season, peacocks shed their feathers and regrow a longer, fuller train.

Ready to draw your own? Start with a curving line for the head, neck and lower body. Then, draw a second line for the bird's back. Sketch a curving, pointed beak and add a series of lines with circles on top of the head. Give your peacock a wing, as well as an eye that's separated from the rest of the face inside a triangular shape. Now, it's time to form the tail by drawing a series of leaf-shaped feathers extending from the body and curving around below it. Continue adding more until the train looks full, then add extra details inside each feather, like ovals, circles, dots or anything you like. Finally, use vibrant colors to bring your peacock to life.

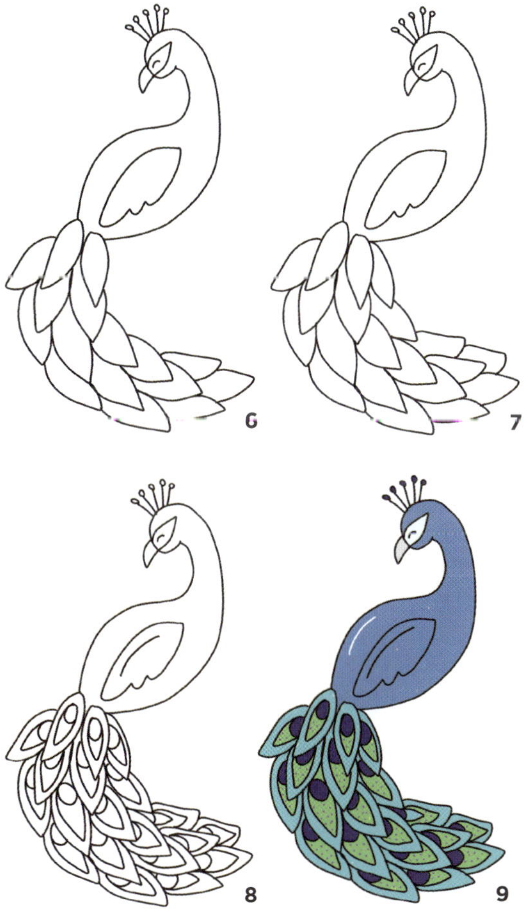

PEAHEN

Unlike their male partners, peahens aren't very colorful birds. Their necks are a pretty shade of blue-green, but the rest of their bodies are gray or brown. Peahens make their nests on the ground and prefer walking over flying.

Begin your peahen doodle with a wavy line for the head, neck and back. Then, sketch a curve for the bird's lower body. Add a series of lines with circles on top extending from the head and give your peahen an eye and a beak. Separate the eye from the rest of the head with a triangular shape. Sketch a wing inside the body area. Finally, connect the lines at the back of the body by adding a "u" shape for the tail feather. Add legs and feet, then color your peahen.

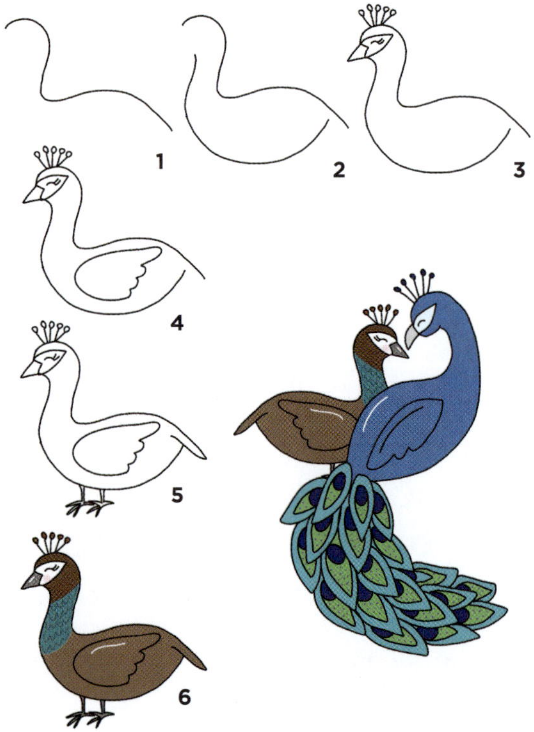

CAPYBARA

The world's largest rodent is the capybara, a semiaquatic herbivore. Capybaras are excellent swimmers, able to hold their breath for five minutes underwater, and they're also able to run on land at speeds up to 21 miles per hour (34 kph). They're in the same family as guinea pigs.

To doodle a capybara, start with a "c" shape that extends upward at the top for the back of the head. Add a curving line for the front of the body that tucks into your "c" shape and forms a tail. Draw a flat head with a wide, blunt nose and a small, pointed ear. Add a second ear, as well as front legs and webbed feet. You'll also want to sketch a little back foot underneath the body. Draw an eye, a nostril, and a smile and add detail lines inside the ears. Then, color your capybara light brown with darker ears, feet and nose.

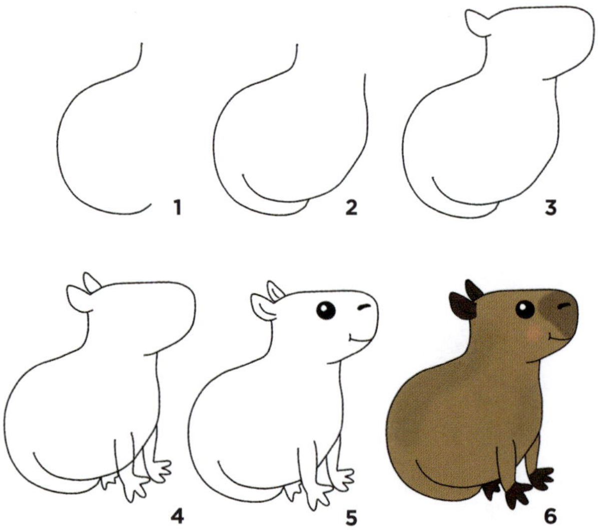

BLUE MORPHO BUTTERFLY

One of the world's largest butterflies is the blue morpho, which has a wingspan ranging from 5 to 8 inches (13 to 20 cm). The wings are an iridescent blue, due to microscopic, light-reflecting scales. The underside of the wings, which are brown with spots that look like eyes, are designed for camouflage. They blend in with surrounding foliage, and the eye spots can trick predators into thinking they belong to a much larger creature.

To doodle this special butterfly, start by forming a long, thin body shape with a small, oval head on top. Add two large upper wings, then draw two "u" shapes for lower wings that connect to the bottom of the body. Draw antennae and add scalloped lines on the wings to separate the blue area from the border. Draw lines from each scallop in toward the body and add eyes. Finally, color the wings blue with a black border. For more detail, you can add darker blue shading to the inner area of the wings and white spots around the border.

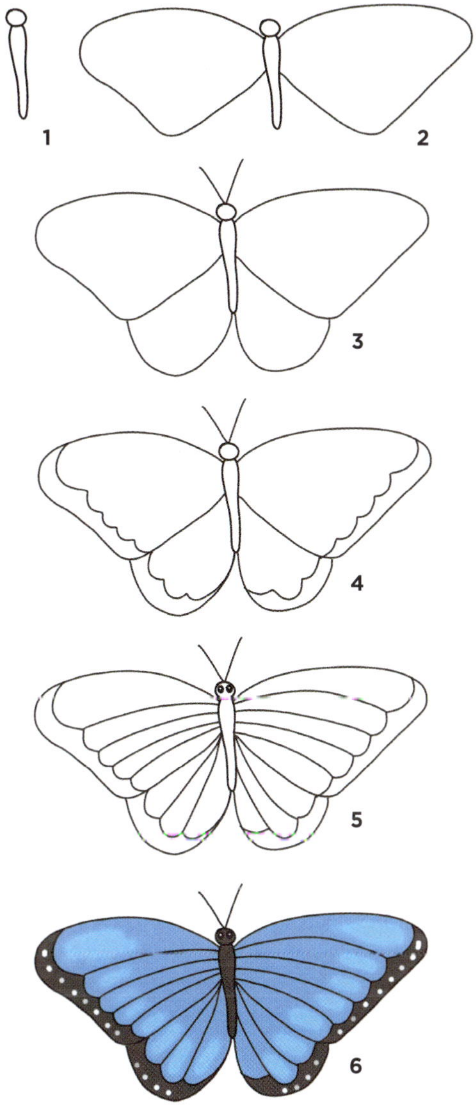

practice here

MONARCH BUTTERFLY

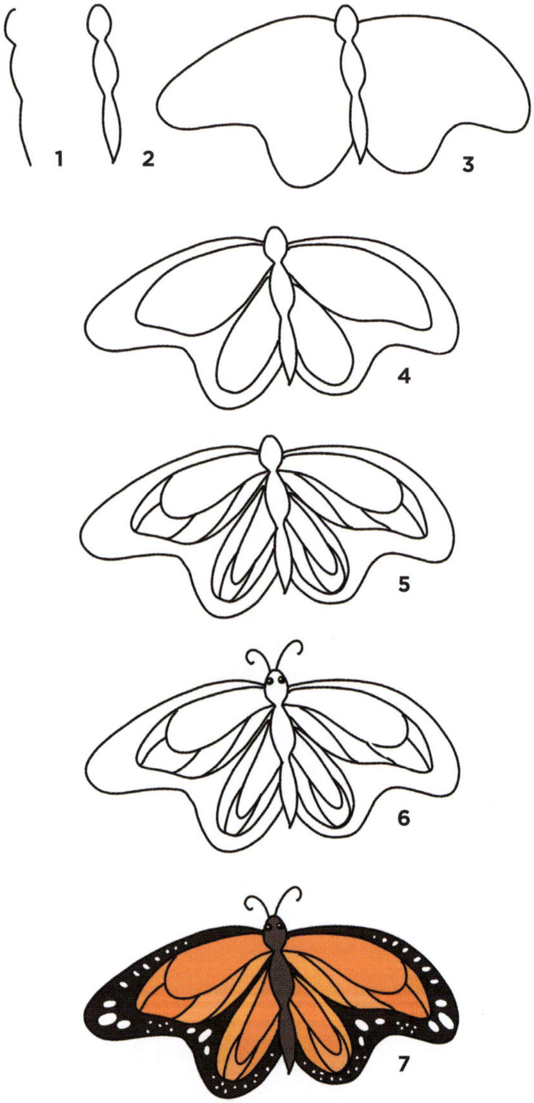

One of the monarch's most notable achievements is its migration. Every spring, adult monarchs travel from Mexico and California (where they spend the winter) to locations in the northern United States and Canada, then travel back again in the fall. This journey is more than 3,000 miles (4,828 km) each way. A monarch's bright colors are a warning to predators that it's poisonous, due to a steroid found in their bodies from the milkweed they ingest as caterpillars.

Start drawing a monarch by making a vertical line with three bumps. Draw a second line to the right of the first one, mirroring the bump shapes, to create the body. Sketch a pair of large wings, then start dividing the wings into geometric sections. You can draw these lines and divisions in any way you like. Add eyes and short, curved antennae. Color the butterfly, keeping the outer edges of the wings black and the inner parts yellow and orange. Use a white gel pen to add white spots inside the black border for extra detail.

practice here

POISON DART FROG

Known as the "jewels of the rain forest," these tiny, brightly colored frogs can be quite dangerous. In fact, the golden poison frog is one of the most toxic animals on the planet. The toxins that poison dart frogs secrete from their skin have been used on the tips of hunters' weapons. Only the frogs themselves and one species of snake are immune to their poison.

Start your poison dart frog drawing by sketching a wavy line that forms the back, eye area and nose. Add a bent back leg and a webbed foot. Then, draw a front leg and foot and connect the two legs with a short line for the stomach. Draw a second front foot and a bumpy line inside the body to show the frog's other eye and the texture of the back. Add an eye, a second back leg, a smile and a small nostril. The most fun part is coloring your frog using a combination of bright, vibrant shades of red, yellow, blue, orange and/or green.

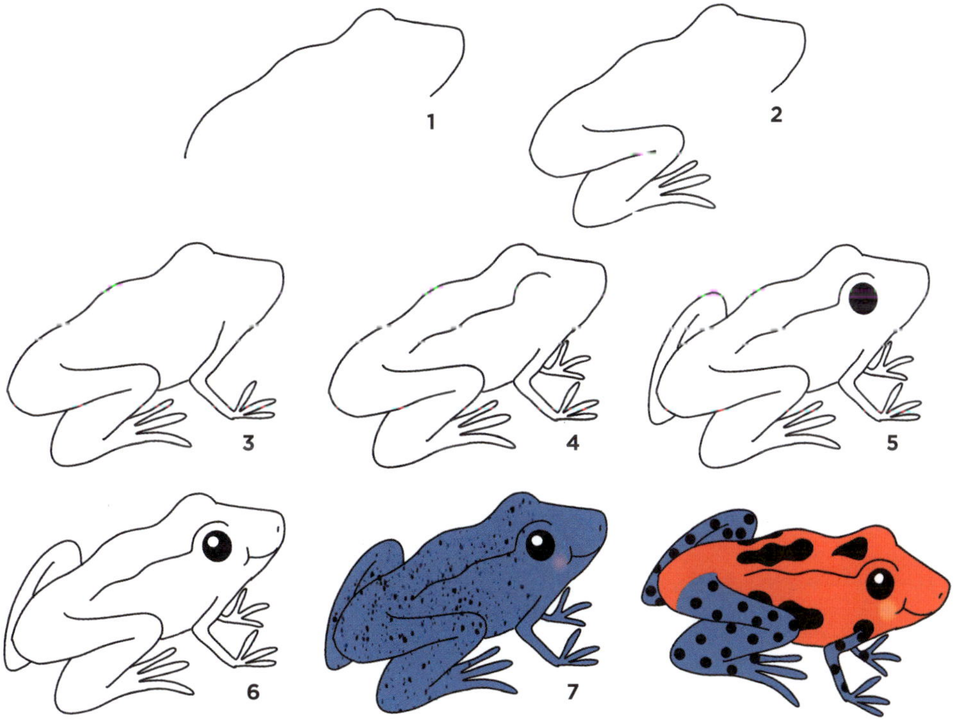

BAT

Bats are flying mammals and there are more than 1,100 species of them worldwide. They play a big role in controlling the insect population, since they're able to eat their body weight in insects every single night. A single bat can eat 1,200 mosquitoes in an hour, which is helpful for everyone!

To doodle this nocturnal creature, start with an oval-shaped head attached to an oval-shaped body. Next, add small, pointed ears. Sketch the top of each wing extending out from the sides of the body. Add a bumpy line to form the bottom of each wing and connect it to the lower part of the body. Divide each wing into three sections. Add feet made up of three small "u" shapes, then give your bat a face. I chose to make mine asleep. Add color to finish your doodle. To take your drawing to the next level, sketch a branch and position your bat hanging from it upside-down!

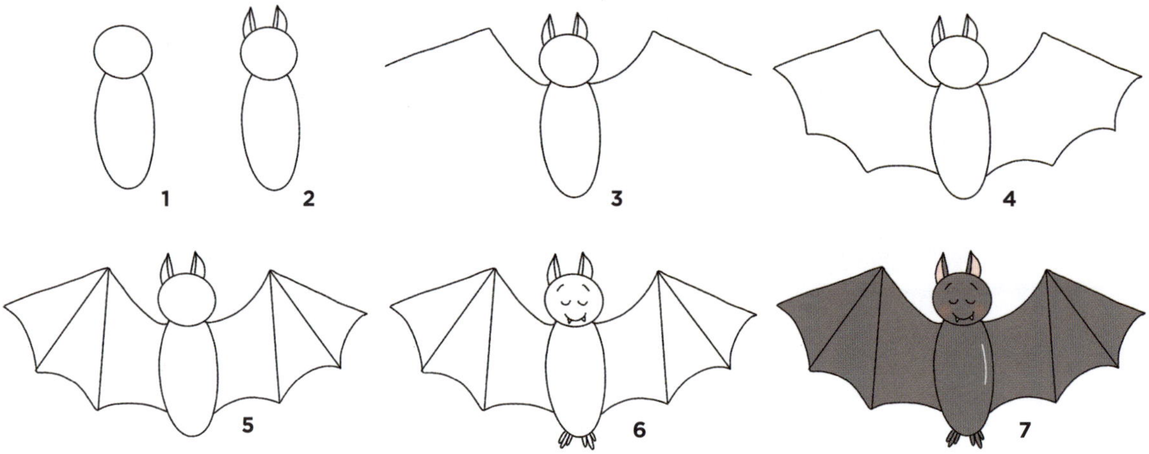

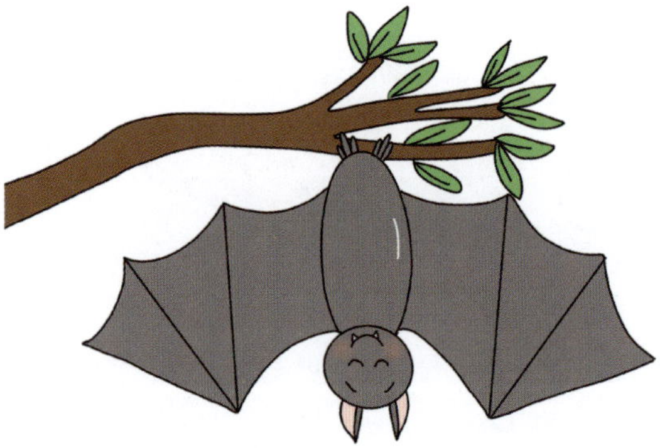

practice here

IN THE HABITAT

BROMELIAD PLANT

Bromeliads are tropical plants known for their bright, spiky blooms and long sword-shaped leaves. They're epiphytic, which means they have the ability to grow on rocks, trees or other plants, as well as in the soil.

To doodle this type of plant, start by sketching two overlapping curved shapes that are rounded at the bottom and pointed at the other end. Next, draw a second set of these shapes coming out of the center of the first set. Repeat this process until you have whatever size bloom you want (mine has four sets). Then, begin drawing long, thin, curved shapes for the leaves that are also pointed on the ends. Continue adding these shapes, overlapping one another, until you have a full-looking base. Color your bloom in a bright, tropical shade and the leaves in various shades of green. Feel free to add highlight lines to the leaves and bloom for more detail.

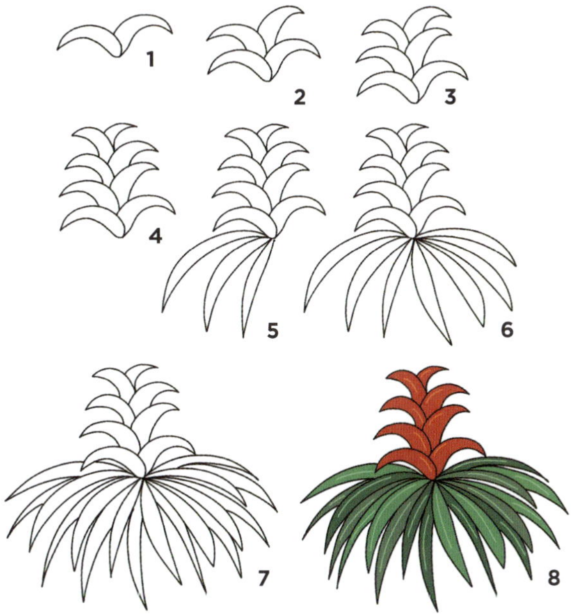

MONSTERA LEAF

Another name for a monstera is the "Swiss cheese plant," because of the holes in its wide, heart-shaped leaves. These distinguishing holes are called fenestrations.

To draw your own monstera leaf, start with a basic rounded heart shape, then draw a series of slightly curving shapes inside it, along both side edges. Your slits/holes can be as wide or large as you like. Erase the parts of the original shape that overlap your fenestrations. Finally, add some lines on the inside of the leaf for veins. Color your leaf a vibrant shade of green.

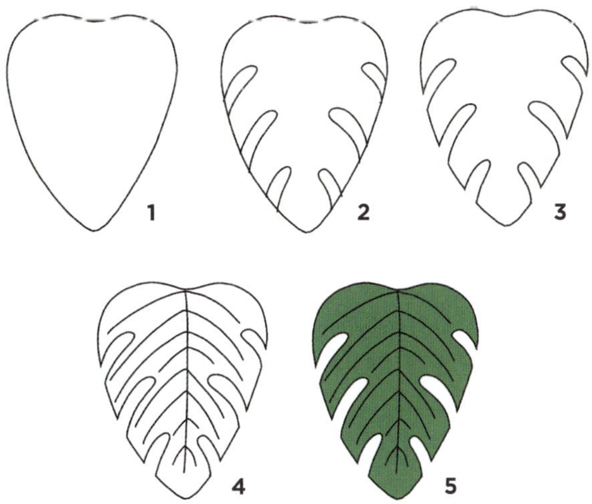

GIANT LILY PAD

Giant water lilies, or Victoria amazonica, *are native to the tropical regions of South America. They can be as large as 10 feet (3 m) in diameter with 16-inch (41-cm) flower blooms. These lily pads can hold animals, as well as a child or a small adult, up to 140 pounds (64 kg).*

The first step in drawing the lily pad is to form a large, thin oval with a small opening on one side. Draw a "v" shape in the opening. Next, add three overlapping teardrop shapes to begin forming the flower. Add three more petals around the base of the flower, then continue drawing more petals behind the existing ones to give the bloom fullness. Erase the overlapping lines on the petals. Draw curving lines around the lily pad to create a dimensional effect, then add dots and detail lines for more realism. Color your lily pad green and the flower white, yellow, pink or any other shade you choose.

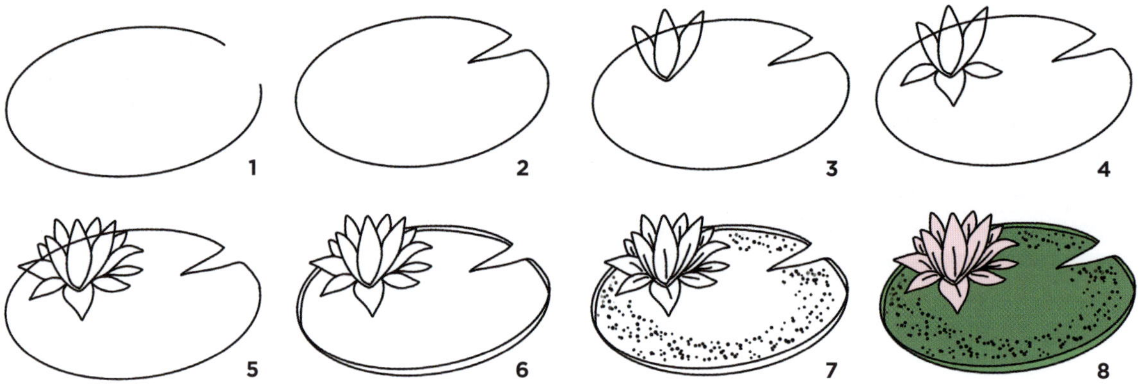

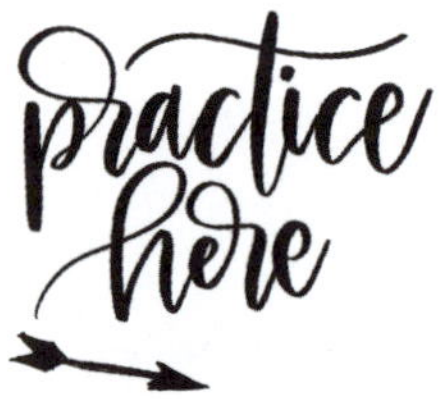

HIBISCUS FLOWER

When you think of a tropical flower, the hibiscus is probably the first thing that comes to mind. The large, bright blooms are eye-catching, but did you know the plant can be medicinal as well? Extracts, teas and supplements made from hibiscus can be used to treat liver problems and high blood pressure, along with a variety of other ailments.

Start your hibiscus doodle with four curving lines extending out in different directions from a center point. Starting with the top two, add a wavy line and form large, wide petal shapes. Repeat for the bottom two lines, creating two more petals. Finally, draw a waving line to form a large top petal. Next, draw two long lines extending out from the center of the flower to create a thin stamen. Add a bumpy oval shape on top of the stamen and draw details like dots inside and tiny circles extending from it. Draw a pair of leaves with veins. Color your flower in any bright vibrant shades you like. Add some darker shading close to the flower's center, as well as some detail lines for a more realistic effect.

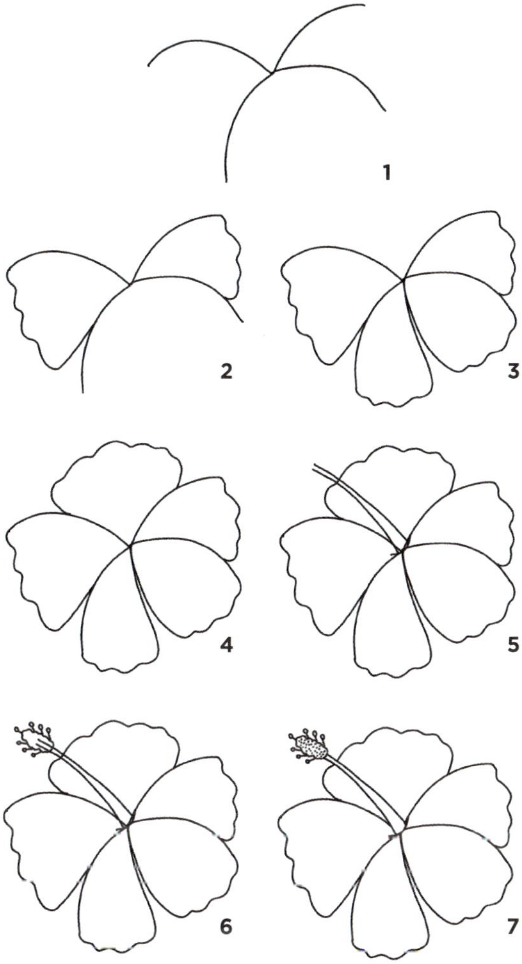

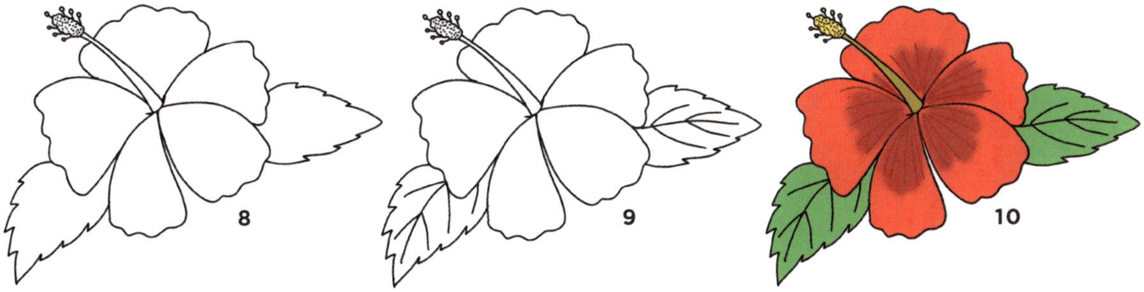

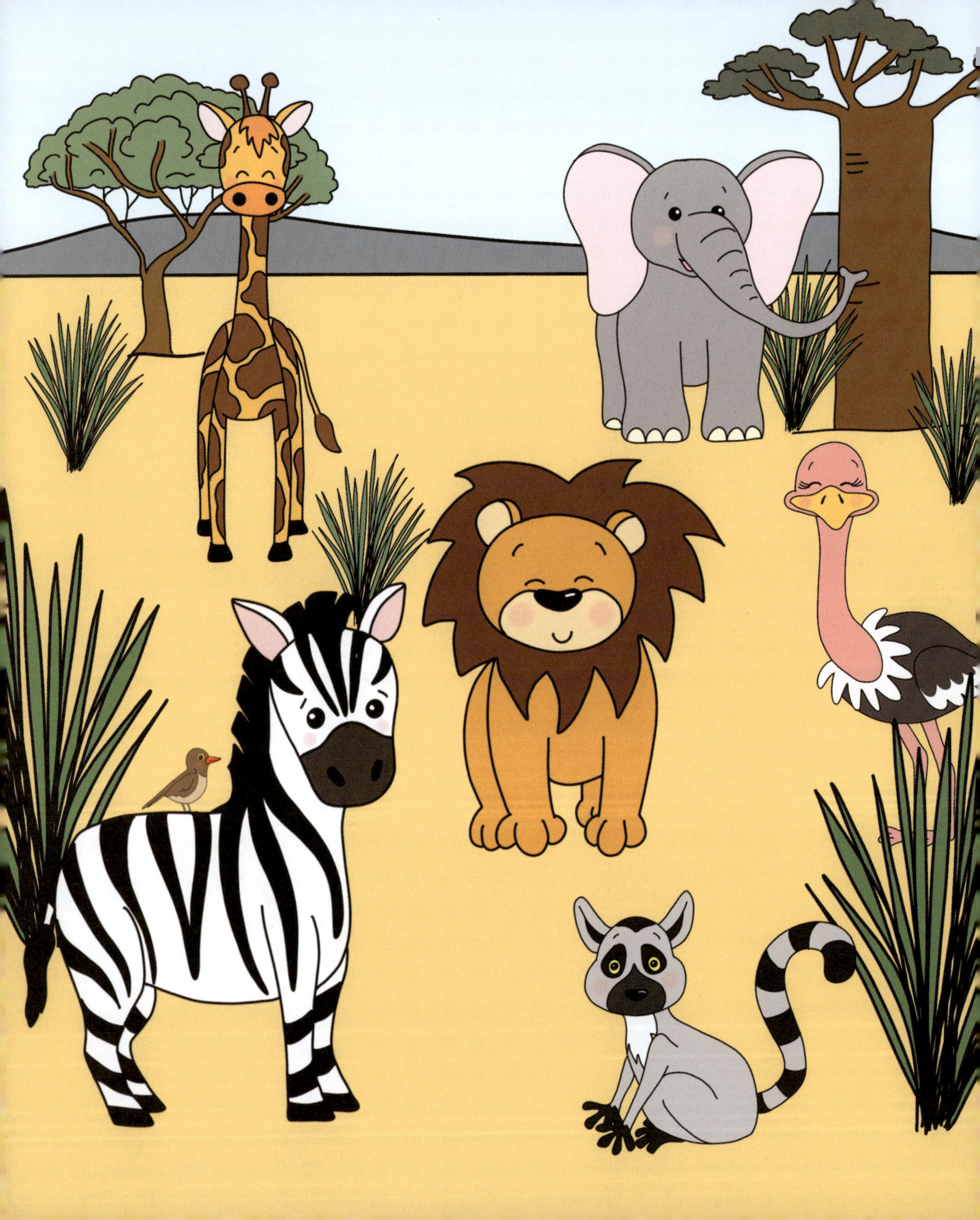

IN THE
Savanna

Savannas are located in tropical regions near the equator and are characterized by a continuous grass cover that's occasionally interrupted by brush or a tree. They're often transition areas between rain forests and deserts. The climate in savannas is typically hot and dry, with only short seasons of significant rainfall. Savannas can be found in Asia, South America and Australia, but the most well-known is in Africa, thanks to the large mammals who call it home. Let's take a trip to the savanna and meet some of these fascinating creatures . . . and, of course, learn to draw them!

LION

Known as the kings of the jungle, African lions are social animals that live in groups called prides. Their roars can be heard almost 5 miles (8 km) away, warning intruders to stay away from their territory. The older a male lion gets, the darker and more impressive his mane becomes, showing dominance within the pride.

To draw a lion, start with a round face and small, rounded ears. Add a series of "zigzags" surrounding the head and ears for the mane. Draw curving lines below the head for the front of the body and separate it into a pair of front legs and a stomach. Add paws below the legs. Draw back legs and paws and add a face including eyes, eyebrows, a nose, a mouth and lines to divide the upper and lower parts of the face. Finally, color your lion to give it character.

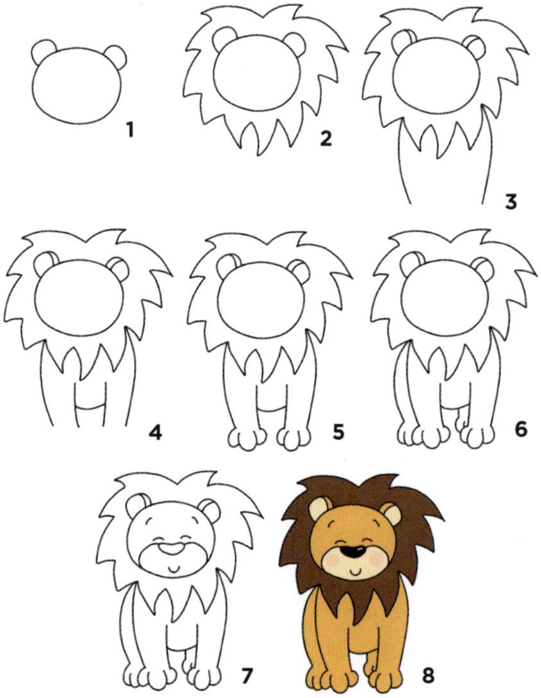

LIONESS

Female lions do the majority of the hunting, while the males stay back to defend the territory and "babysit" the cubs. Lionesses prefer to hunt at night and especially during storms, when the noise and wind make it easier to sneak up on their prey. When the food is brought back to the pride, the males eat first, then the females and cubs.

To sketch a lioness, draw a round face with a semicircle extending below it for the chin. Add small, rounded ears, then draw a nose and a mouth in the lower section of the face. Draw lines extending down from the head for the front and back legs and add paws at the bottom of each. Draw a line for the stomach and a curving tail. Color your lioness a shade of light brown or yellow.

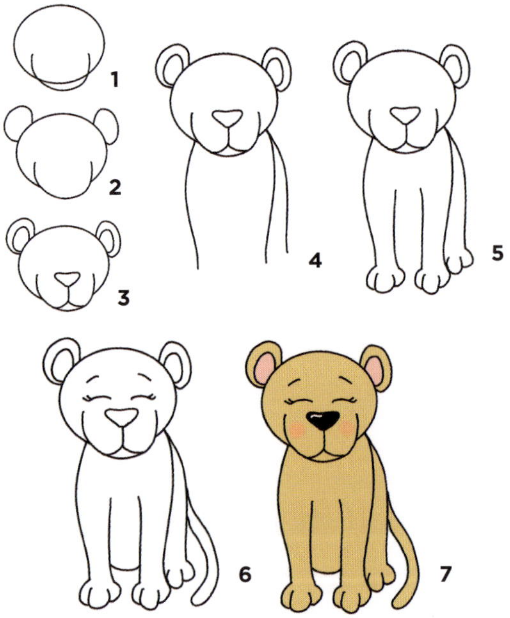

LION CUB

Although grown lions are strong, capable predators, lion cubs are born quite defenseless. They're small and vulnerable, with no teeth, and unable to open their eyes and fully see for the first several weeks of their lives. That's why lionesses keep their cubs hidden for at least six weeks, until they're old enough to follow the pride. Lion cubs need their mothers' care until they're two years old, at which point they can be independent, but they remain close as part of the same pride.

Drawing a lion cub starts with a round head and a pair of small, rounded ears divided into inner and outer sections. Next, add a "u" shape at the bottom of the head and a bean-shaped nose. Erase the spot where the "u" overlaps the face and add a mouth and a tongue below the nose. Draw lines to connect the nose to the sides of the head. Finish the face by adding eyes and eyebrows. Draw a pair of front legs and paws and add a zigzag "v" shape to show fur below the head. Draw curving lines on each side of the body to form back legs and add a pair of back paws. Give your cub a tail with a teardrop shape on the end. Finish your doodle by adding color.

Bonus: Now that you can draw male and female lions and a cub, try drawing them together to form a family or even a whole pride.

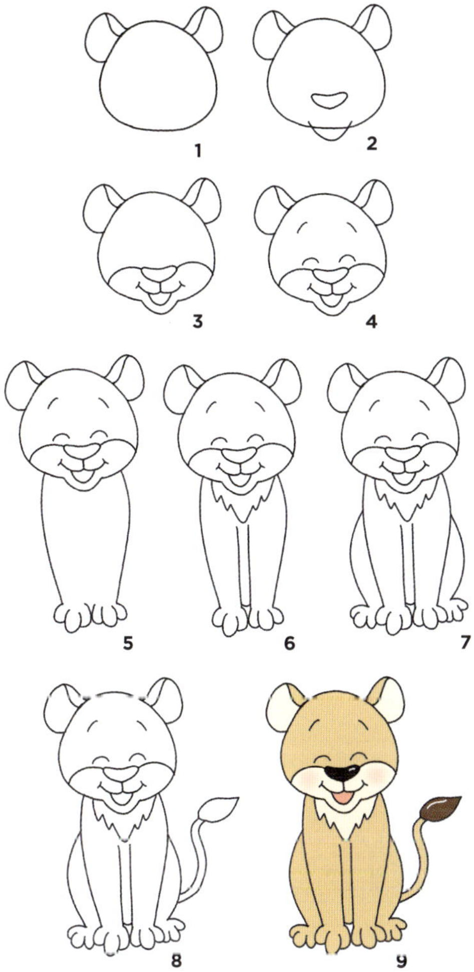

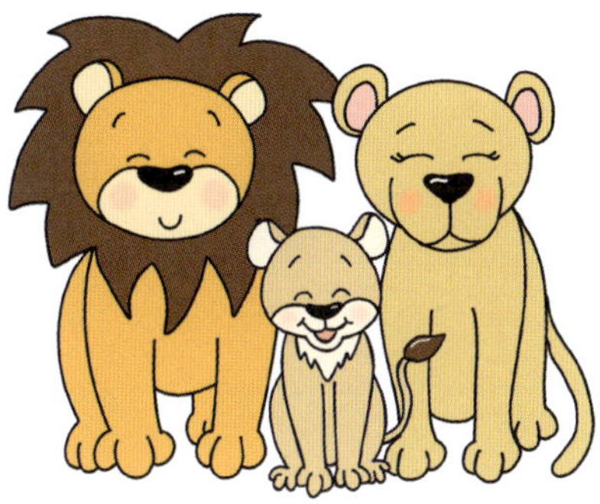

practice here

ZEBRA

Each zebra has a pattern of stripes that's as unique as a human's fingerprints. These members of the horse family are surprisingly fast and can even outrun a lion. When migrating from one feeding ground to another, zebra herds join together into "super herds" that can consist of thousands of animals moving together.

Start your zebra doodle with a long "u"-shaped face and add a pair of small, pointed ears. Complete the head shape and divide the ears into two sections. Separate the lower face area from the rest of the head, then add curving lines for the neck, back and chest. Give your zebra a pair of front legs with hooves. Add the back legs and connect them to the front legs to form the lower body. Sketch a mane on top of the head and on the neck and add a tail. Draw a pattern of stripes all over the body using long, thin "v" shapes. Add eyes and nostrils, then color your zebra doodle.

Practice here

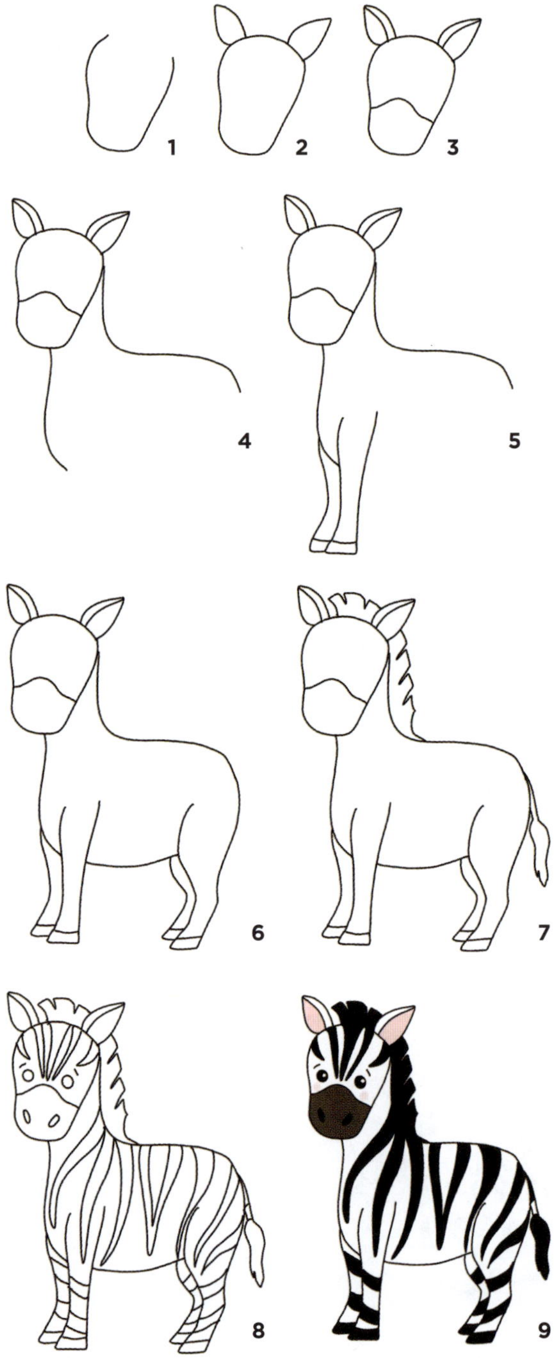

GIRAFFE

Reaching heights of up to 18 feet (5 m), giraffes are the tallest of all land animals. Surprisingly, they need very little sleep—only about 40 minutes every 24 hours, usually divided up into several five-minute "power naps"!

To start your giraffe doodle, draw a semicircle head with an oval at the bottom. Add pointed ears and ossicones, or horns, on top of the head. Draw eyes and eyebrows, as well as two circles inside the nose area. Give your giraffe a long, thin neck and a pair of front legs with a line connecting them to make the body. Add curving lines for the back legs and draw a hoof at the bottom of each leg. Add a patch of zigzag hair on the head and draw a tail. Sketch uniquely shaped spots all over the body and head. Finally, add color to your giraffe.

practice here

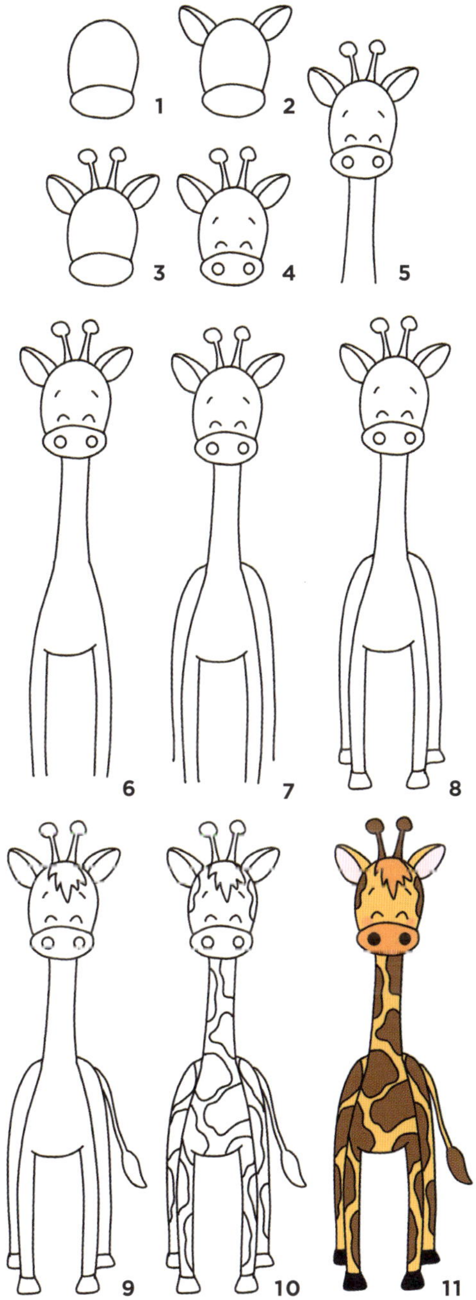

ANTELOPE

Did you know that antelopes are the second-fastest animal in the world? These two-toed herbivores also have quite a remarkable leap! They can jump up to 10 feet (3 m) high and 33 feet (10 m) in distance, which helps them escape from predators. There are 91 different species of antelope in the world. The one we're drawing is the impala, which is native to the African savanna.

Start your antelope sketch with a basic head shape and small, pointed ears. Add a heart-shaped nose and divide the face so that there's a large stripe in the center and a small stripe on the side, with a closed eye in between. Sketch a long neck and the back of the body, then add front and back legs and hooves. Draw the belly and divide the lower half of the body from the rest with curving lines. Add a short tail. Finally, draw a pair of curving horns extending up from the top of the head and pointing inward. Color your antelope, using mine as a guide or in any way you like.

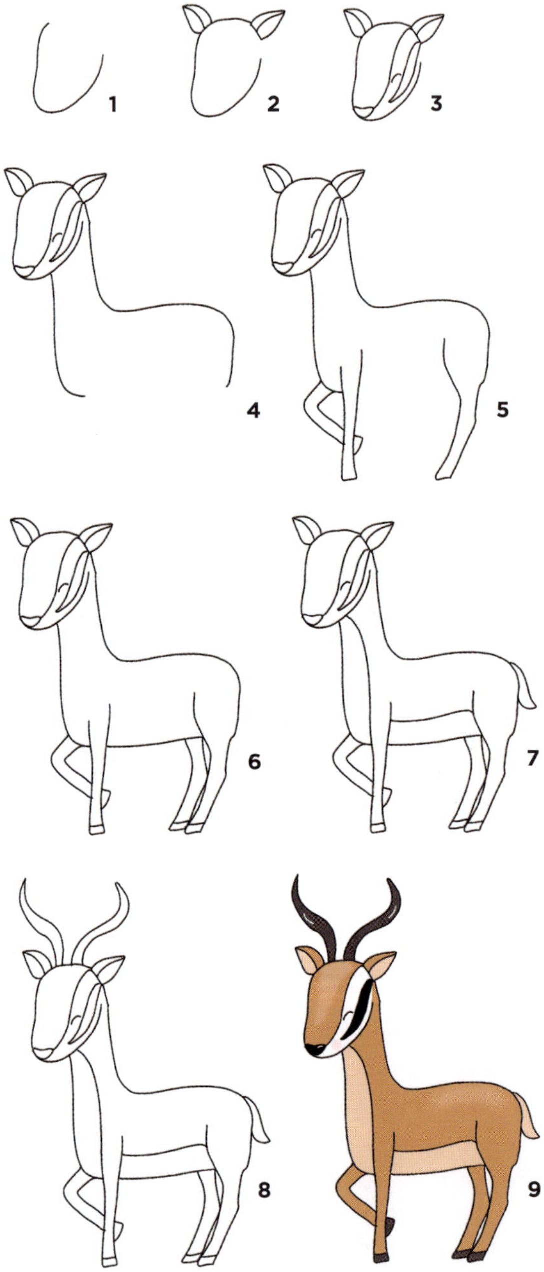

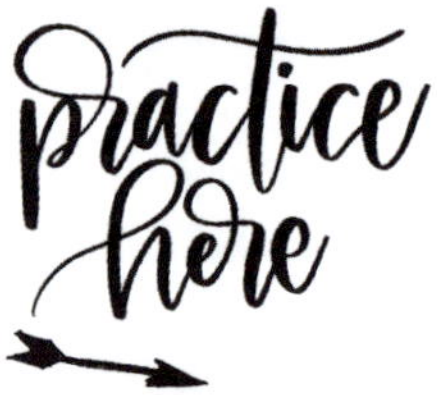

ELEPHANT

African elephants, the largest land animals on earth, can weigh as much as 13,000 pounds (5,897 kg)! While the human body contains over 650 muscles, an elephant's trunk alone has about 40,000. One way that elephants communicate is through rumbling noises that are too low-pitched for humans to hear. Another is by stomping, as they're able to detect seismic vibrations with their feet.

To draw your own elephant, start with a round head and large ears. Add two thick front legs and a short line to indicate the stomach. Draw a back leg, then add semicircles on each foot for toenails. Sketch a long, curving trunk that gets thinner as it reaches the end, erasing any overlapping lines. Give your elephant eyes, eyebrows and a mouth peeking out from below the trunk. Draw a series of texture lines on the trunk to show wrinkles, then color your elephant.

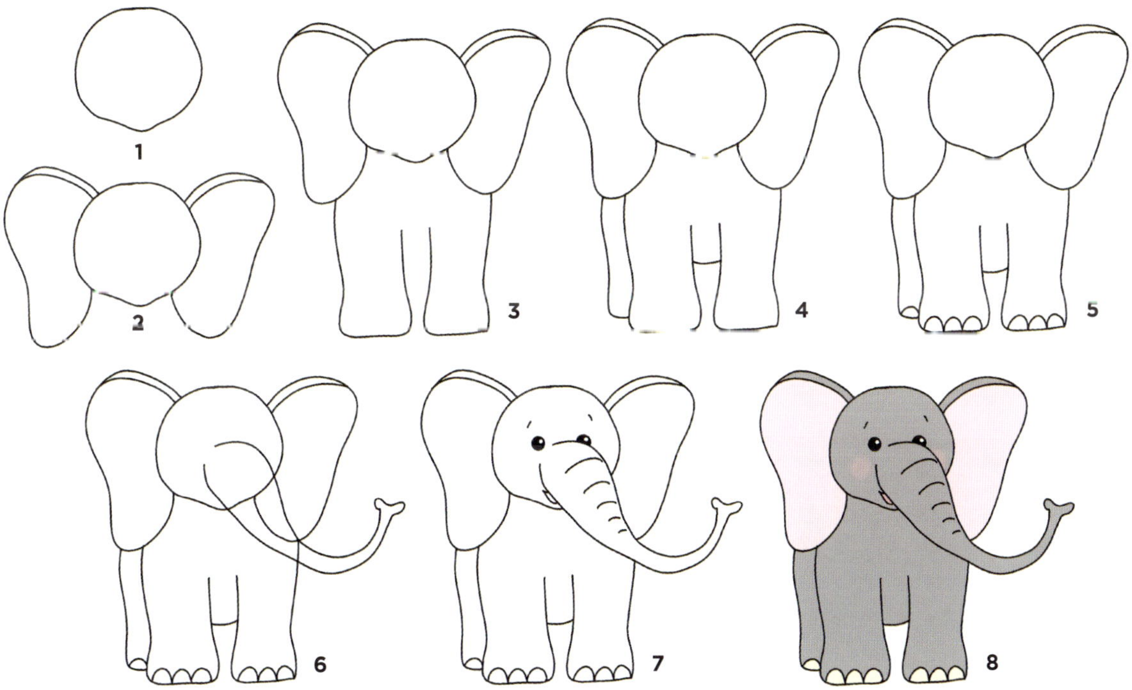

ELEPHANT CALF

Baby elephants, called calves, usually weigh between 115 and 200 pounds (52 and 91 kg) and drink about 3 gallons (11 L) of milk each day. Ninety-nine percent of elephant calves are born at night, so that it's harder for predators to find them. Since they're nearly blind at birth, they rely on their trunks, as well as the guidance of their mothers, to help them find things. Elephant calves love to play and will flap their ears when they're excited. They also make a trumpet-like sound to express joy.

Start your baby elephant drawing with a round head and two very large ears. Divide off the top section of each ear. Then, draw a pair of rectangular front legs. Add an oval-shaped foot on each side of the front legs. Then, draw small scallops on each of the four feet. Add a trunk that ends in a spiral and erase the areas where it overlaps the face. Draw detail lines on the trunk and give your elephant a face. All that's left to do is add color to finish your doodle.

Bonus: Try drawing an elephant calf with its mother!

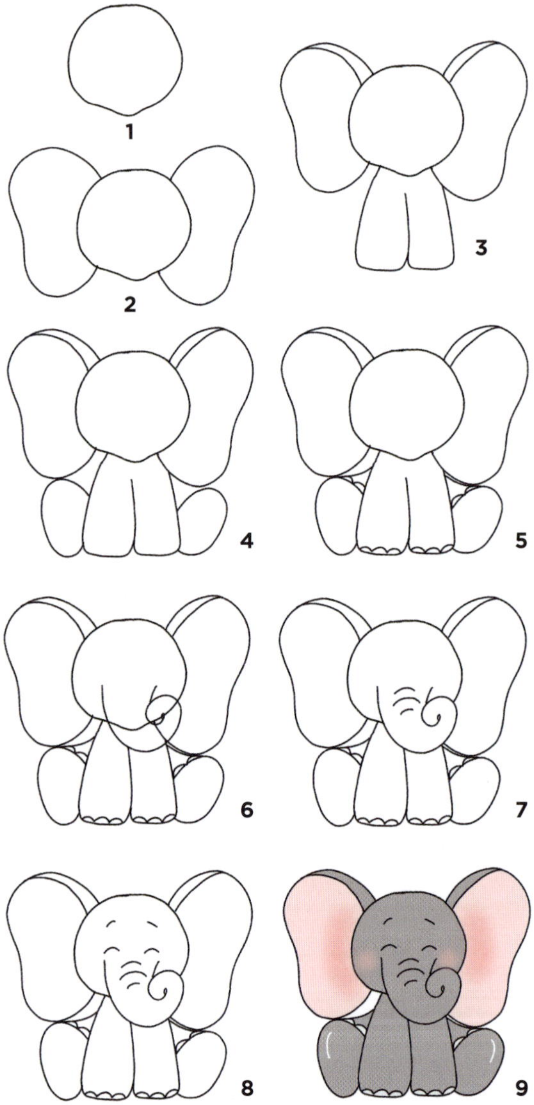

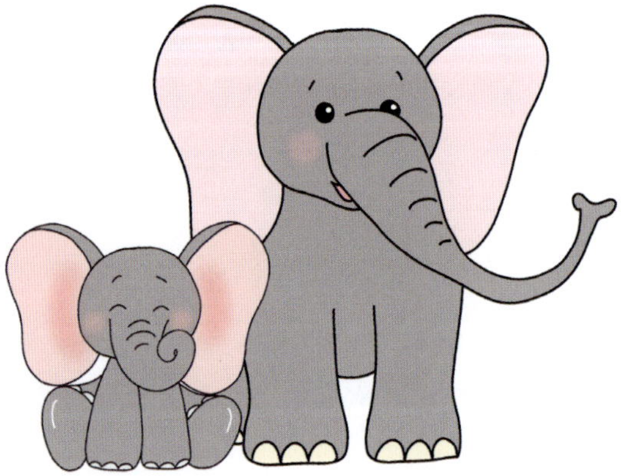

RHINOCEROS

The name "rhinoceros" is a combination of two Greek words, meaning "nose horn." Although most rhinos don't spend much time with other members of their own species, they often form symbiotic relationships with birds called oxpeckers. These birds perch on a rhino's back and feed on the parasites living on its thick skin. In turn, they clean the rhino and can also alert it of potential danger.

To draw your rhino, start with a curving line that ends in a point for the outline of the face. Add a pair of small, pointed ears. Next, sketch a bumpy line for the back. Add a pair of curving triangles on the head for horns (erasing the lines that overlap) and draw the rhino's lower head. Add a pair of thick front legs and connect them to the head with a short curving line. Draw the back legs and connect them to the front legs to complete the body. Add scallops on the feet and a short tail. Give your rhino an eye and inner ear areas, then draw some detail lines all over the body to show the wrinkly texture of the skin. Finally, add color to complete your rhinoceros.

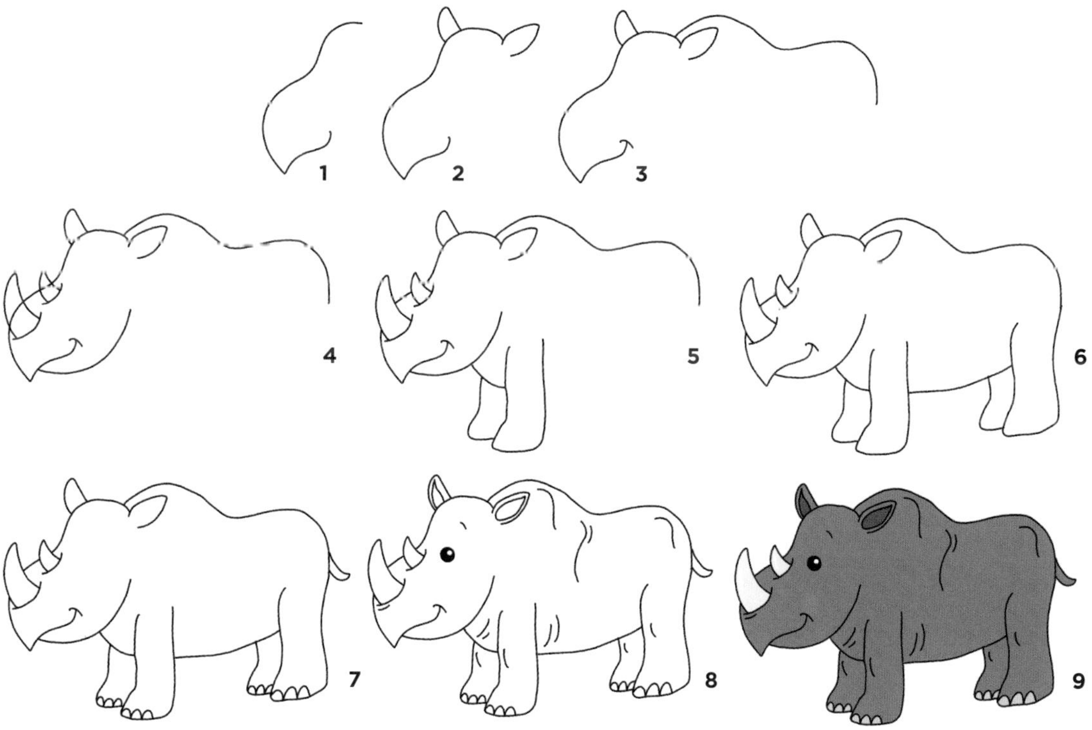

OXPECKER

Oxpeckers are small birds that are native to the African savanna. They're only 7 to 9 inches (18 to 23 cm) in size and weigh less than 2 ounces (57 g), but they can eat hundreds of bugs each day. Oxpeckers spend most of their time perched on large animals like hippos, rhinos and zebras, feeding on the insects and parasites located on their bodies.

To doodle this interesting bird, start with a semicircle head and add a pointed beak with a line inside. Sketch a curving line for the neck and lower body, then add a line for the bird's back. Draw a long tail with two thin feathers. Next, sketch a wing and draw a scalloped detail line inside. Give your bird three concentric circles in the eye area, the center of which will be the eye itself. Draw a line dividing the lower portion of the body from the face and upper body. Add legs and feet, then color your oxpecker. These birds are brown with cream-colored bellies, yellow and orange patches around the eyes and red beaks.

Bonus: Try drawing your rhino with an oxpecker or two hitching a ride on his back!

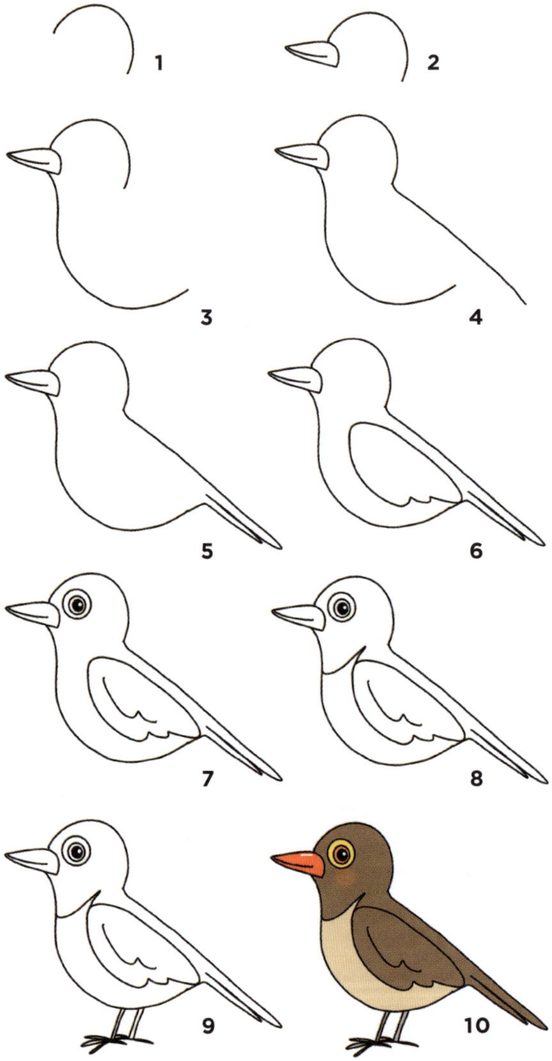

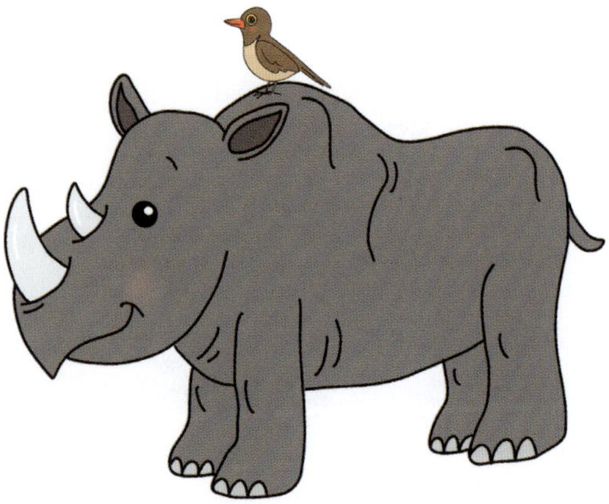

practice here

WARTHOG

The tusks of a warthog are actually teeth that have grown out of their mouths and curved upward. These are used for self-defense against predators and in fights with other warthogs. Although they enjoy spending time wallowing in the mud, warthogs actually will groom one another in social groups.

Begin your warthog sketch by drawing a semicircle head and a rounded triangle snout. Connect the triangle to the head, then draw a curving horn on each side of the snout. Add a pair of pointed ears and divide them into two sections. Draw a small area below the snout for the lower jaw. Sketch a curving line for the back and draw lines for the chest and front leg. Sketch the lower part of the body and back leg and add a second front leg behind the first one. Give your warthog a tail, then draw a wavy oval mud puddle all around the lower body, with detail lines inside. Draw a series of zigzags on top of the head and down the back for hair and add facial details. Complete your drawing by coloring it in any way you like.

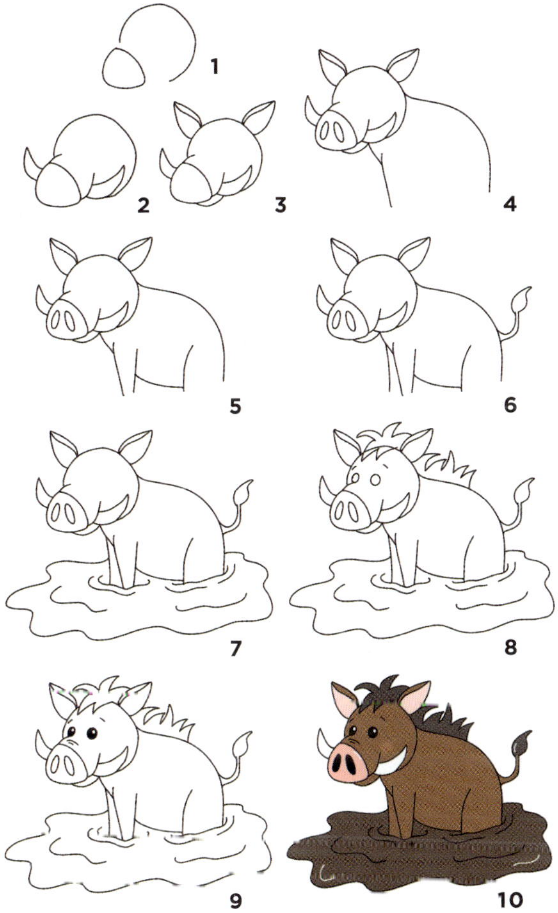

practice here

HIPPOPOTAMUS

The name "hippopotamus" is Greek for "river horse." Hippos have an excellent sense of smell but poor eyesight. Their eyes, ears and nostrils are located on the top of their head, which allows them to see, hear and breathe while the rest of their body is submerged in water. Although they spend most of the day in water, hippos can't swim or float!

The first step in drawing a hippo is to make a sideways "3" shape for the cheeks. Add a curving line on top for the head and a pair of small, pointed ears. Draw a small rectangle below each cheek for teeth. Sketch a large semicircle to the right of the head for the body and add two thick front legs. Draw a line for the stomach and add a pair of back legs, making sure each foot has a few toenails. Add a face and a short, pointed tail, then color your hippo.

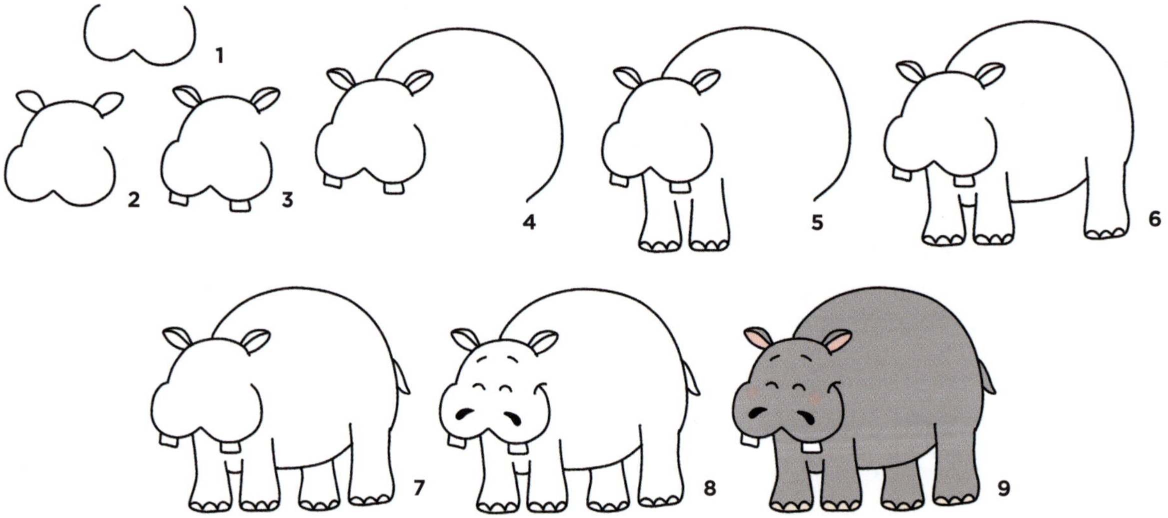

practice here

CHEETAH

Cheetahs are able to run almost 70 miles per hour (113 kph), which makes them the world's fastest land animal. The cheetah's tail actually plays a role in its speed, acting as a counterbalance for the running animal.

Draw your own cheetah, starting with a round head and two rounded ears. Add a nose and a semicircle for the chin. Erase the area where the lines overlap. Divide the face into an upper and lower section and draw a mouth below the nose. Finish the face with eyes, eyebrows and a pair of curving lines running from the side of the nose up over each eye. Draw a jagged "v" shape below the chin for a patch of fur, then add the front legs and paws. Sketch curving lines for the back legs, then add paws, dividing them from the rest of the legs. Draw a curving tail extending out to the side. Finally, draw spots on the body, tail and head. Color your cheetah to bring your doodle to life.

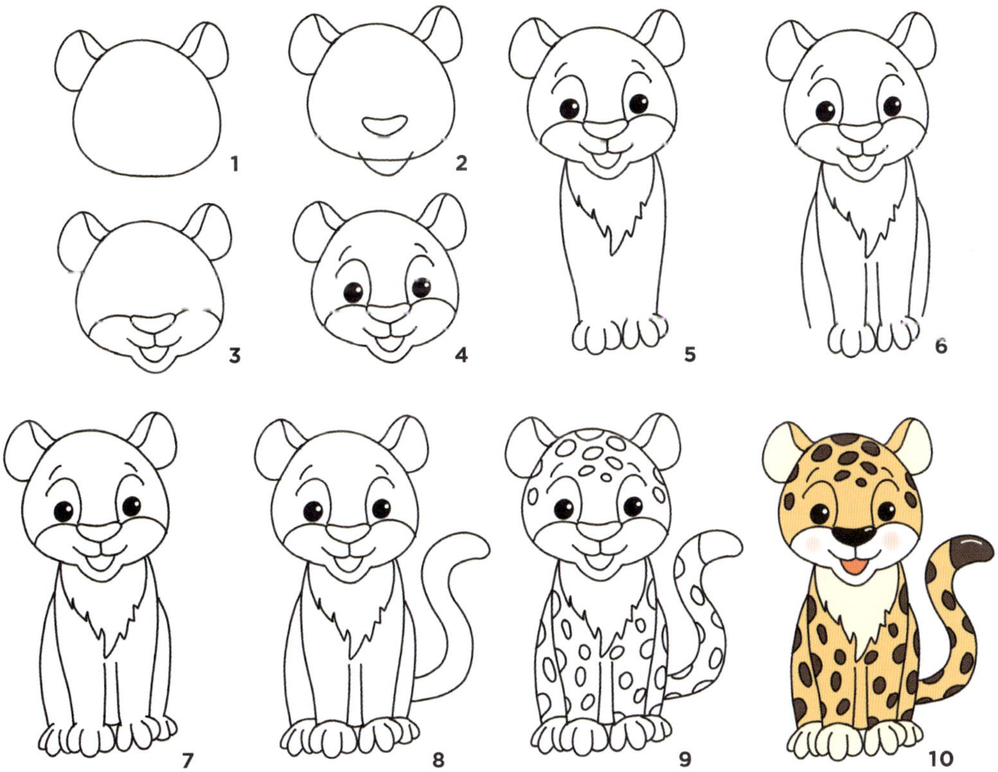

LEOPARD

Did you know that due to specially adapted retinas in their eyes, leopards can see seven times better than humans in the dark? These elusive big cats are hard to trace in the wild and sometimes use trees to escape from predators, hide their kills and gain a good vantage point where they can watch for prey.

Start your leopard doodle with a round head and a semicircle chin. Add short, pointed ears, a nose and a mouth. Draw a curving line extending from the side of the head to form the leopard's back. Next, draw two long, curving lines below the leopard for a tree branch. Sketch a paw to the right of the face and an arm to the left. Add a back leg and paw. Draw a long, rounded tail, erase all overlapping lines, then add eyes and eyebrows. Finally, add rosette spots by drawing curving lines and dots. Color your leopard a shade of yellow or tan with black, orange and/or brown spots.

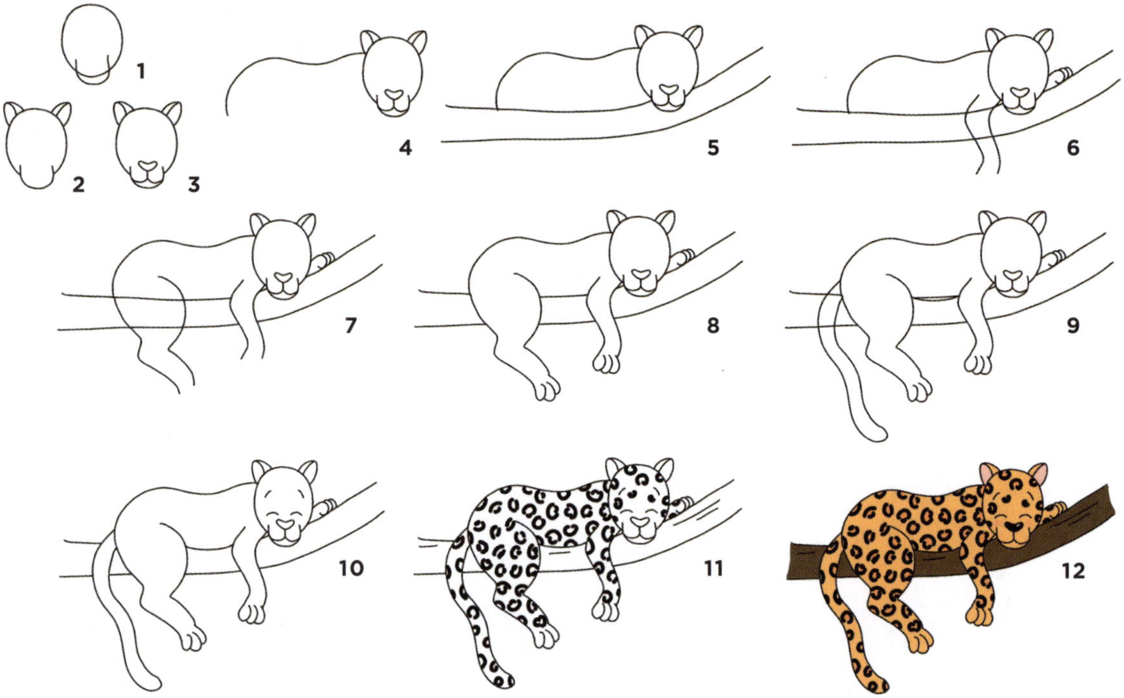

OSTRICH

An ostrich can grow as tall as 9 feet (3 m), with its neck accounting for almost half of its height! Because ostriches can weigh up to 300 pounds (136 kg), they're too heavy to fly, so they've adapted to living on land. They can run about 43 miles per hour (69 kph), which makes them not only the largest living birds on the planet but also the fastest animals on two legs.

To draw your own ostrich, start with a semicircle and a wavy line. Add a "v" shape below the wavy line to turn it into a beak, then add curving lines on either side of the beak to finish the head. Draw a long, slender neck that curves slightly to the right at the base. Next, draw a paisley-shaped body that connects to the neck. Sketch a series of bumps around the base of the neck, as well as for the tail, to indicate feathers. Draw a wing on the side of the body, then add long, thin legs and webbed feet. Give your ostrich eyes, eyebrows and markings on the beak, then add color to finish your doodle.

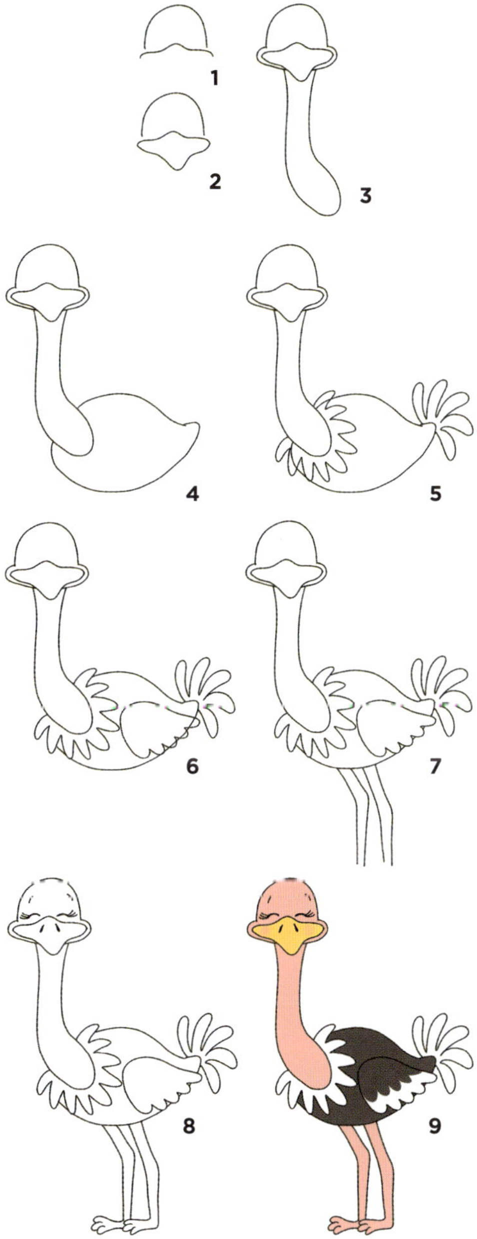

practice here

LEMUR

Lemurs are intelligent primates and the smartest ones tend to be the most popular among their peers. Those who display new skills receive affectionate attention from the rest of the group. When two male ring-tailed lemurs have a disagreement, they resolve it by having a "stink fight," where they run their tails through their scent glands to transfer a foul odor to the fur, then wave them at each other until one of them backs off.

To doodle a lemur, start with a pear-shaped face and two long, pointed ears. Divide the face with a "v" shape near the top of the head, two egg shapes where the eyes will be and a pointed section for the nose area. Add eyes, a nose and eyebrows. Draw a curving line for the lemur's back and zigzag lines for the chest. Sketch an arm with rounded fingers, then a second arm and a hand behind the first. Draw a curving line for the back leg and add toes beneath it. Draw a long, curling tail. Divide the tail into sections, then color your lemur, using mine as a guide.

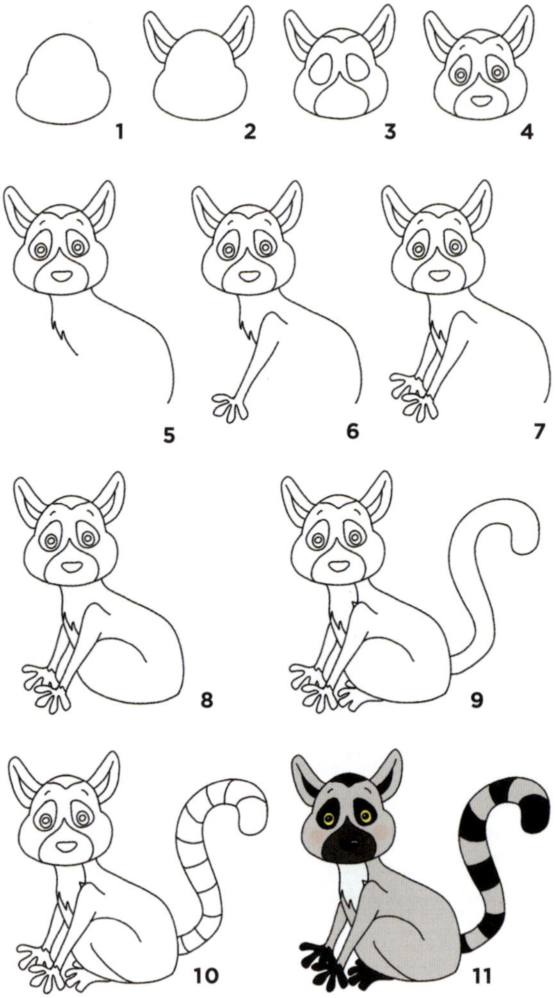

practice here

AARDVARK

Aardvarks are nocturnal, spending their days sleeping in burrows (which are often inside termite mounds) and their nights searching for food. An aardvark's tongue is almost 12 inches (30 cm) long, which means it can eat up to 50,000 ants and termites in a single night.

To draw this unique animal, start with a curving question mark–shaped line for the head and nose and add a set of pointed ears. Sketch the bottom of the head and draw a circle at the end of the nose for a snout. Add two short front legs below the head and a curving line on each side to form the rounded body. Draw the back legs and a line for the stomach, then add a long, pointed tail. Add details like toenails, holes in the snout, a curved line dividing the head, an eye, an eyebrow and a smile. Finally, add color to your doodle.

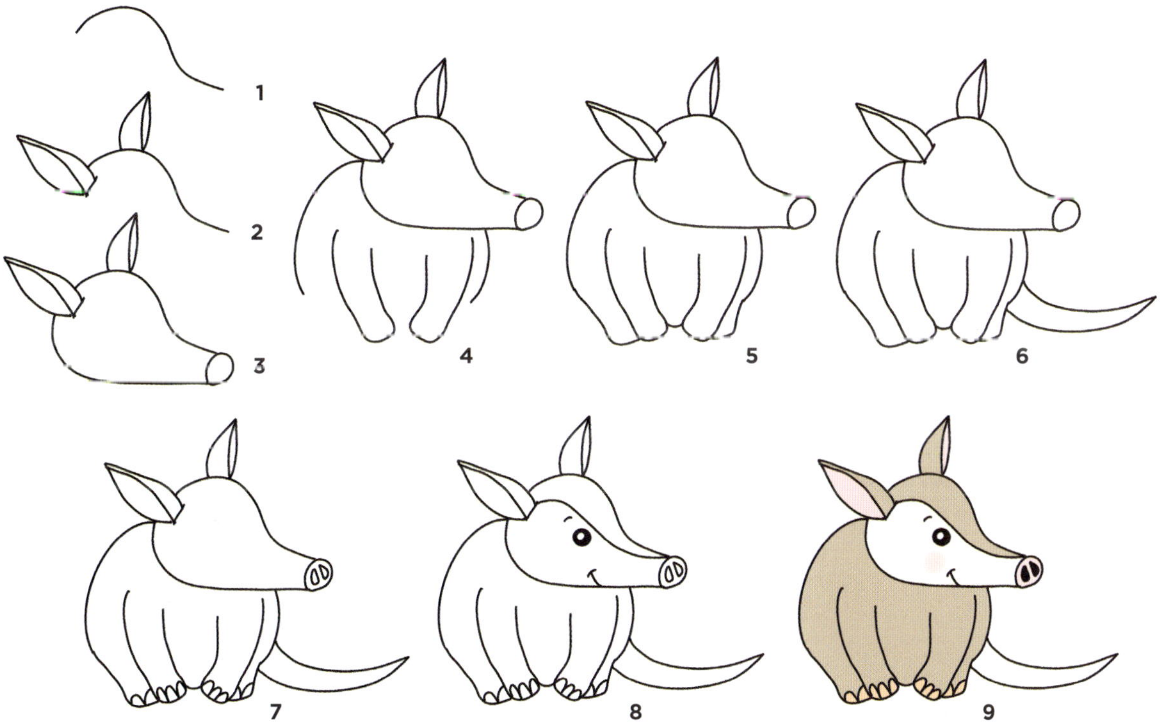

IN THE HABITAT

ACACIA TREE

Not only is the acacia tree an important part of the food chain, as the habitat of many different mammals, birds and insects, it's also the main source of gum arabic. Why is that important? Gum arabic is used in paints, watercolors, candy, medicines, cosmetics, silk and paper.

To doodle this special tree, start with two wavy lines that are farther apart at the bottom. Add a second set of lines branching off in the opposite direction. Continue adding branches, coming off of the main two, until you're satisfied with the structure of your tree. Then, add a dome-shaped top using scalloped lines. Add more scallops inside the top to show the texture of the leaves. Finally, add thin lines connecting the larger branches to the top to represent smaller branches. Color your tree brown and green or color it black to create a silhouette on the landscape!

practice here

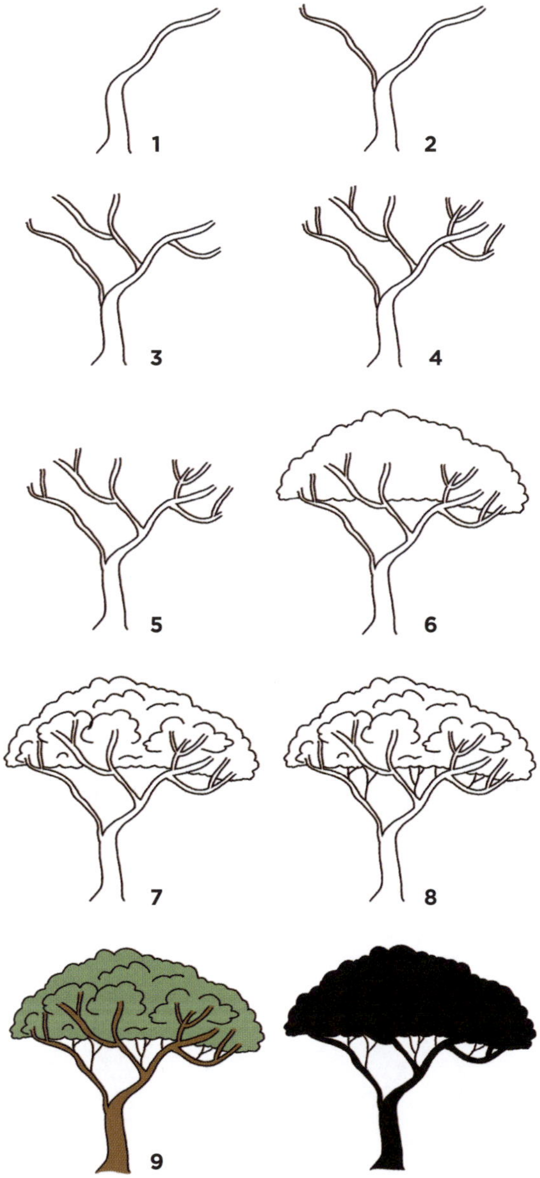

BAOBAB TREE

Known as the "tree of life," the baobab tree stores huge amounts of water in its large trunk (up to 30,000 gallons [120,000 L]!), so during the dry season, elephants and other animals will chew the bark to stay hydrated. This tree can reach up to 100 feet (30 m) in height and 46 feet (14 m) in diameter. The various parts of the tree can be used to create rope, cloth, soap, rubber, glue and medicine and its fruit can be eaten or blended into a drink.

Start your baobab doodle with two widely spaced vertical lines. Add several small branches on top, then surround the branches with multiple scalloped shapes to represent leaves. Draw detail lines on the trunk, then color your baobab tree.

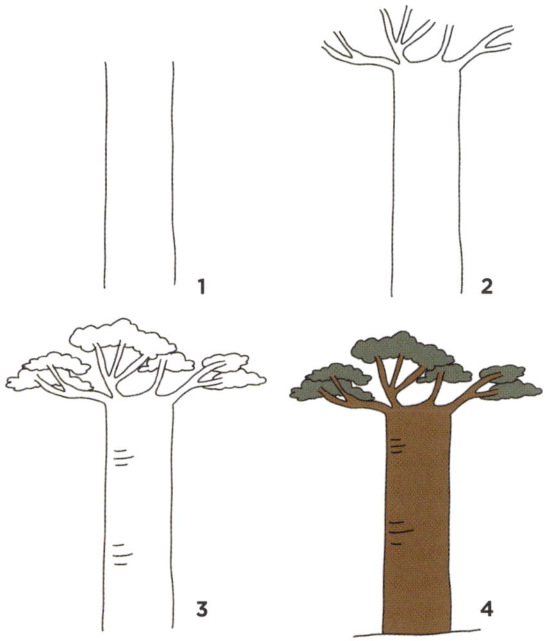

ELEPHANT GRASS

Elephant grass requires very little water and few nutrients, so it's able to thrive in the African grasslands. This grass is rough to the touch and can reach heights of almost 10 feet (3 m). It provides food for elephants and other large animals, while providing shelter and a hiding place for smaller animals on the run from predators.

To draw elephant grass, start by sketching a series of very long, thin leaf shapes that are close together at the bottom. Continue drawing more and more of these shapes, varying the height and curving some out to the sides until you have a full patch of grass. This can be as large or small as you want it to be. Color your grass green or yellow.

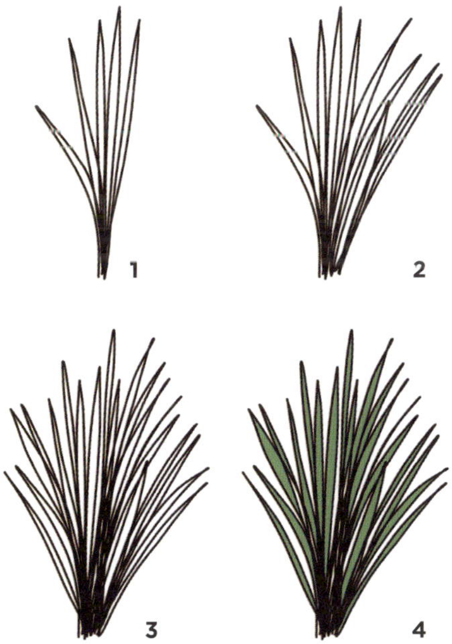

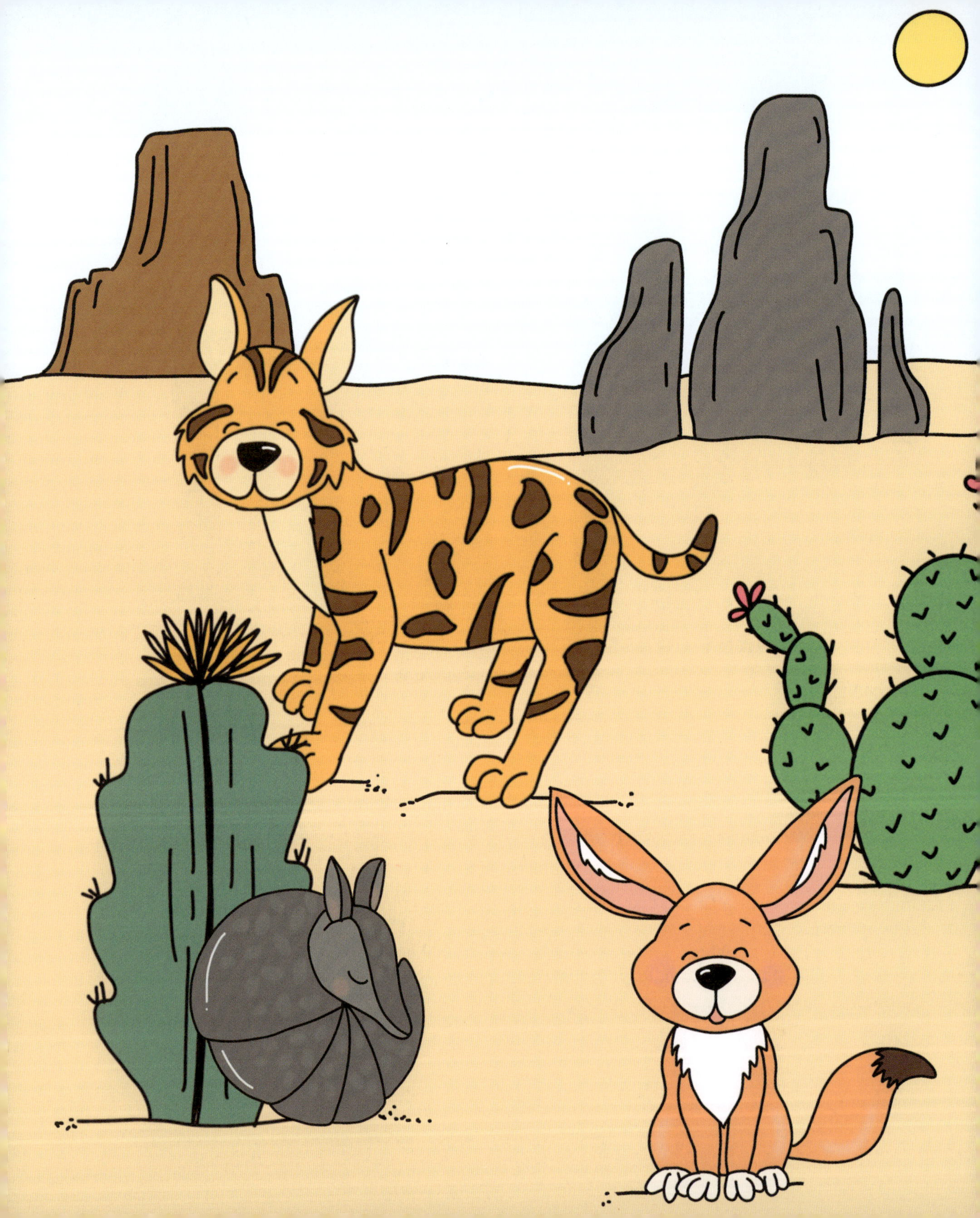

IN THE Desert

Around one-third of the planet is covered by deserts, which are areas that receive very low (less than 16 inches [41 cm]) precipitation each year. There are two types of deserts: hot and cold. The largest deserts in the world, the Antarctic and Arctic deserts, are incredibly chilly with temperatures around -56 degrees Fahrenheit (-49°C). The Sahara, on the other hand, typically ranges between 104 and 116 degrees Fahrenheit (40 and 47°C) and is the site of the second-hottest recorded temperature on the planet (after Death Valley in California), 136.4 degrees Fahrenheit (58°C)! Despite the harsh conditions, deserts are actually diverse ecosystems that are home to a variety of reptiles, mammals and insects. Let's learn about some of them and add them to our doodle repertoire.

ROADRUNNER

Roadrunners are terrestrial birds found in North America. They can only fly short distances, and unlike other birds, they build their nests on the ground. In order to survive nighttime desert temperatures, roadrunners actually lower their body temperatures by 10 degrees at night.

To sketch a roadrunner, the first step is drawing the long, thin beak. Next, add the front of the body, head and back. Draw a large wing and a long, narrow tail with bumps on the end to represent feathers. Below the main body, draw the area where the legs will connect, then add legs and feet. The feet should have two toes pointing forward and one pointing backward. Add a bumpy line above the head to form the feathered crest. Finish your doodle with details like the eye, feather detail lines, a curved line down the body, the lower section of the beak and a patch behind the eye. Finally, add color.

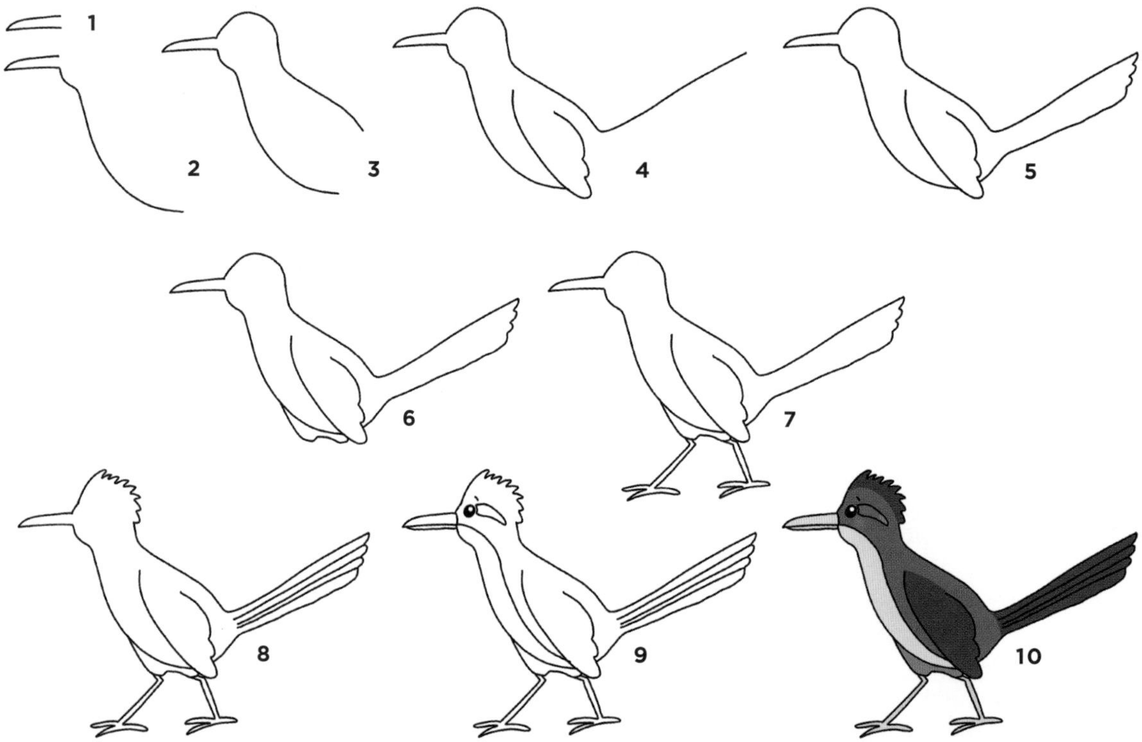

QUAIL

Quail are small birds, only measuring between 5 and 8 inches (13 and 20 cm) in size. Although they can fly, they prefer not to. Instead, they primarily walk and make their nests on the ground among shrubs or bushes. Male quail are called cocks or roos, females are called hens and babies are called chicks. One of the most notable things about the common quail is the male's unusual call, a song that sounds like "wet my lips."

To draw a quail, start with a curving line for the front of the body, then add a second curving line above it to form the outline of the head and back. Sketch a large wing with scalloped feathers and connect it to the rest of the body, forming a tail. Draw a small beak and a pair of legs and feet. Add a plume on top of the head and two thin teardrop-shaped markings on the face. Add an eye and a marking around the eye. Draw scalloped lines on the body for a feathery texture, then color your quail.

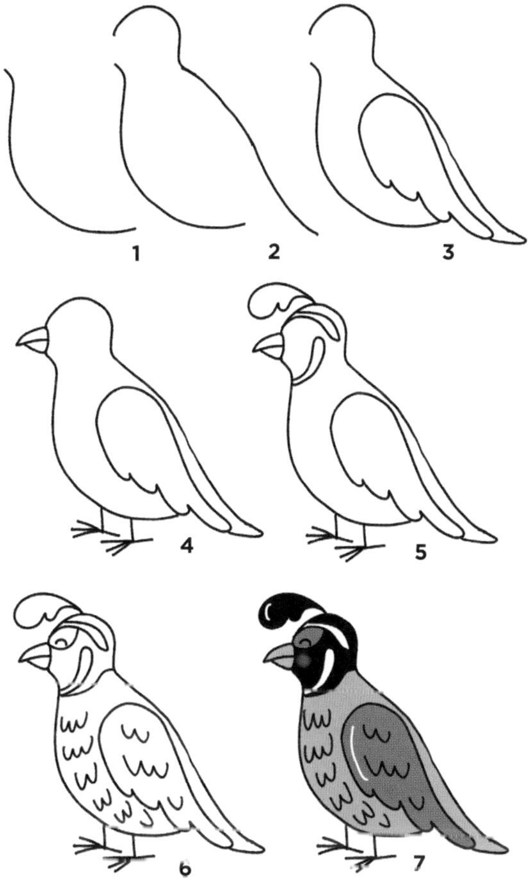

practice here

ANTELOPE JACKRABBIT

An antelope jackrabbit is a large-eared hare with long, powerful hind legs. It gets its name from its similarities to the antelope; both animals are agile, fast and able to leap quickly out of danger. Antelope jackrabbits can jump 10 feet (3 m) in a single bound and will confuse predators by hopping in a zigzag pattern. Their extraordinarily large ears are useful not just for hearing but also for helping to regulate their body temperature.

To doodle this fascinating hare, start with an oval-shaped head. Add a "u" shape inside and slightly below the head and draw a curving "v" for the nose. Erase the areas where the "u" shape overlaps the head and sketch a line connecting the nose to the bottom of the "u." Draw curving lines to form the jackrabbit's back and chest. Add a curving back leg and a foot, then draw a pair of front legs and feet. Connect the front leg to the back leg and draw an "L" shape to suggest the other back leg. Add a small tail. Give your jackrabbit a large pair of ears and divide them into two sections. Add eyes and eyebrows and separate the chest area from the rest of the body. Finally, color your doodle!

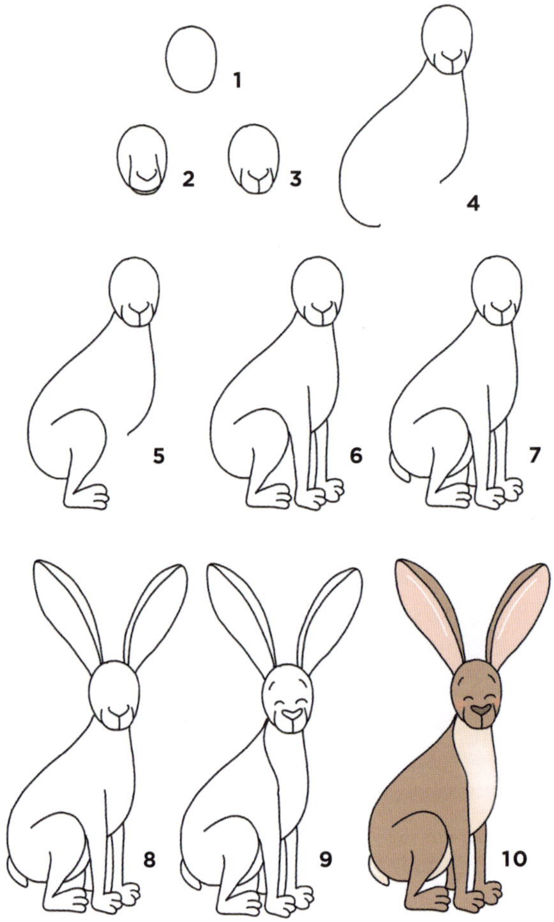

practice here

ARMADILLO

Armadillos are the only mammals with shells. Some species (three-banded armadillos) are able to curl up into a ball when threatened by predators, but all species use their shells as body armor. Nine-banded armadillos, the type found in the United States, almost always give birth to identical quadruplets!

To draw an armadillo, start by sketching a head shape with a long, thin nose. Next, add short, pointed ears, then create the first band of its armored shell. Doodle a series of curving shapes that form the rest of the shell. Under the head, draw the front of the body and two legs with feet. Add another set of legs, giving all of the feet lines for claws. Sketch a belly and a long, pointed tail. Finally, add a face, along with other details like segmenting the tail and dividing off a portion of the head. Color your armadillo, adding spots on the shell area for extra detail.

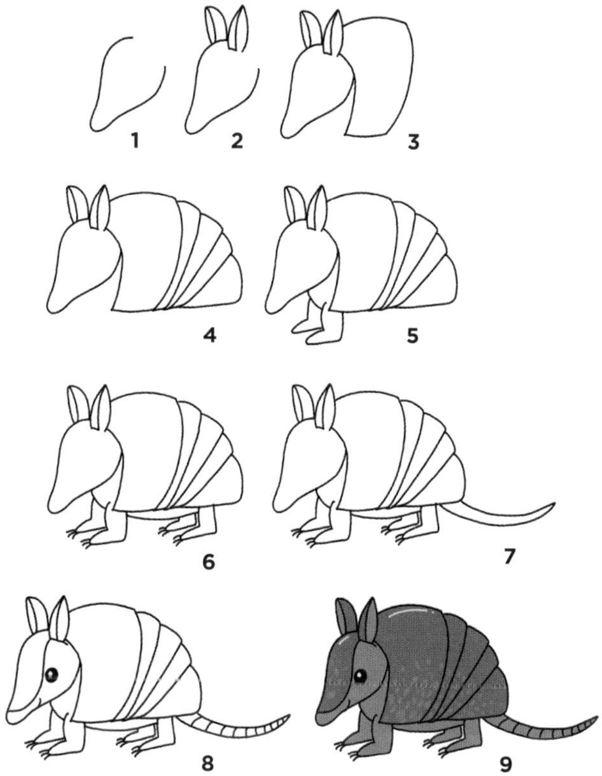

ARMADILLO—SLEEPING

The name "armadillo" means "little armored one" in Spanish. When armadillos are born, their shells are soft with a leathery texture, which becomes hard and bony over the next few days.

To add some variety to your armadillo doodle, try drawing it curled up in a ball! Start with the same head and ear shapes, but this time when you draw the shell, gently curve the sections around to form a circle. The last section should wrap around, going under the armadillo's head. For this version, you don't need to show the legs, feet or tail; just add a closed eye and color your sleeping creature.

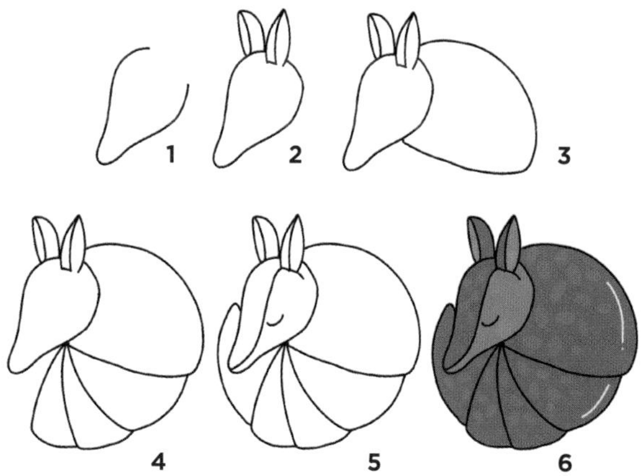

COYOTE

Coyotes have incredible survival instincts, changing their diets and even controlling how many pups they have in a litter based on food availability. They can hear sounds from a quarter of a mile away and are able to detect the sound of a mouse moving under 7 inches (18 cm) of snow. Coyotes also have excellent night vision and smell.

Our coyote doodle is busy howling at the moon, so we'll start the drawing with a curving line for the head and back. Next, sketch the back leg and foot in a seated position. Add ears and the muzzle, which points up to the sky. Erase the overlapping lines and draw the bottom jaw and neck, then sketch the front leg and paw. Doodle a long, fluffy tail and add zigzags to the ear, chest and tail to show the furry areas. Divide off the muzzle and chest from the rest of the body. Give your coyote a face, then add color to finish your masterpiece.

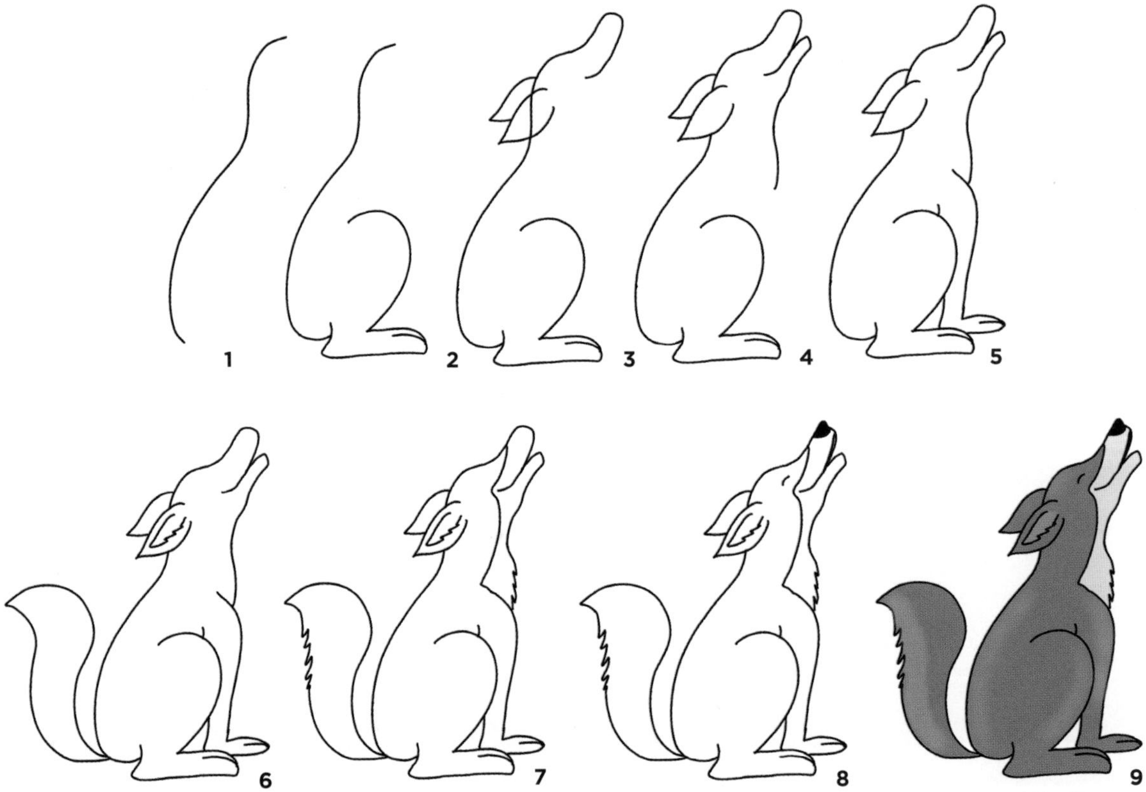

FENNEC FOX

The fennec fox is the smallest member of the fox family, measuring just 7 to 16 inches (18 to 24 cm). Its enormous ears are about half the size of its body and are actually useful for cooling off. This adorable animal has adapted to its environment and can go for long periods without drinking water, getting hydration through food instead. Fennec foxes purr when they're happy and can emit a musky smell from scent glands in their tails when they feel threatened or stressed.

Start your doodle of this adorable animal by sketching the face shape. Next, draw a triangle below it, using zigzag lines to indicate fur. Add two front legs and paws, then sketch wavy lines for the sides of the body. Draw two more paws and a thick, curving tail. Section off the tip of the tail with a zigzag line. Doodle two enormous pointed ears with furry areas inside, then add a muzzle and a nose. Finish adding face details, then color your fennec fox.

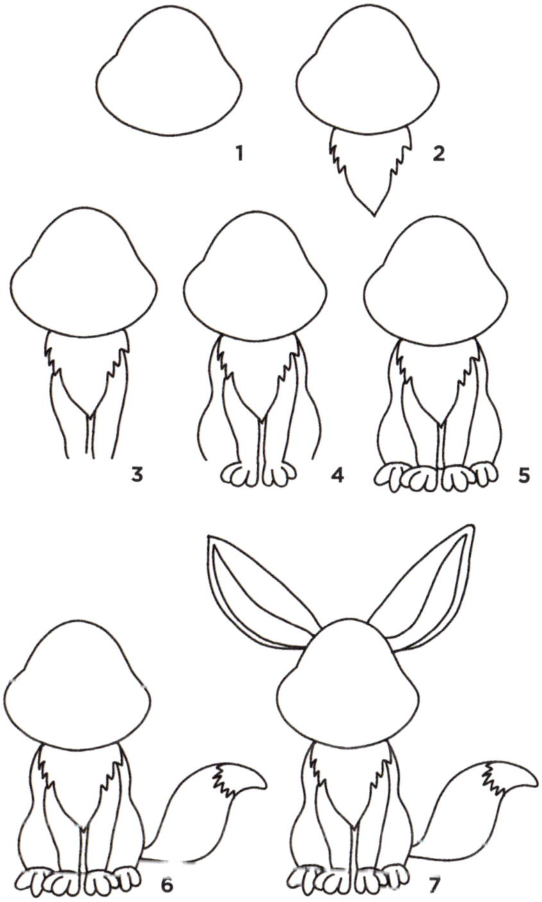

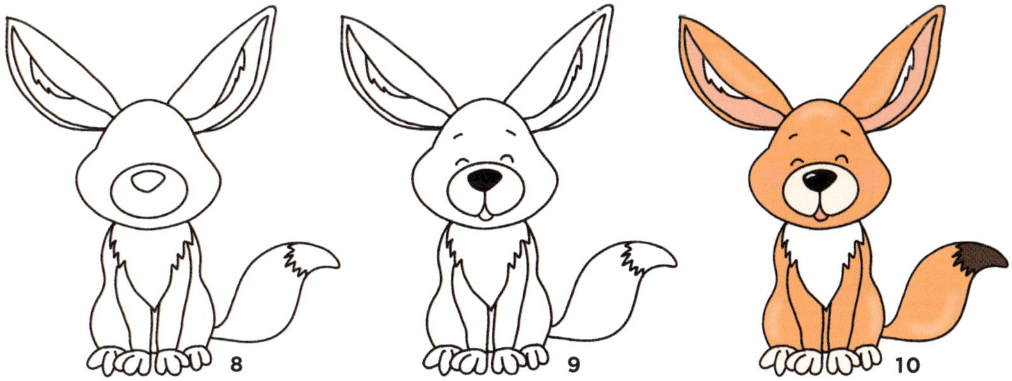

MEERKAT

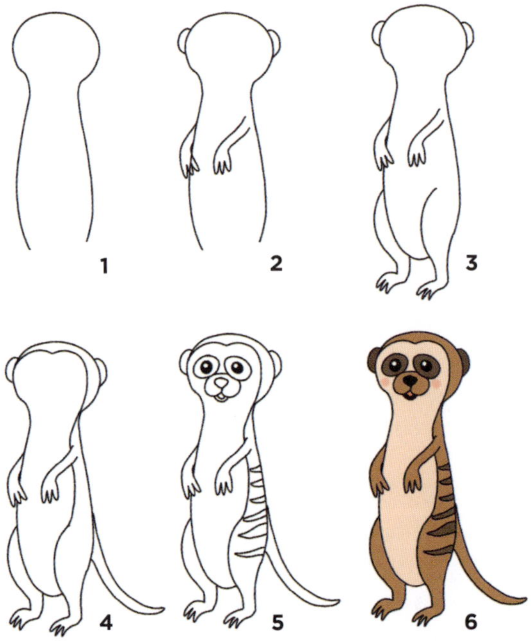

Meerkats are social animals, living in family groups called mobs. Within these mobs, all members share the responsibilities of gathering food, caring for young and watching for predators. They live underground in burrows and only go aboveground during daylight hours. The dark patches around the meerkat's eyes serve to protect them from the sun's bright glare.

Start doodling a meerkat by sketching a round head and a long, thin body. Add small, rounded ears on either side of the head and short arms with a few fingers on each hand. Add short legs and feet and erase any lines where the arms and legs overlap the body. Draw a curving line to section off the face and belly from the rest of the body and add a tail. Doodle details on the face, including those dark patches around the eyes. Sketch stripes on the back, then color your meerkat.

COATIMUNDI

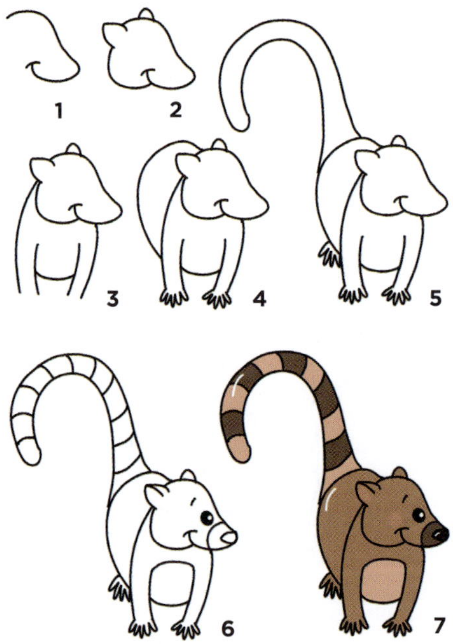

Coatimundis, with their long, ringed tails, are members of the raccoon family. Their name comes from a combination of words in the Tupian (South American indigenous) language that describes the way they sleep with their noses tucked into their bellies.

Start your coatimundi sketch by doodling the top of the head, a nose and a smile. Then, draw the jaw and a pair of short, pointed ears. Draw two front legs and a belly just under the head, then add toes. Sketch a curved line for the back end of the body, along with another set of toes. Next, add the signature long tail, divided by horizontal stripes. Finally, draw facial details and section off the belly, then color your coatimundi.

RINGTAIL

The ringtail, a member of the raccoon family, is the state mammal of Arizona. Resembling a cross between a cat and a raccoon, these adorable animals have large ears and striped tails that are as long as their bodies. Ringtails are excellent climbers and can even scale vertical walls in search of the best places to build their dens. Some early American settlers kept ringtails in their homes to hunt mice, earning them the nickname "miner's cat."

Begin drawing your ringtail with a round face and a pair of slightly pointed ears. Divide the ears into inner and outer sections. Sketch curving lines for the chest and the back/hind end of the body. Draw a pair of short front legs with small paws. Add a back leg and a paw and connect the front and back legs to finish the body outline. Draw the other back foot, then add a long, striped tail. Draw two circles inside the face where the eyes will be and an oval below them. Sketch eyes, a nose and a mouth. Finish your doodle by adding color.

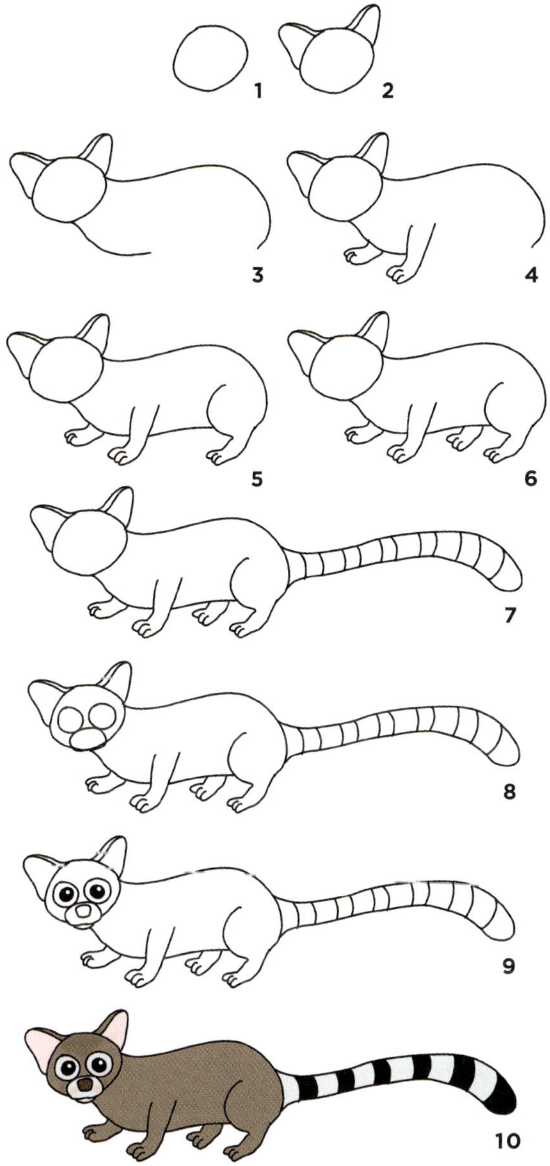

Practice here

IGUANA

There are many species of iguanas around the world that live in a variety of habitats and climates. Desert iguanas are able to withstand high temperatures and they burrow in the sand, often under creosote bushes, the flowers of which are their favorite food. Desert iguanas hibernate during the winter, then come back out in the spring to mate.

To draw an iguana, start with a curving line for the head and back that comes down in a spiral for the tail. Add a smile and the bottom jaw, along with the flap of skin attached to it. Draw the belly, then finish the curling tail. Add three legs and feet, erasing the lines where the legs overlap the rest of the body. Finish with details on the head and face, as well as spikes and stripes on the back and tail. Then, color your iguana to finish the doodle.

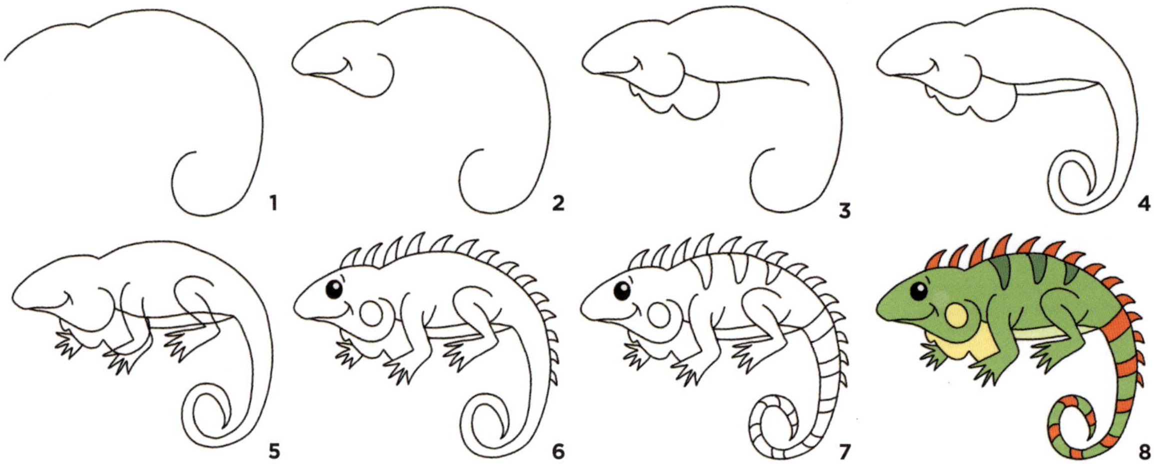

practice here

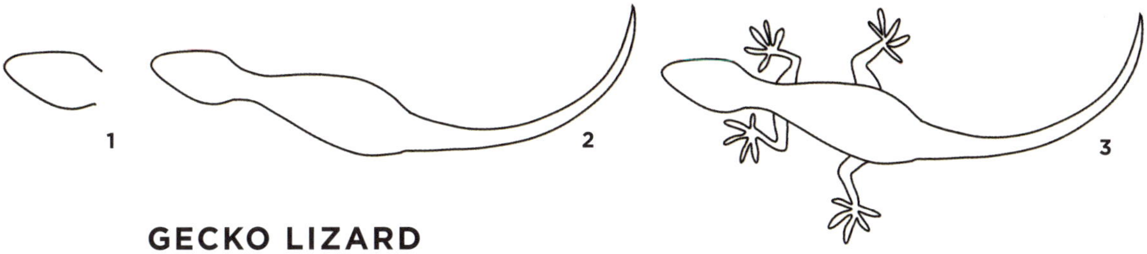

GECKO LIZARD

A variety of lizard species can be found in the desert, one of which is the gecko. These nocturnal reptiles store fat in their tails, which can actually be detached and regenerated if necessary! Most geckos have clear protective coverings over their eyes to protect them from dust and sand. Their toes are covered with tiny hairlike hooks, which allow them to climb smooth and even vertical surfaces.

Draw a gecko by first sketching the head shape as viewed from above. Next, form the body and a long, thin tail. Draw four legs, which protrude from the body at various angles, and add five long, thin toes at the end of each leg. Then give your lizard eyes and any other details like lines or scales on its back. Finally add color, including shading and spots, to make your drawing look more realistic. Geckos can be a variety of different colors, so feel free to personalize your drawing with whatever shade you like.

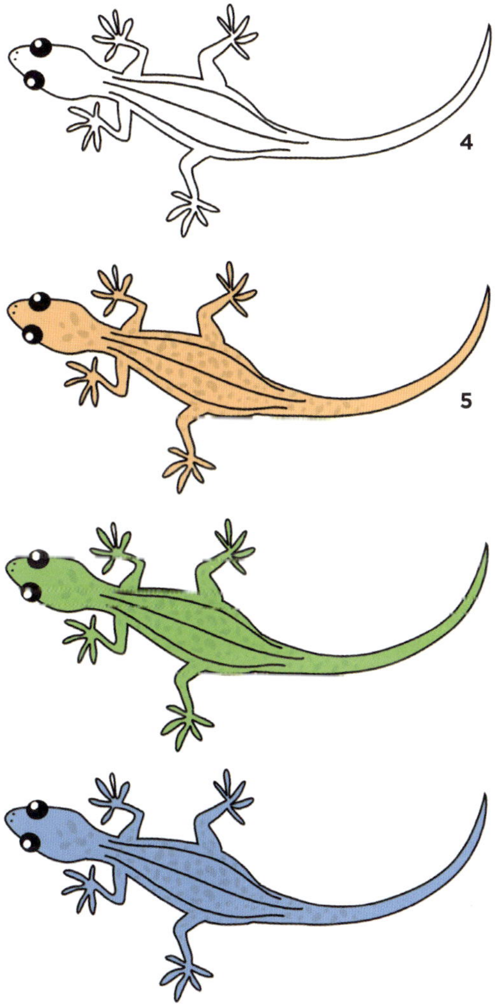

practice here

SCORPION

Scorpions are uniquely adapted to survive in harsh, dry climates. Believe it or not, they can go for a full year without food. Although many people think of scorpions as insects, they're actually arachnids, cousins of spiders, mites and ticks. Their most distinguishing trait is a narrow, segmented tail with a stinger that's used to immobilize prey.

Start your scorpion doodle with a pointed head shape, followed by two bumpy lines that will outline the body. Connect the lower points of the lines to form the separate sections that compose the body. Next, add a series of shapes that curve around to form the segments of the tail, making sure that the last one ends with a point. Add four legs on each side of the body and a pair of pincers in the front. The final step is to add eyes and and detail lines to the head and face. Color your scorpion brown, gray or black.

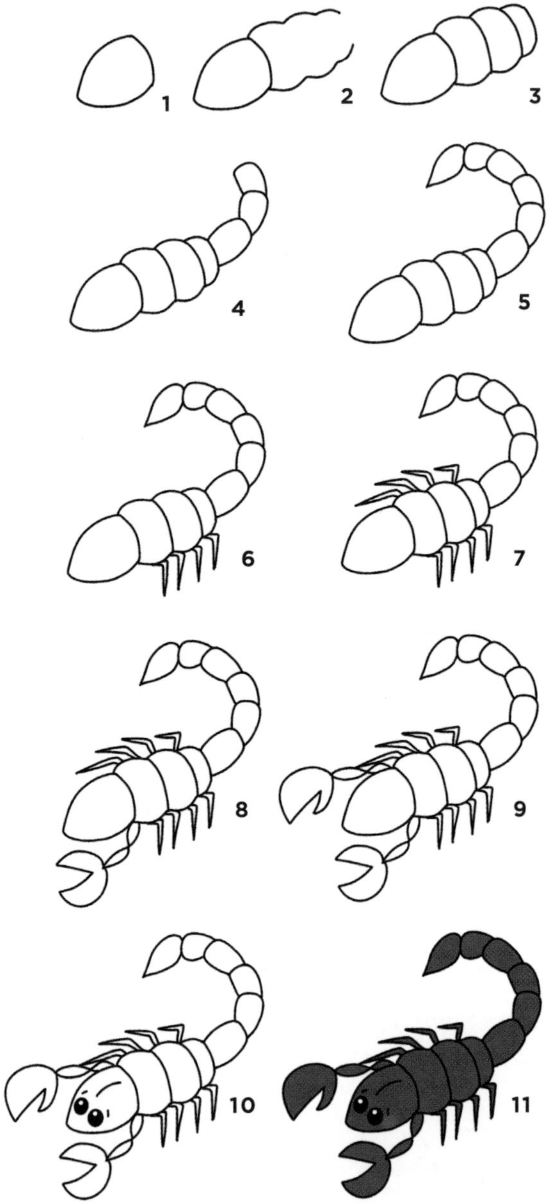

practice here

RATTLESNAKE

Although rattlesnakes are the largest venomous snakes in North America, they're actually rather shy and reclusive, only attacking when they feel threatened. The loud rattling noise made by shaking the keratin rattle at the tip of their tails is meant to ward off predators by signaling danger.

To doodle a rattlesnake, start with the head shape, which is wider in the back and pointed in the front. Next, add curving lines to form the first part of the body. To show that the snake is curled up, draw a series of four rounded triangles that sit on top of one another. Erase any lines that overlap. Draw the end of the tail coming out on the side, adding a stack of small ovals to the tip for the rattle. Sketch lines to divide the body into stripes and add eyes, nostrils and a tongue. Finish by coloring your snake.

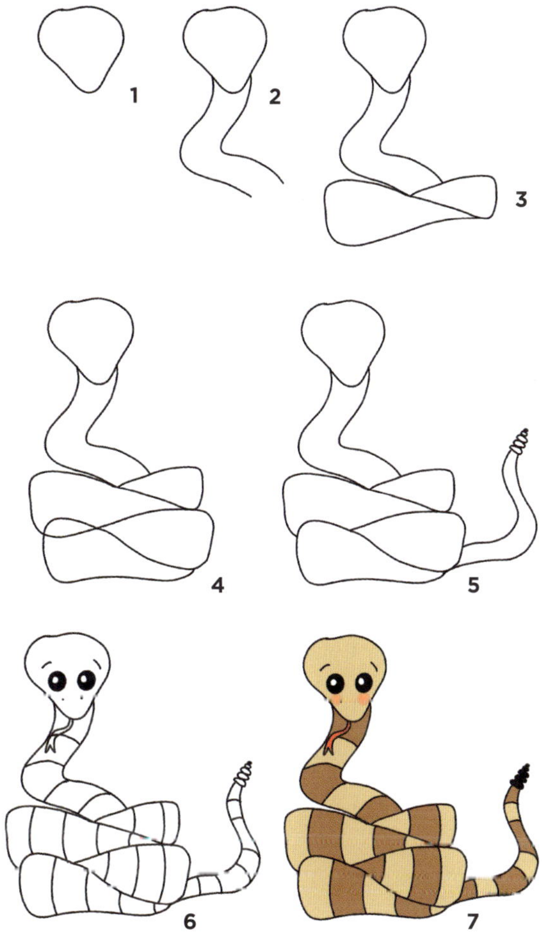

practice here

CAMEL

The name camel comes from an Arabic word meaning "beauty." A camel's hump is used for storing fat, which is then converted into food or water when necessary. Arabian camels have one hump; Asian camels have two. These large animals can drink up to 50 gallons (200 L) of water at a time in the desert and can run at speeds up to 40 miles per hour (64 kph).

The first step in drawing our camel is sketching the head, complete with a smile. Add two small ears, a jaw and the camel's long, curving neck. Next, draw the large, rounded hump. Give your camel two thin front legs, followed by a belly and two back legs. Make sure you show off the camel's knobby knees! Draw a tail and face details, then color your doodle.

Bonus: To make your camel more colorful, let's try a variation where the hump is covered with a bright blanket. Draw your camel as before, then add three lines to show the edges of the blanket that drapes over its back. Now, the fun part is to give the blanket a design! You can create any pattern(s) you like, including stripes, zigzags, polka dots or a combination of several different ideas. Add tassels along the bottom edge by drawing small circles with rounded triangles just below them. Choose a few cheerful colors to fill in your design.

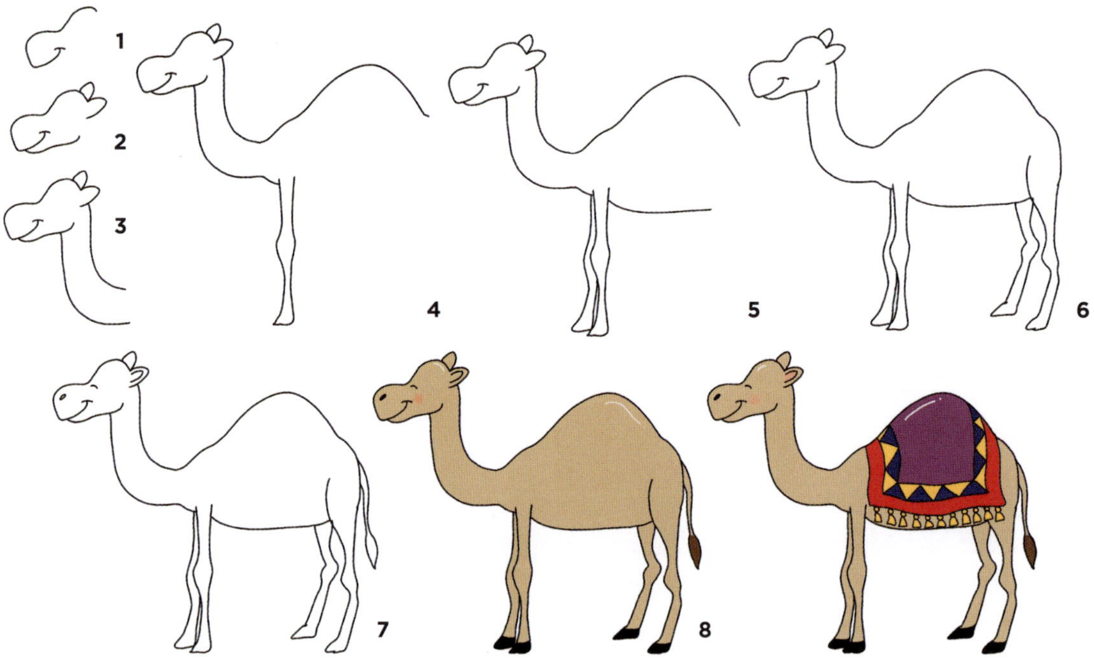

IN THE HABITAT

PRICKLY PEAR CACTUS

The fruit of a prickly pear cactus has many health benefits, including the ability to boost immunity, reduce cholesterol and protect the liver. This cactus can also be used medicinally to treat stomach problems, sunburn, cuts, bruises, the common cold, constipation and diabetes! Unlike the towering saguaro, the prickly pear cactus is less than 6 feet (2 m) tall, sometimes even shorter than 12 inches (30 cm).

To draw this cactus, start with a central shape that resembles a wide upside-down "u." Next, add smaller versions of the same shape, one on the side and one on top of the original shape. Continue adding even smaller "u" shapes branching off of the existing ones. When you're happy with the look of your cactus, sketch small three-petaled flowers on the topmost branches. Draw spines by making short lines all around the outer edges of the cactus and tiny "v" shapes inside. Color your cactus green with bright pink blooms.

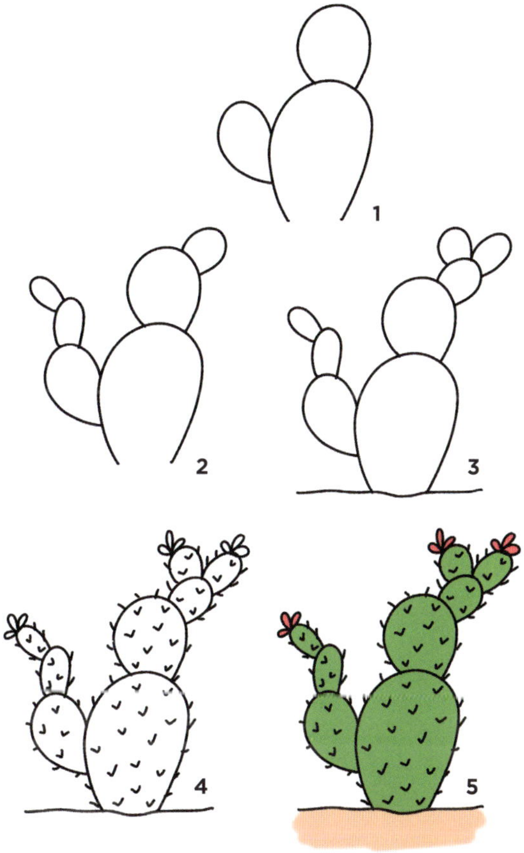

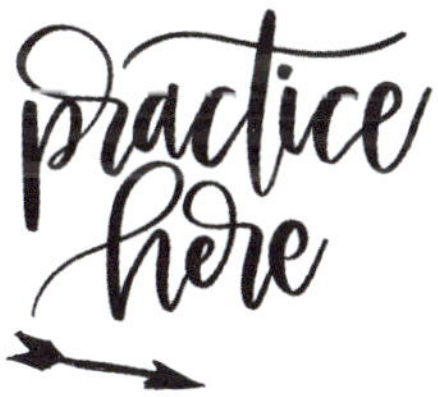

SAGUARO CACTUS

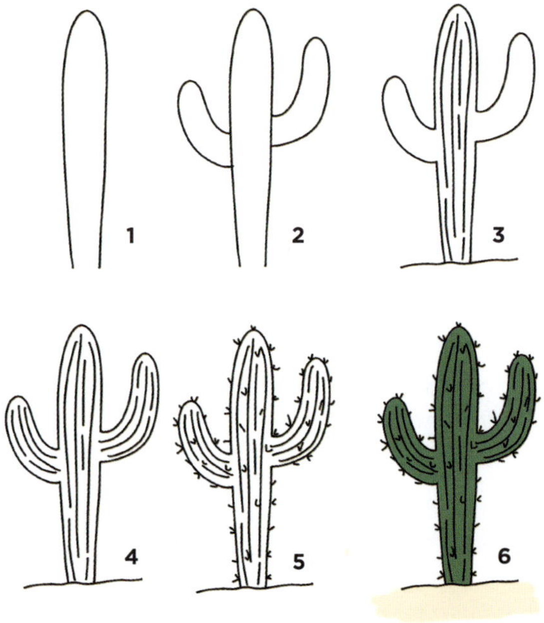

Although the saguaro is a slow-growing cactus, it can eventually reach heights between 40 and 60 feet (12 and 18 m)! It's the largest cactus type found in the United States, specifically in the Sonoran Desert. A saguaro has one deep taproot that can extend about 3 feet (1 m) underground, while the rest of its roots are only 4 to 6 inches (10 to 15 cm) deep.

To doodle a saguaro cactus, start with the center section, a tall upside-down "u" shape. Next, add a curving arm to each side. Sketch detail lines inside the cactus shape, then draw tiny lines and "v" shapes around the outline and inside for the spines. Color your cactus in your favorite shade of green.

SAN PEDRO CACTUS

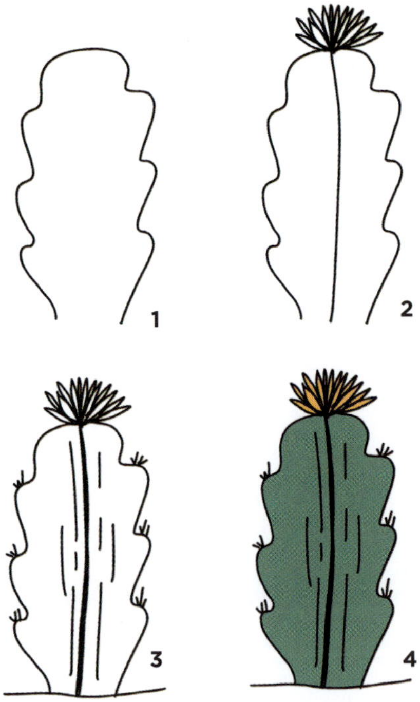

A San Pedro cactus is a tall column that can eventually reach between 10 and 19 feet (3 and 6 m) in height. Its blooms, which appear at night, are very large and fragrant.

The first step in drawing this cactus is to create a shape with rounded bumps on either side. Add a vertical line through the center of the shape and a flower with many pointed petals on top. Finally, sketch a few detail lines inside the cactus and a series of short spines on each of the bumps. Color your cactus green and the flower white, yellow or any color you like.

LANDFORMS

Although we often imagine the desert to be a flat area, they are actually home to a variety of landforms, including rock formations and even mountains. Made from everything from crystal to sandstone, these formations are natural wonders that lend a unique beauty to the landscape.

Just as each landform is different from the next, your doodles can take on a huge variety of sizes and shapes. Experiment with rounded and flat lines and try sketching formations that are one large shape, as well as several smaller shapes grouped together. Add detail lines to show the texture of the landform's surface, then finish your doodles with color. Some landforms are shades of gray, while others are brown or even red-orange.

TUMBLEWEED

A tumbleweed can actually be one of several kinds of plants that dries out and detaches from its roots, then rolls around on the ground as the wind blows it. This is actually how the plants disperse their seeds. One of the most common tumbleweed plants is the Russian thistle.

Since this particular drawing doesn't have any areas to fill with color, I suggest either drawing with your brown marker from the start, or sketching in pencil, then tracing over your doodle with your desired marker. To draw this wandering plant, start with a "c" shape. Add several more of the same shapes inside, continuing to fill the space with overlapping lines. Draw a short stem at the bottom and sketch short lines coming off of some of your "branches." Tumbleweeds are typically brown, although they may have a bit of green as well.

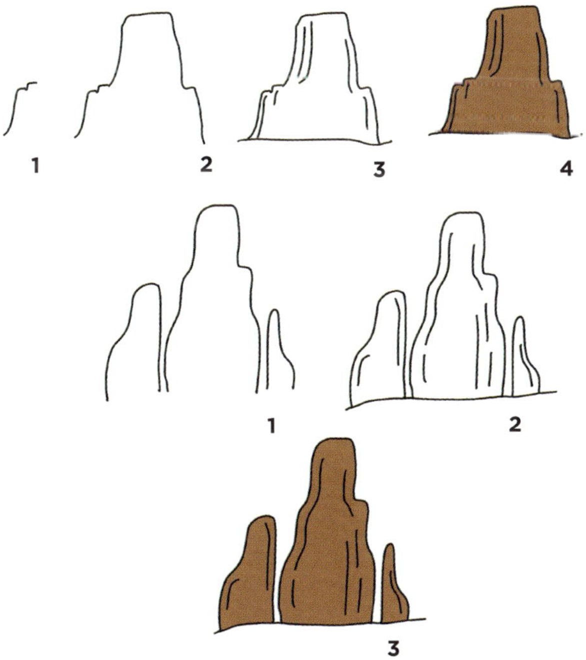

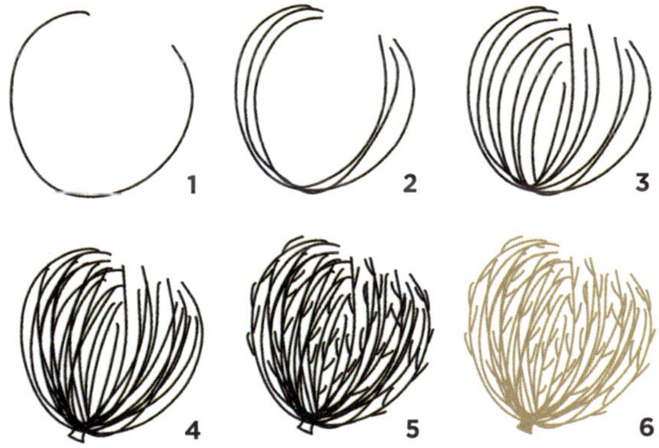

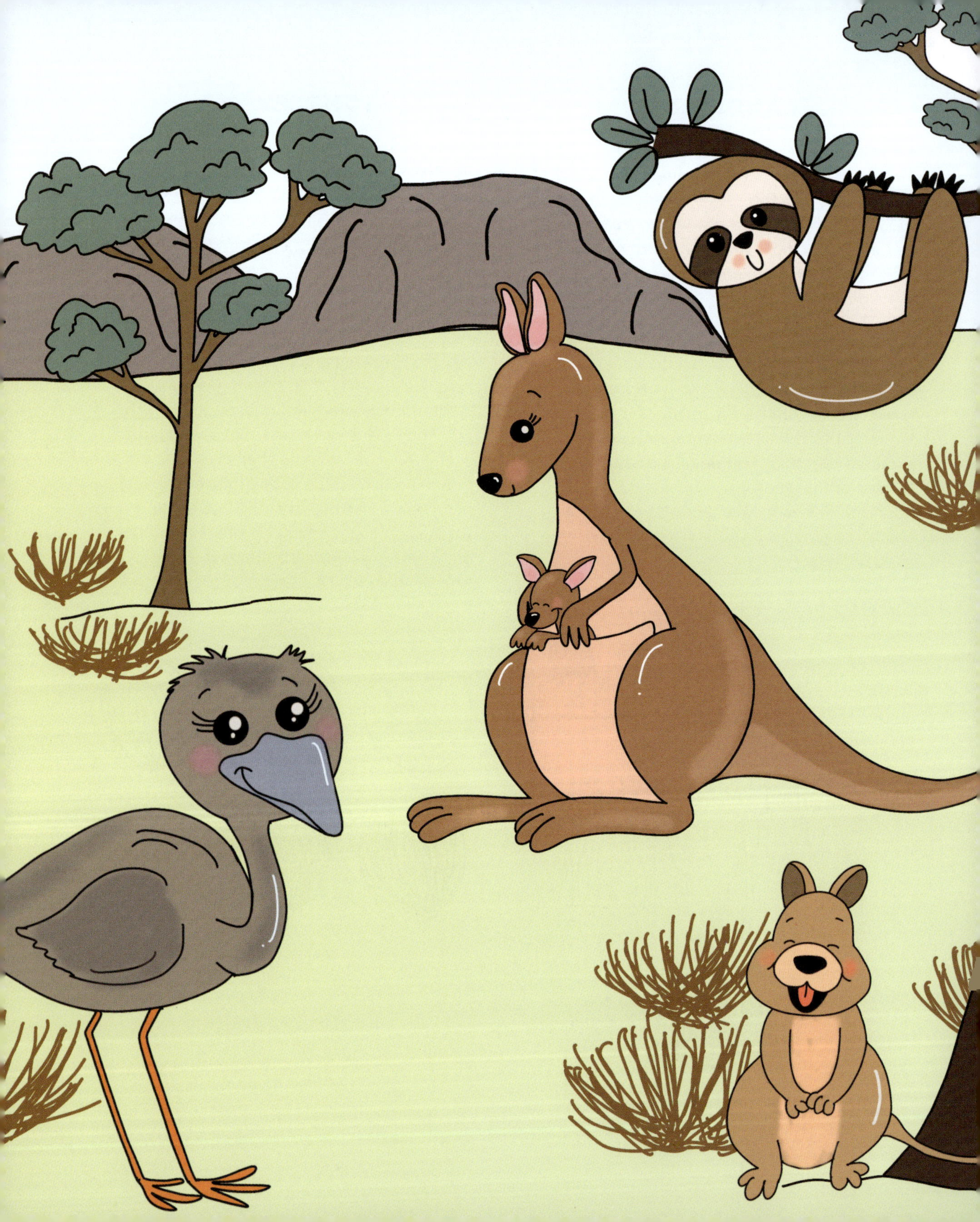

IN THE Outback

The landscape and climate of Australia make it the perfect home for a variety of unique animals, some of which aren't found anywhere else in the world. It's extremely dry, with about 35 percent of the country rarely getting any rain, and large areas of desert that are unusable for agriculture. The distinctive trees and plants of the region are perfect habitats for many marsupials and birds. Let's take a look at some of the fascinating animals of the outback and learn to draw them as well!

KOALA

Koalas have unique fingerprints, as well as unique nose prints, which is how biologists identify and track them in the wild. Although they look like bears, koalas are marsupials with pouches like kangaroos. They're nocturnal animals and they love eating from eucalyptus trees all night long.

Start drawing your koala by sketching a shape for the head and two very large, rounded ears. Next, add a curving line for the back and draw an arm extending out to the right. Add a leg and foot, a tummy, ear details and a tail. Then, draw a face, complete with a large nose. Finally, add a tree trunk with branches and leaves for your koala to climb, then color your drawing.

Bonus: For extra fun, draw a baby koala using the same steps, but smaller, on the mama koala's back!

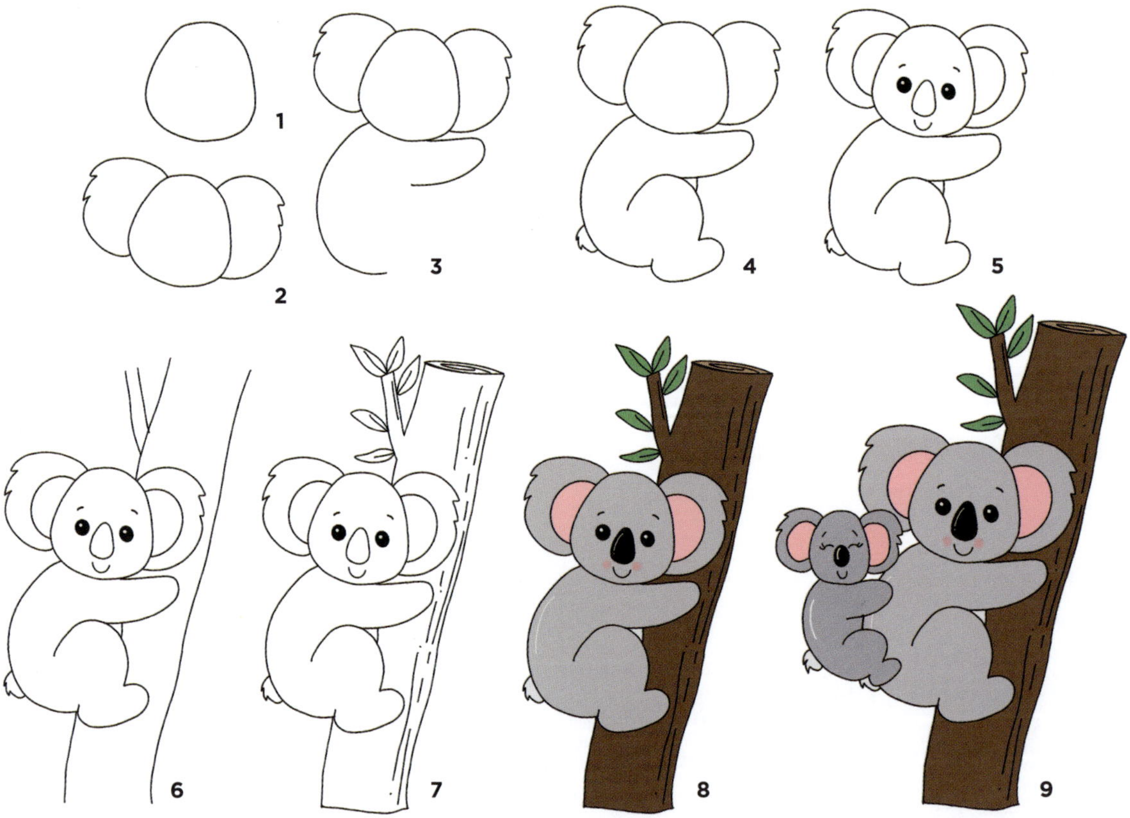

KOOKABURRA

Kookaburras are small birds known for their loud, distinct call, which sounds like laughter. They tend to sing (or laugh) most at dawn and dusk, and their sound can be mistaken for other animals, including donkeys and monkeys!

To doodle this unique bird, start with a round head and a long, thin beak. Next, add a paisley-shaped wing. Draw a curved line for the rest of the head and a rounded body. Add a long, thin tail. Divide the tail with wavy lines and add a boxy area around the eye. Finally, add detail lines to the wing and draw a branch with leaves for your kookaburra to sit on. Color your drawing using white, gray, brown, black and blue for a realistic look.

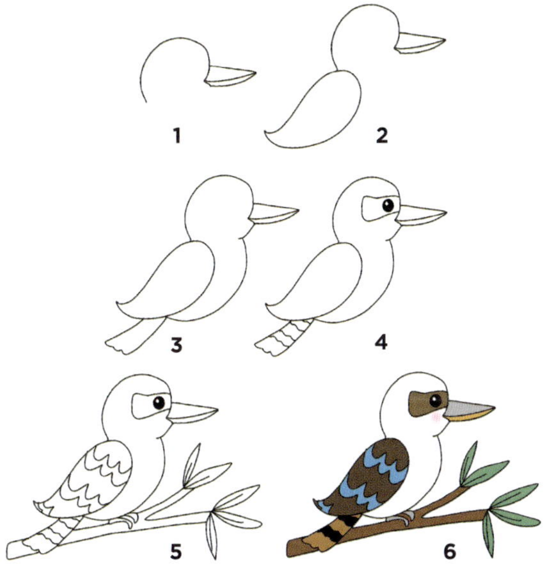

KANGAROO

Not only do kangaroos show a tendency to use one hand over another, the majority of them are left-handed! These amazing marsupials can hop about 6 feet (2 m) in the air and cover a distance of 25 feet (8 m) in a single leap.

Our mama kangaroo doodle starts with one pointed ear and a head. Add a second ear, then make a curving line extending downward to form the back of the head, neck and body. Draw two curving lines for the legs and add large feet. Add a long tail and a pair of very short arms. Next, draw detail lines inside the ears and give your kangaroo an eye, a nose and a smile. Finally, divide off the stomach area and add a line for the pouch. Color your kangaroo in shades of brown.

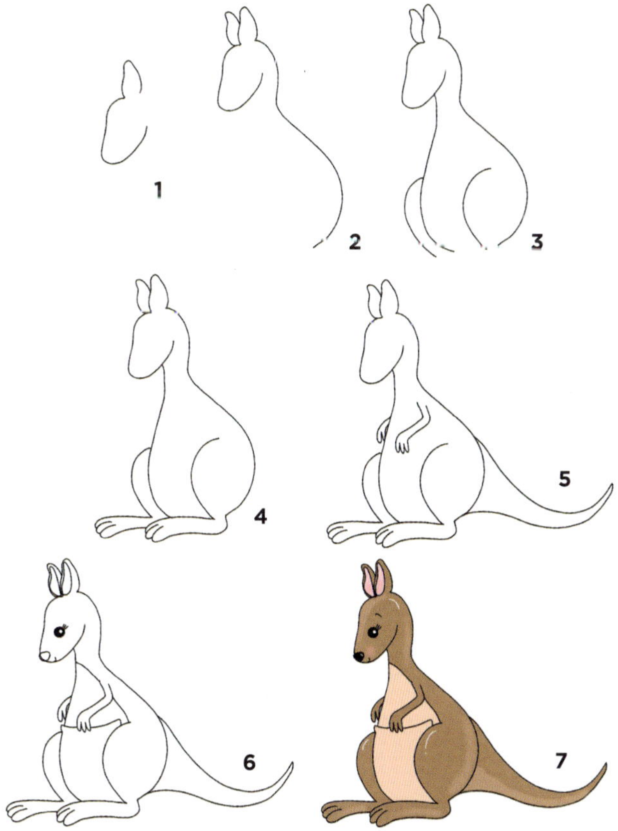

KANGAROO BABY (JOEY)

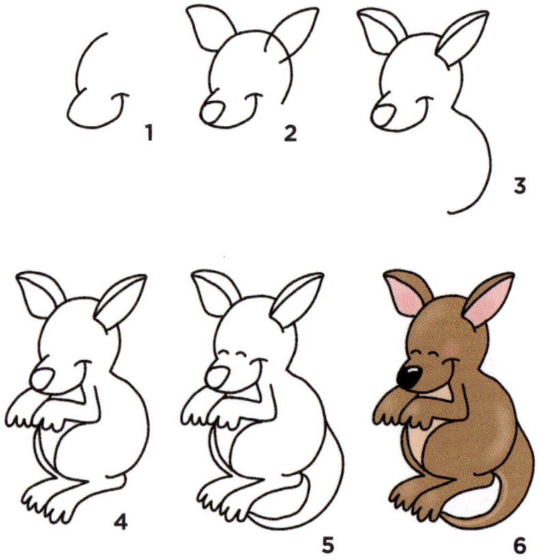

When a baby kangaroo, also called a joey, is born, it's only about the size of a grape! It crawls through the mother's fur and into her pouch, where it continues to grow and develop. After four months, the baby can leave the pouch for short periods of time, but it takes ten months before the joey is mature enough to leave its mother for good.

To draw a joey, we're going to start with the front of the head and add two pointed ears. Add a nose and a cheerful smile. Make a "3" shape for the back of the head and the body, keeping it much smaller and more compact than the mama kangaroo. Add an arm and hands, then a stomach, two legs and feet. Finally, add a tail and eyes, then color your baby kangaroo.

Bonus: You can doodle your joey on his own, jumping next to his mama or tucked safely in her pouch! Also, this doodle makes a good representation of a wallaby, which is very similar to a kangaroo but slightly smaller.

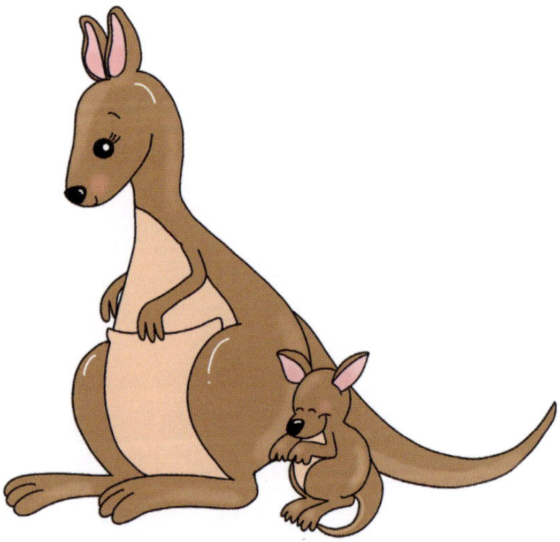

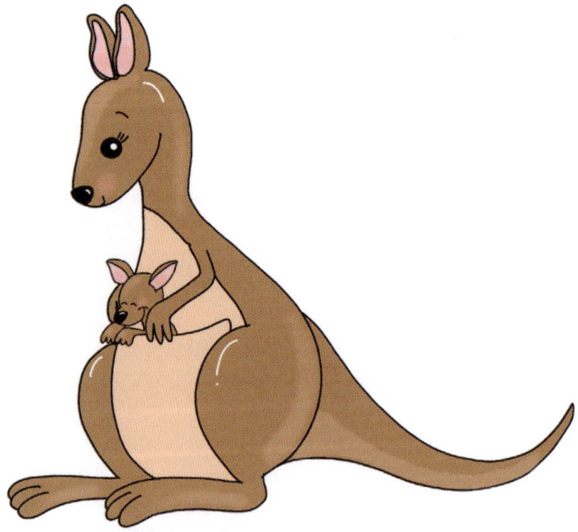

EMU

Emus are the second-largest birds in the world, and although they're unable to fly, they make up for it by running at speeds of up to 30 miles per hour (48 kph). An emu's stride while running can be almost 9 feet (3 m) long! The average emu is about the size of a human, around 5.7 feet (1.7 m) tall, and weighs 69 to 82 pounds (32 to 37 kg).

Our emu sketch starts with an oval head and a raindrop-shaped body. Connect the head to the body with a thin, curving neck, then add a wing. Give your emu a large smiling beak, eyes and eyebrows, erasing any overlapping lines. Sketch two long, thin legs and feet. To add texture, erase a few spots on the head and wing and replace your lines with zigzags that represent feathers. Finally, color your creation.

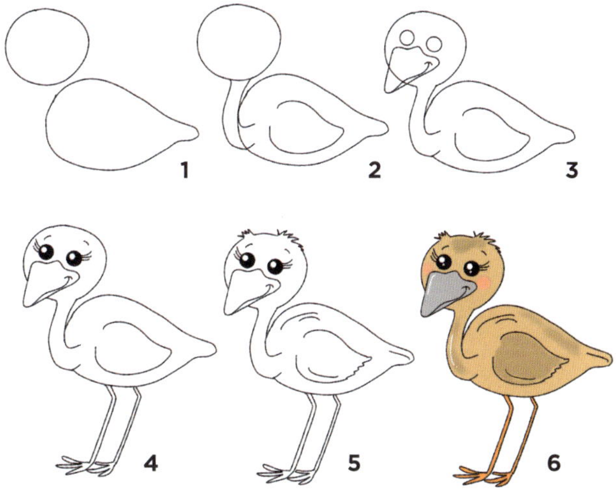

FRILLED-NECK LIZARD

The frilled-neck lizard is named for the large, colorful membrane of skin that can be erected around its neck to intimidate predators, attract a mate or mark its territory. These reptiles are solitary tree dwellers and are sometimes also called "bicycle lizards," because of their ability to run on just two feet.

To draw this lizard, start with the head shape, which is rounded at the bottom with two bumps on the top for the eyes. Next, sketch that famous frill around the head. Add a body and a long, thin tail. Sketch legs and toes, then add a face with large eyes and an open mouth. Divide the tail into stripes and add detail lines around the frill. Finally, color your lizard. The frill is often a lighter color than the body and tends to be red or orange.

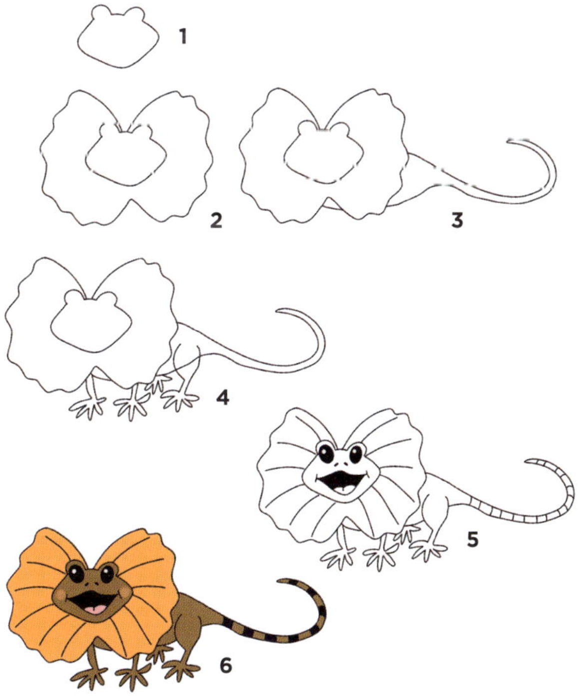

CROCODILE

Crocodiles have the strongest bite of any animal in the world, up to 3,700 pounds of force (16 kN)! However, their jaw opening muscles are quite weak and can be held shut using something as simple as a rubber band—or your bare hands . . . if you dare! Because a croc's upper and lower jaws are the same size, all of its teeth are visible even when its mouth is closed.

To draw a crocodile, we're going to start with the thick pointed tail and back. Next, add the head shape, which has a bump where the eye goes, and a long snout. Add the bottom jaw and two legs. Draw the stomach, then add spikes to the back and feet. Separate the underbelly from the upper body and add some detail lines to the lower area. Draw a large eye and a nostril, and don't forget to sketch some of those visible teeth! Finally, add color to bring your crocodile to life.

practice here

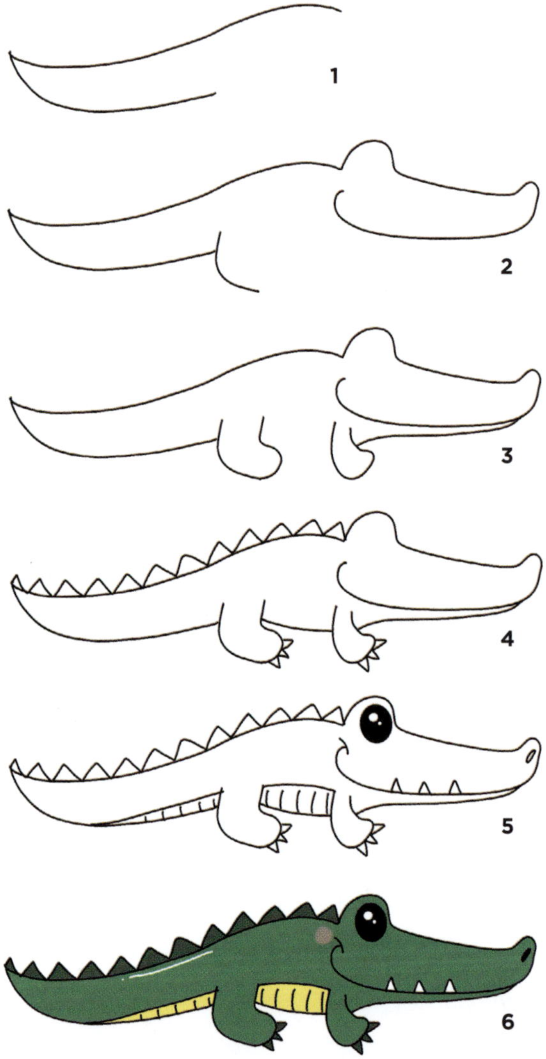

DINGO

The dingo is a wild dog that preys on a wide range of animals, typically hunting at night. The world's longest fence, which is 3,488 miles (5,614 km) long and runs from eastern Queensland to the South Australian coastline, is also known as the Dingo Fence and serves to keep dingoes out of the fertile southeastern part of the continent.

Draw your own dingo by first sketching a head shape, then extending a line down for the front of the body. Add pointed ears and a curving back. Draw a tail wrapping around the front and curved lines for the back leg and foot. Add a nose and divide the front part of the body from the rest with a line. Sketch two front legs and feet, then erase the places where they overlap the original lines of the body. Add an eye, a smile and an eyebrow, then color your dingo. Most dingoes are reddish-brown and white or tan.

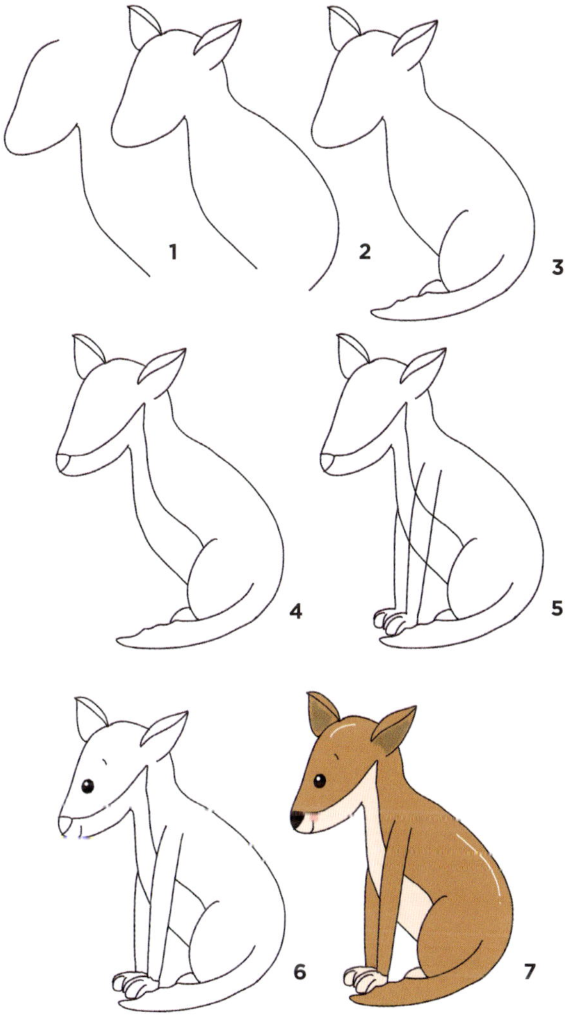

Practice here

SLOTH

Despite sloths' reputation for laziness, they're quite strong; in fact, they're three times as strong as the average human! From birth, a sloth can lift its entire body weight up with only one arm. It takes a sloth no energy to hang from a branch due to specialized tendons that lock in place, which is why they're able to sleep in that hanging position. Sloths are color blind and struggle to see in bright daylight, but they have a great sense of smell.

To draw a sloth, start with an oval head, a curved back and a rounded arm and leg. Connect the head, arm and leg with a line for the stomach. Add a branch for the sloth to hang from, then sketch the back arm and leg behind it. Give your sloth toes and draw details on the face to mark the front section and the patches around the eyes. Add a line to separate the stomach from the rest of the body and a cute face. Finally, color your sloth using shades of brown, black and gray.

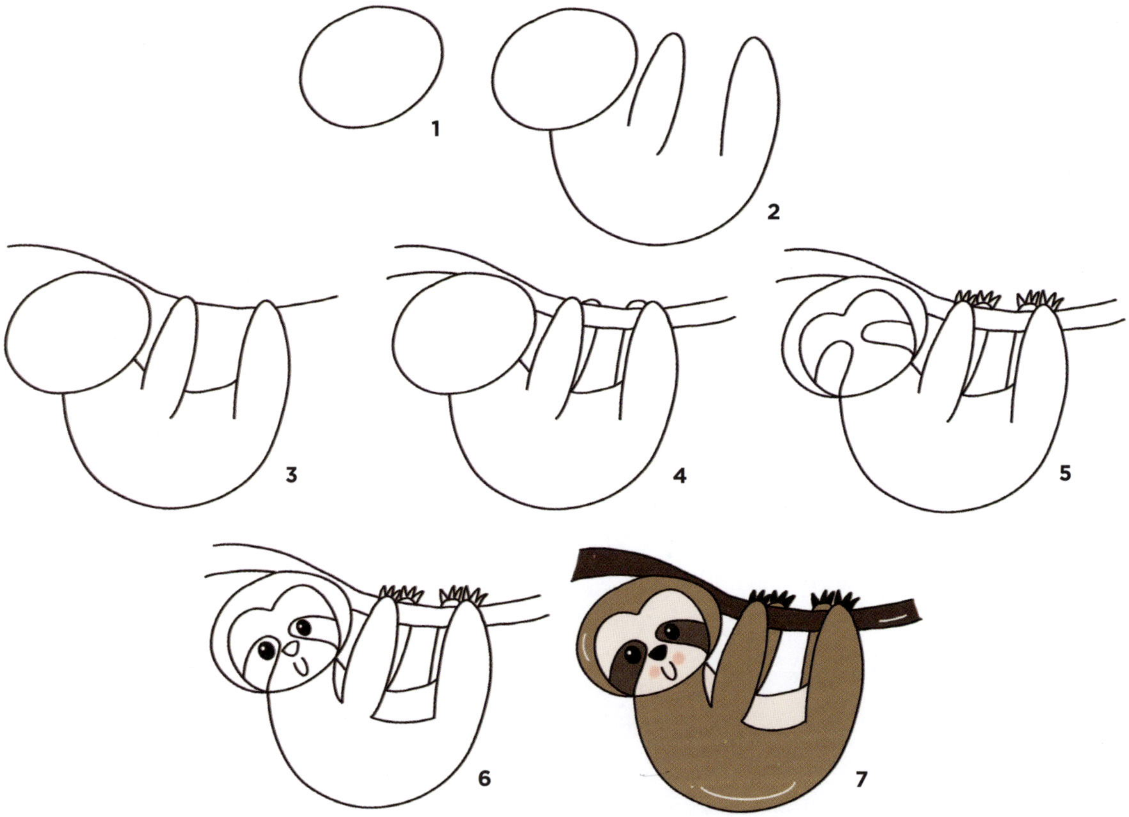

DUCK-BILLED PLATYPUS

The platypus is a fascinating animal that seems to combine the characteristics of many species. It has a bill like a duck, a tail like a beaver, fur and feet like an otter and is a mammal that lays eggs. It's also venomous; males have a spur on their hind foot that can dispense a venom that's very painful to humans.

To doodle this curious creature, start by sketching the duck-like bill. Next, add two curving lines to form the head and body. Sketch two short legs with webbed feet, then erase the areas where those legs overlap the body. Add a long, flat tail, then finish your drawing with a face and detail lines on the feet and tail. The final step is to add color.

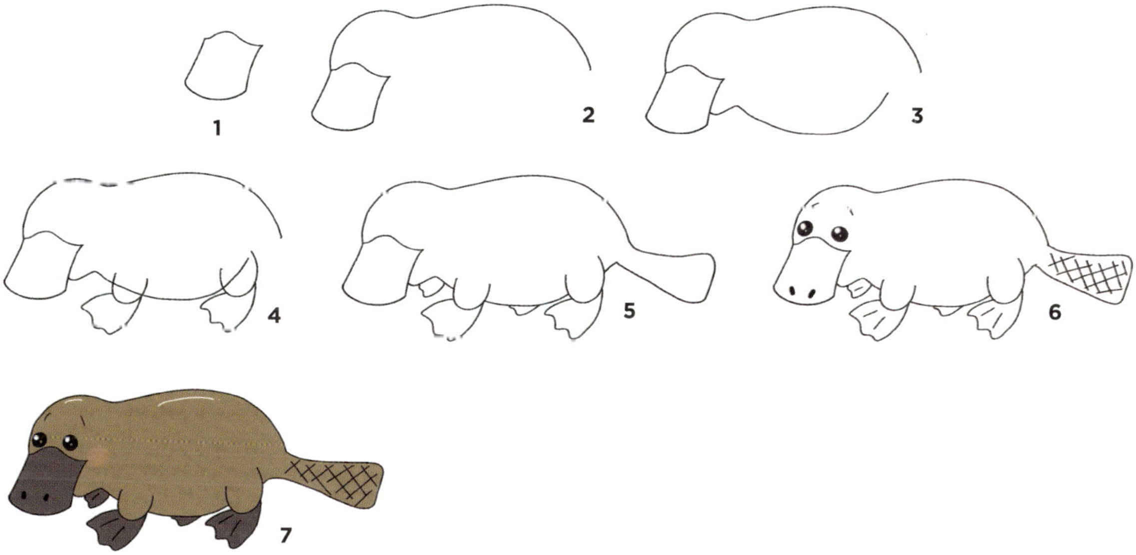

practice here

QUOKKA

Quokkas are known as the "happiest animal on earth," because they look like they're perpetually smiling. Although it's illegal to touch one of these animals, they're unafraid of human interaction and willingly pose for selfies with tourists. Quokkas are herbivores and can store fat in their tails to sustain them during periods of drought.

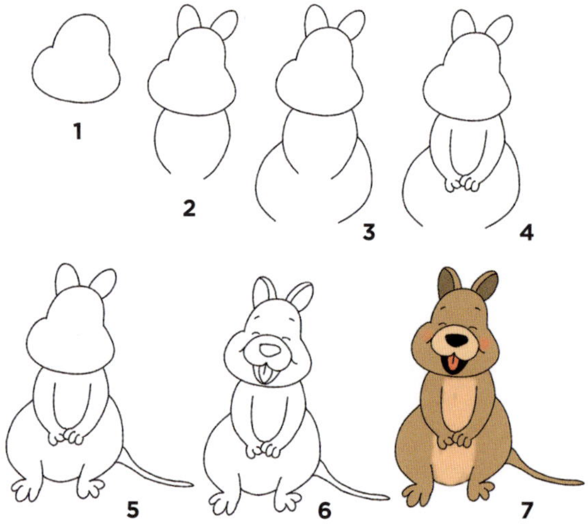

Drawing this cute critter starts with a pear-shaped head and two small, rounded ears. Add two sets of parentheses below the head, one for the arms and another wider set for the legs. Finish drawing the arms and hands and add feet. Draw a tail, then add a face, including a large nose and that special quokka smile! Color your doodle and enjoy the happiest animal on the planet.

WOMBAT

Wombats live in burrows and spend much of their time digging tunnels underground or grazing on native grasses. Although they don't typically run, if they need to, they can reach speeds of about 24 miles per hour (39 kph) to escape from predators. One of the most fascinating wombat facts is that their poop is actually square! Scientists think the cube shape helps wombats mark their territory, because it keeps the poop from rolling away!

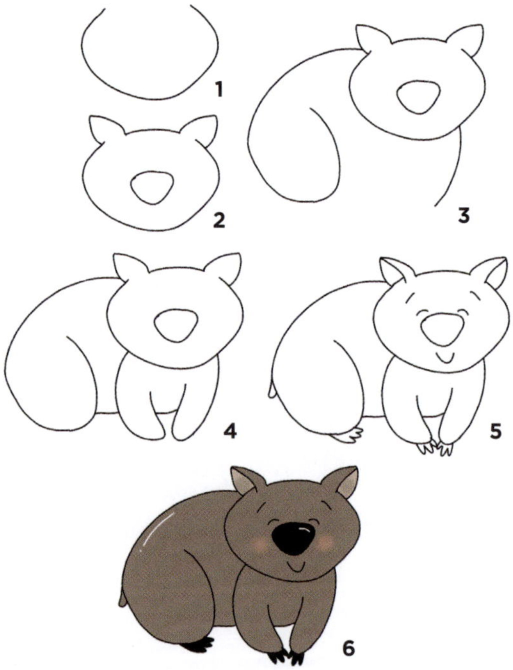

To make a wombat doodle, start by sketching a rounded face with short, pointed ears and a large nose. Add a rounded body, a back leg and arms. Draw hands and feet and a tiny tail, along with a face. Color your wombat in shades of brown or gray.

IN THE HABITAT

AUSTRALIAN CHRISTMAS TREE

The Nuytsia floribunda*, also known as moodjar or the "Australian Christmas tree," is native to Western Australia. It produces an abundance of bright yellow-orange flowers during the summer, which coincides with Christmastime in the Southern Hemisphere.*

To draw it, start with a thin trunk that branches out into a "y" shape. Next, add several main branches, followed by some smaller branches coming off of them. For the flowers, sketch small, puffy cloud shapes at the end of each branch and other places all over the tree. Erase any areas where you have overlapping lines, then add detail lines inside the blooms. Color your tree using bright shades of orange and yellow.

practice here

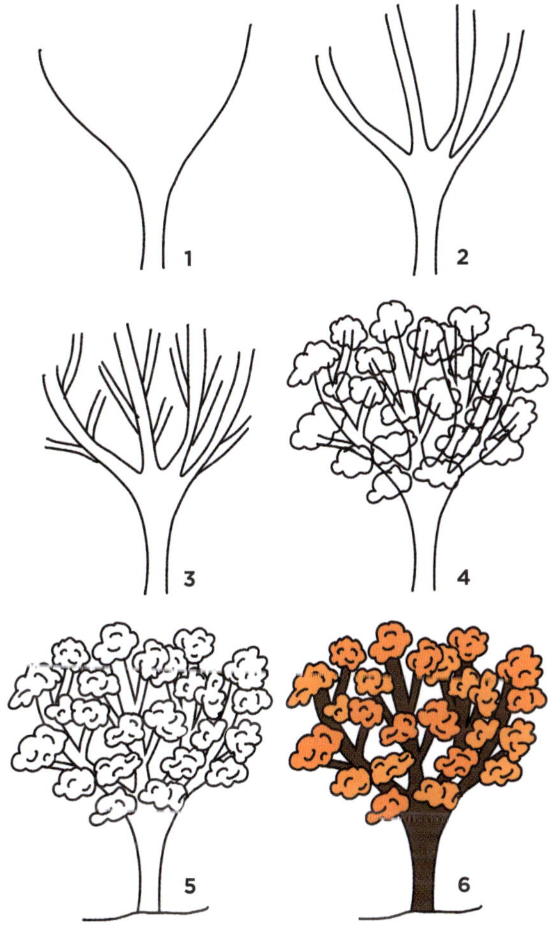

EUCALYPTUS TREE

The eucalyptus tree, part of the myrtle family, is native to Australia. The leaves contain an aromatic oil that's useful in medicines and the wood is commonly used for fuel, buildings and fences. Many species of animals make their homes in these trees and use their leaves for food.

To sketch one, start with a tall, thin trunk that splits into three main branches. Add smaller branches to those main ones wherever you like. Then, add two more lower branches a little farther down the trunk, erasing the lines where the branches intersect. For the leaves, draw a large cloud shape at the top of each set of branches. Erase the overlapping lines, then add some bumpy detail lines to show texture and color your tree.

practice here

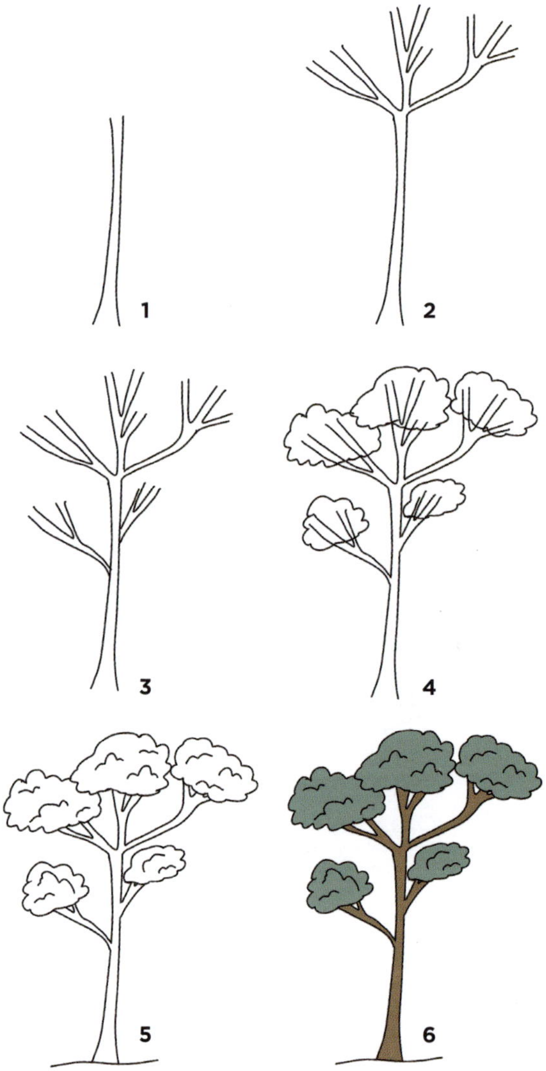

BRUSH

Parts of the ground in the outback are covered with low shrubs and grasses, which are easy to add to your landscape sketches.

Just make a wide "u" shape, then start adding more "u" shapes inside. You can do this with a brown marker and leave the sketch as is for desert areas or wintertime. To give the brush some greenery, use a green marker to add some bumpy lines all over the branches.

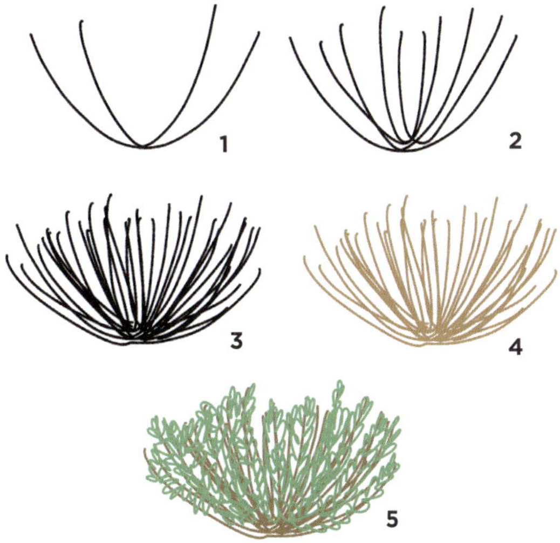

ROCK FORMATIONS

The landscape of Australia contains some incredible rock formations, like Uluru/Ayers Rock and the Pinnacles.

It's easy to add rock formations of all sizes and shapes to your drawings as part of the environment for Australia's animals. Start by deciding how wide and tall you want your rock to be. Then, sketch a basic shape, keeping in mind that the lines should be wavy rather than smooth and straight. Add some detail lines to show crevices and texture, then color your rock in shades of brown, red or gray.

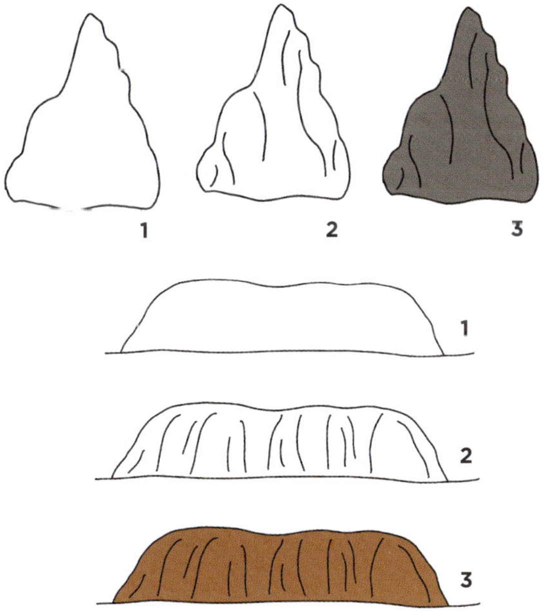

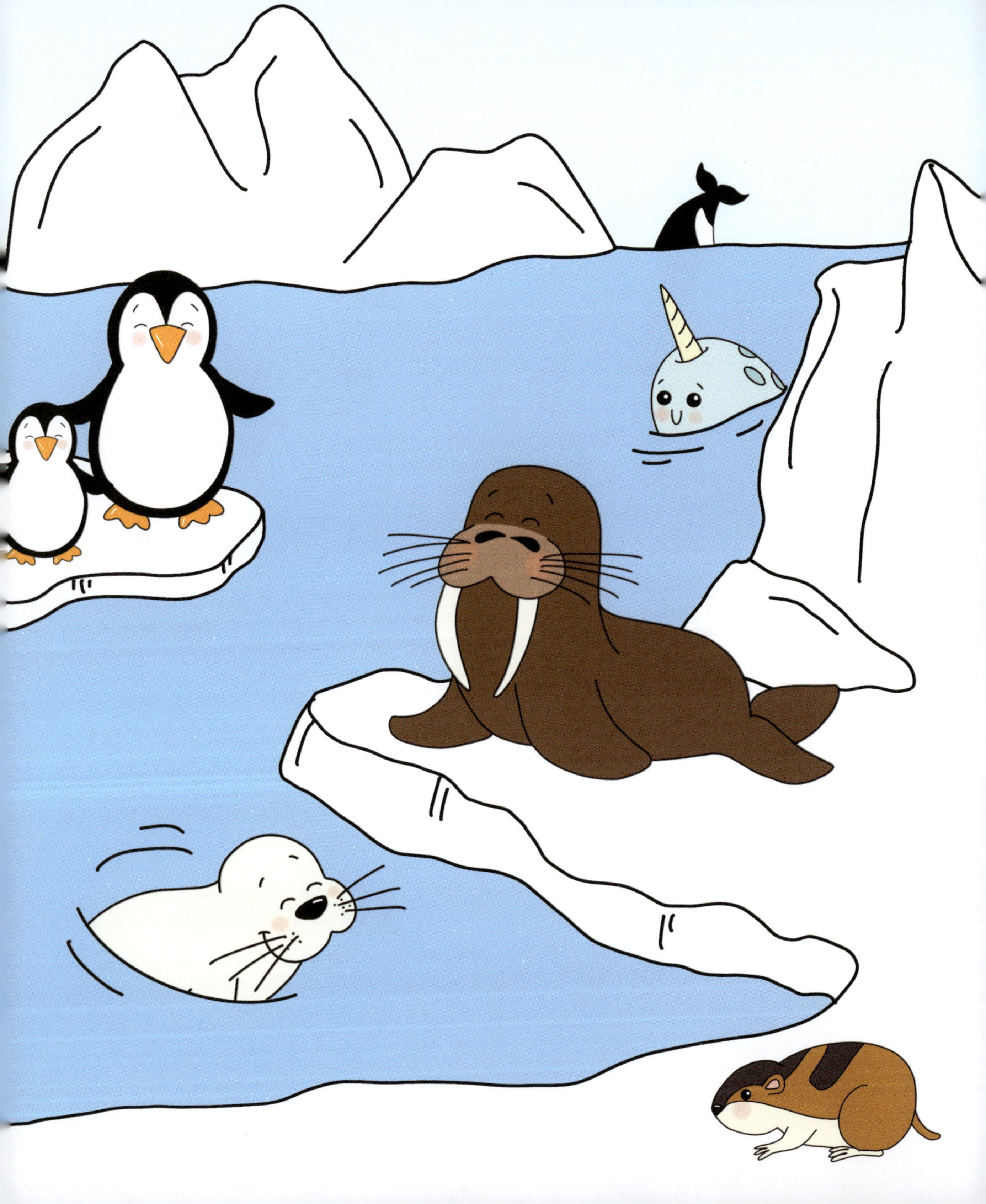

IN THE Arctic

The Arctic, which is the northernmost part of the Earth located above the Arctic Circle, gets its name from the Greek word for "bear," *arktos*. This is because of the constellations Ursa Major (Great Bear) and Ursa Minor (Little Bear), which are seen in the northern sky. Because of the earth's tilt, this part of the globe spends part of the year in almost continual darkness and part of the year in almost continual sunlight. In spite of the harsh environment and freezing temperatures, there are people who choose to live in the Arctic—four million of them, in fact! This region is also home to some amazing animals, including the narwhal, which can't be found anywhere else in the world. Let's find out more about the mammals, rodents and other creatures who inhabit the Arctic.

ARCTIC FOX

Known as the "clowns of the tundra," Arctic foxes have cheeky, playful personalities. But it's not always fun and games. These animals are hardy survivors, able to survive temperatures as low as -58 degrees Fahrenheit (-50°C). They're also skilled hunters that will eat almost anything, including rodents, fish, birds, berries and insects.

To start your Arctic fox doodle, draw the head shape, then add a pair of pointed ears. Next, draw lines for the front and back of the body and sketch a zigzag "v" shape below the head to show a furry patch on the chest. Draw lines for the front legs, then make a tail that wraps around the body, stopping at the front leg. Sketch a paw on that leg and erase any lines that overlap with the tail. Add a curving line to suggest the back leg. Give your fox eyes, a nose and eyebrows, as well as a patch of fur on top of the head. Erase any overlapping lines, then color your doodle.

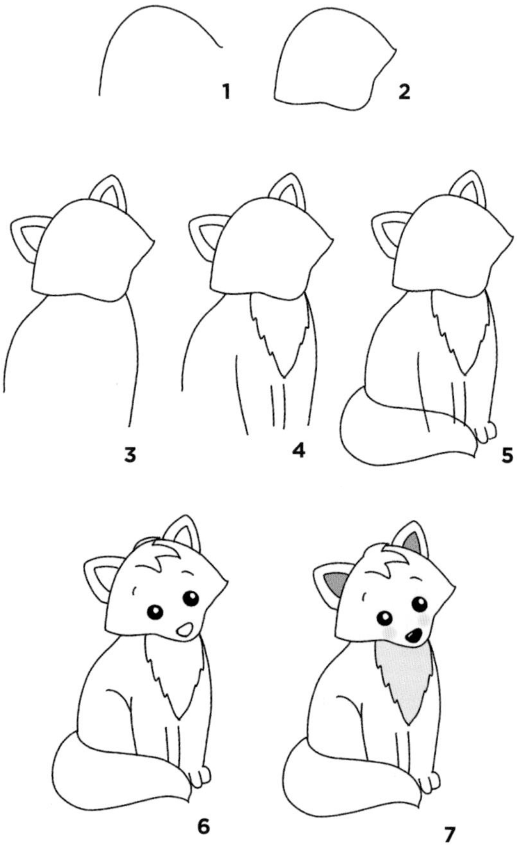

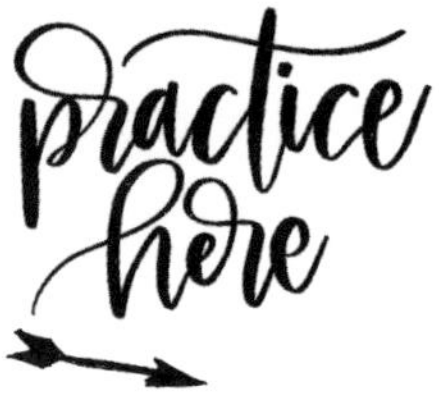

POLAR BEAR

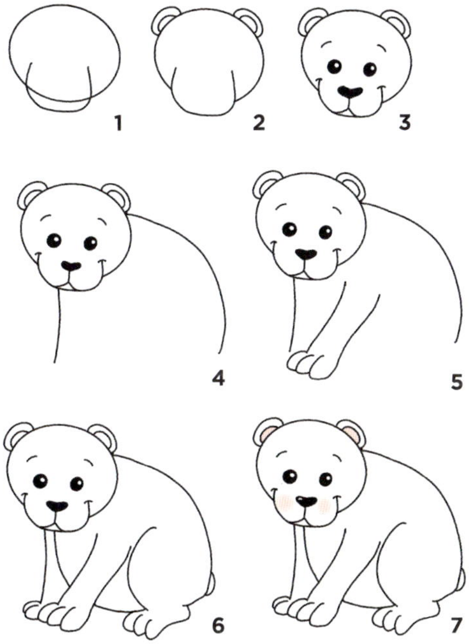

Polar bears are the largest meat-eating animals on earth! They can grow up to 8 feet (2 m) long and weigh as much as 1,600 pounds (726 kg). Beneath their fur, polar bears' skin is actually black, which helps them absorb the sun to stay warm.

To start your polar bear doodle, draw an oval head with a "u" shape overlapping the bottom. Erase the overlapping line, then add a pair of small, rounded ears. Give your bear a face, including eyes and a heart-shaped nose. Sketch a curving line for the back and a straight line extending below the head for the front leg. Add another front leg with a paw. Give your bear a back leg and add a paw to it as well as to the other front leg. Draw a line for the belly and add a short, rounded tail. Finally, color your polar bear.

PENGUIN

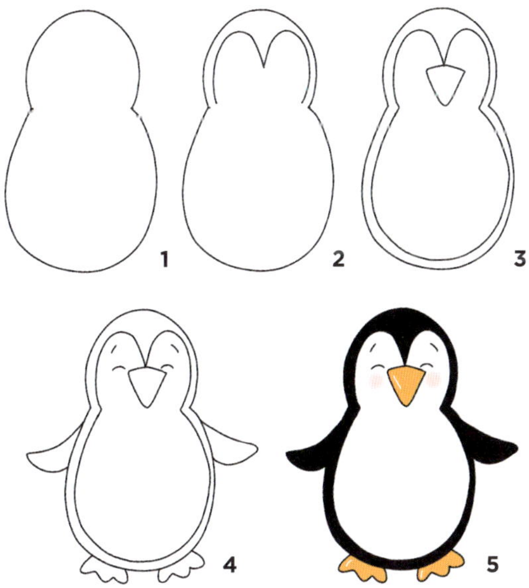

The "tuxedo" coloring of a penguin is actually a form of camouflage when swimming. From above, their backs blend in with the dark color of the water, and from below, their white bellies blend in with the appearance of the water's sunlit surface. Penguins drink a lot of salt water, but they have a special gland located above the eye to filter the salt out of their bloodstream when they sneeze.

Begin your penguin doodle with a body shape that looks like an "8." Add a rounded "M" inside the head, then draw a triangle beak below the center point. Draw a curved line inside the bottom half of the body to separate the belly from the part that will be colored black. Add fins and feet, as well as eyes. Finish your doodle by coloring your cheerful penguin.

PUFFIN

Atlantic puffins are small diving seabirds nicknamed "sea parrots," because of their bright, colorful beaks. Their diet consists of small fish that they hunt underwater. Puffins are able to flap their wings up to 400 times in a minute, which allows them to fly at speeds around 55 miles per hour (89 kph).

Start your puffin doodle with a "C"-shaped head and a large, pointed beak. Add curving lines for the front and back of the body that meet in two points for a tail. Sketch a wing, as well as a large "U"-shaped section inside the head. Then, divide the belly from the rest of the body. Divide the beak into sections, drawing a "v" slightly to the right of the point, then a boomerang shape to the right of that. Also, sketch a small semicircle inside the head near the beak. Draw an eye and sketch a curved triangle around it. Finally, doodle the legs and webbed feet. Color your puffin using mine as a guide for a realistic look or choose any colors you like.

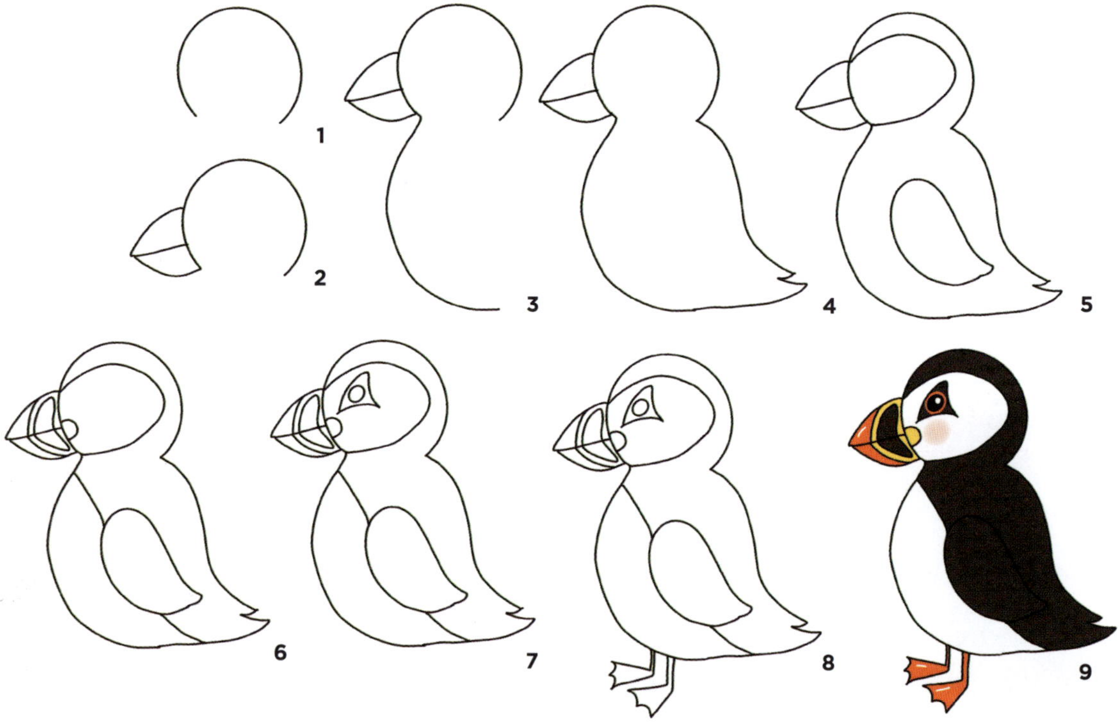

SNOWY OWL

Snowy owls are among the heaviest owl species, because they need a large number of feathers to insulate their bodies from the cold Arctic temperatures. These predators feed on other Arctic species like lemmings, hares, ducks and birds, swallowing their prey whole. Special bristles on their beaks help snowy owls to sense and locate objects. Male snowy owls are usually totally white, while females' white feathers are marked with dark bar-like patterns.

To draw your owl, start with an arc for the head and a large "u"-shaped body. Add a pair of large eyes and a long, thin beak. Draw a pair of wings on the sides of the body and erase the areas where the lines overlap. Add small feet and a pair of parallel lines for a tree branch. Sketch scalloped detail lines on the chest and wings to suggest feathers. Add zigzag lines to separate the head from the chest and draw a wavy line on each side of the beak. Finally, go back to your scalloped detail lines and double them, creating a space for you to color them. Leave the owl's body white but add gray inside the detail lines. Color the rest of the doodle, including the eyes, feet and branch.

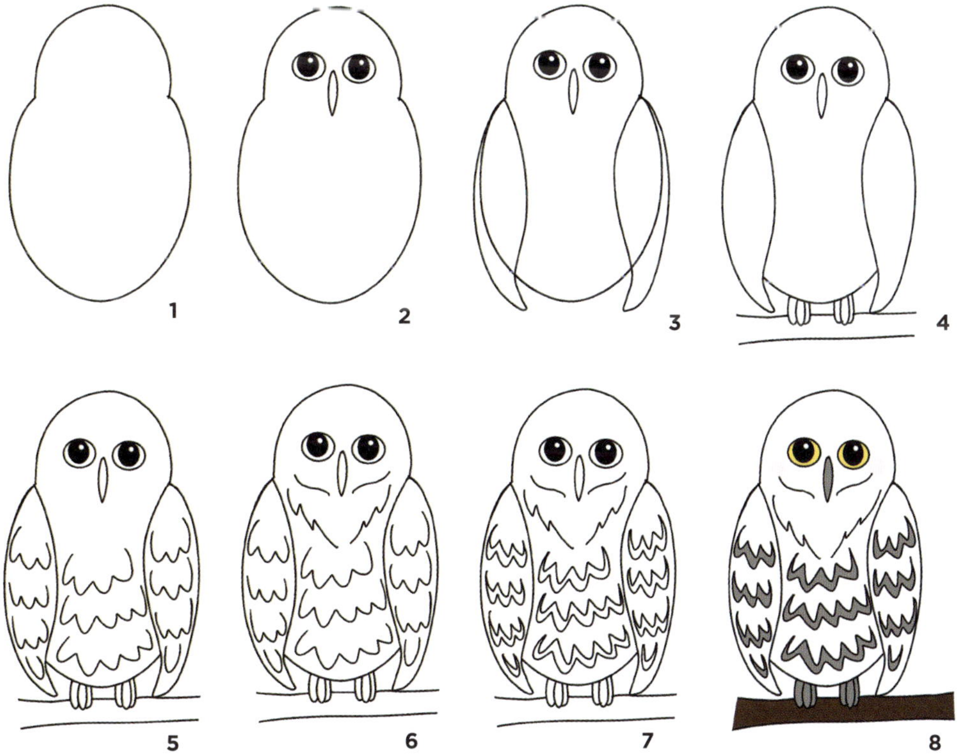

ORCA

Despite the fact that they're called killer whales, orcas actually aren't whales at all—they're dolphins! Orcas have no natural predators and even have been known to hunt sharks and large whales. While they have excellent sight and hearing, scientists believe orcas have no sense of smell.

To start an orca doodle, make a curving line for its back, then draw a second line for the lower part of the body. Sketch a dorsal fin and two lower fins, erasing any overlapping lines. Next, draw a tail that divides into two pointed sections. Divide the belly area from the rest of the body, then give the orca its distinctive markings, like an oval behind the eye, and a curving section near the tail. Add an eye, then color the top part of the orca black, leaving the other sections white.

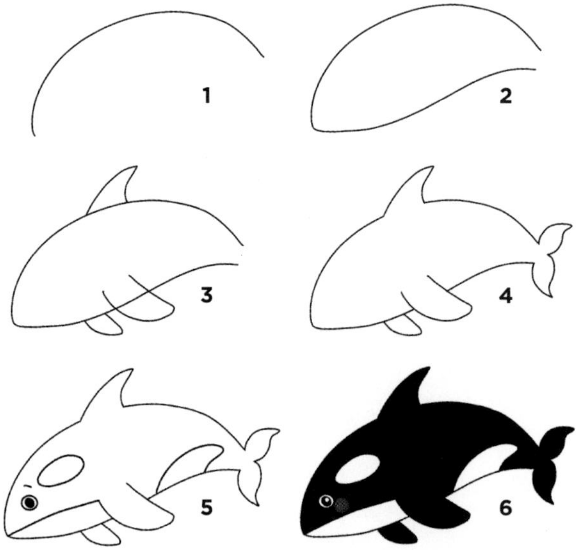

BELUGA WHALE

Belugas are extremely vocal, using more than 30 distinct sounds to communicate with one another. They also communicate by blowing bubbles in particular ways! Although belugas are quite slow, only able to swim 2 to 6 miles per hour (3 to 10 kph), they do have the unusual ability to swim backward.

To draw your own beluga, begin with a curving line for the back and the melon-shaped head. Next, sketch the beak shape and curve it up into a smile. Draw a curving line for the lower part of the beak and body. Next, add a tail and two fins. Erase any areas where the front fin overlaps the body. Give your whale facial features, then color your drawing.

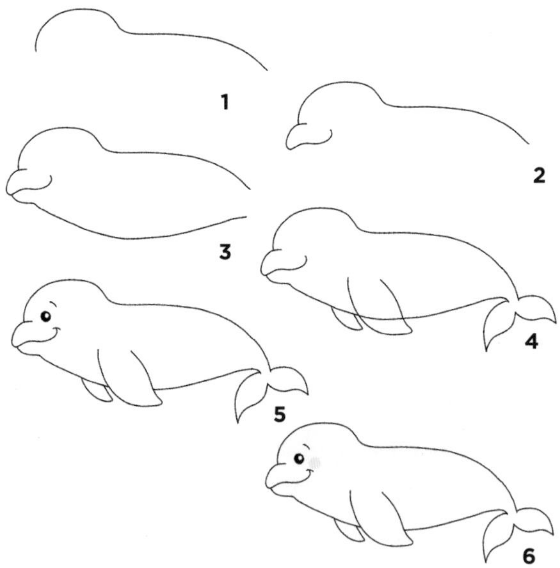

NARWHAL

Thanks to their long tusks, narwhals are known as the "unicorn of the sea." These tusks are actually very long canine teeth that spiral out of the narwhal's upper lip and can reach lengths up to 8 feet (2 m)! Narwhals are very deep divers, sometimes going more than 3,000 feet (914 m) below the surface.

To doodle your own narwhal, sketch a paisley shape that's open at the tip. Add a long, thin triangle for the tusk, erasing where it overlaps with the body. Next, draw a tail that divides into two parts. Sketch a fin for your narwhal, then draw a curving line to separate the belly area from the rest of the body. Finally, add details like spots, lines on the tusk and a smiling face to complete your doodle. Now, all that's left to do is add color.

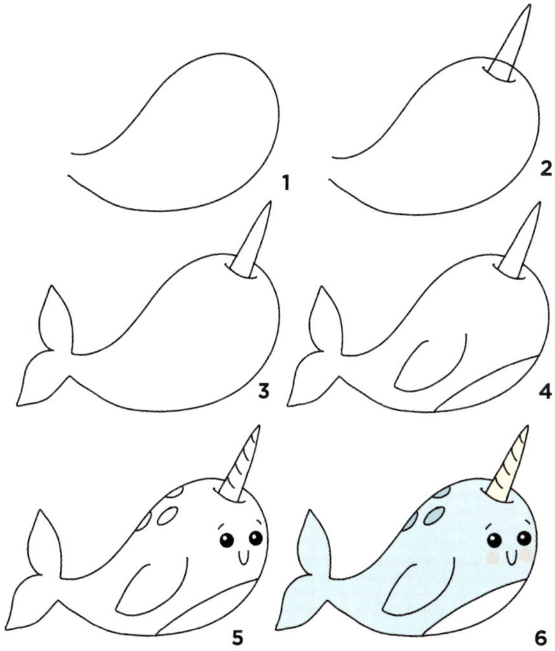

SEAL

Seals prefer to spend the majority of their time in the ocean and can even sleep underwater. They only come on land out of necessity to escape marine predators, mate and molt. In their natural habitat, seals can live 25 to 35 years.

To draw your own seal, start by sketching a semicircle head with a rounded "w" below it. Next, doodle the curved back and the chest. Draw a flipper, then add a line for the belly area. Connect the top and bottom of the body with a tail that divides into two sections. Give your seal eyes, a nose and other facial details, including whiskers. Finally, add color to your drawing.

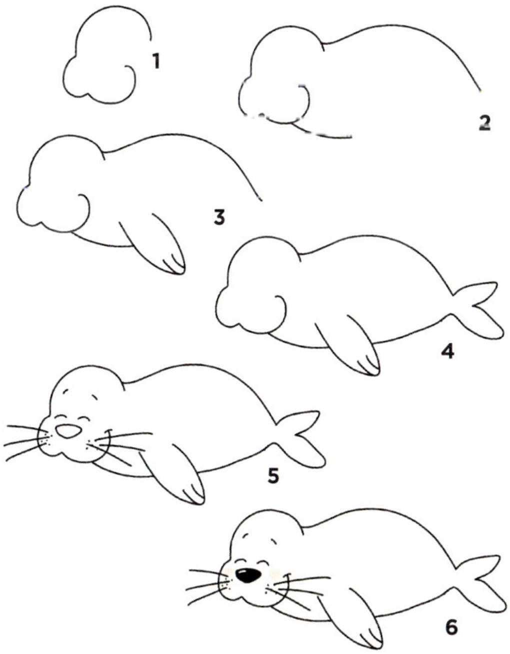

WALRUS

Did you ever wonder why walruses have long tusks? One reason is that they actually work like ski poles! Walruses can dig them into the snow, ice or sand and use them to help pull the rest of their thick bodies out of the water. The tusks are also helpful for breaking through ice to create breathing holes on the water's surface.

Are you ready to draw your own walrus? Start with a semicircle head that extends down into a curving neck. Next, add a large, rounded "w" shape for the mouth and nose area. Draw the back and chest areas, then give your walrus two large flippers. Finish drawing the body and sketch a two-part tail. Doodle nostrils and whiskers, as well as two long, pointed tusks, erasing the area where they overlap the body. Finally, add eyes, eyebrows and color to finish your sketch.

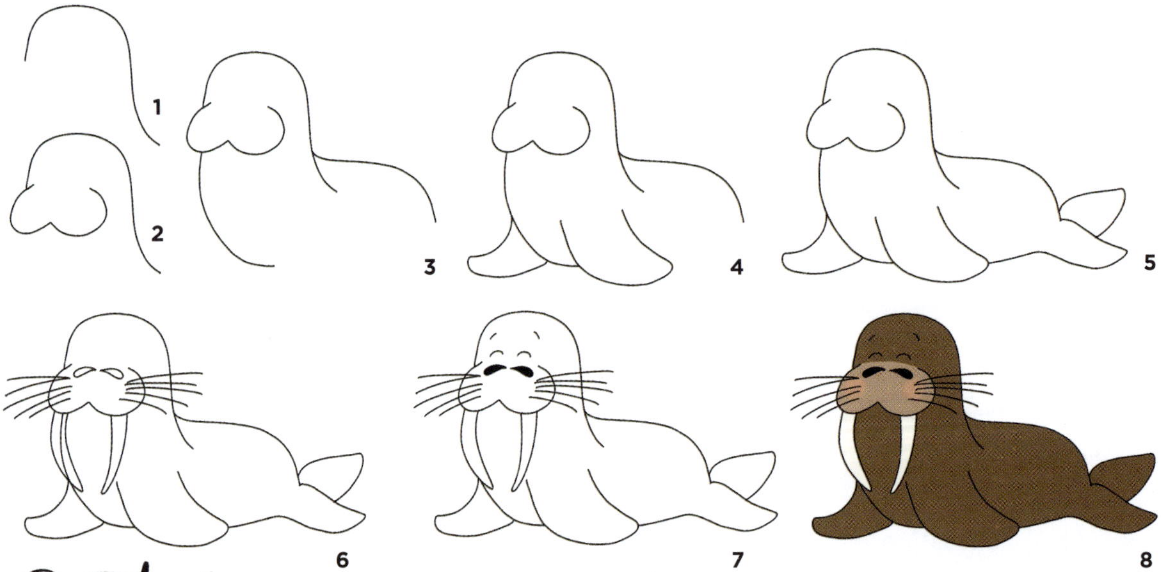

practice here

CARIBOU/REINDEER

You may know caribou by their other name, reindeer, but did you know that both males and females have antlers? Over the summer, caribou migrate north as part of one of the largest land migrations on the planet. Since they cover so much distance, it's helpful that they're excellent swimmers.

To doodle a caribou, start with a long, thin shape for the head. Add a small ear and a curving line for the caribou's back. Draw a zigzag line below the head for the patch of fur on the chest and sketch a line for the front leg. Continue sketching all four legs, as well as a line for the belly. Add a hoof at the bottom of each leg and a small tucked tail. Draw a line to divide the lower part of the body from the upper part. Now, it's time to sketch large curving antlers that branch off into four fingerlike sections on each end. Doodle facial details, then it's time to color your caribou.

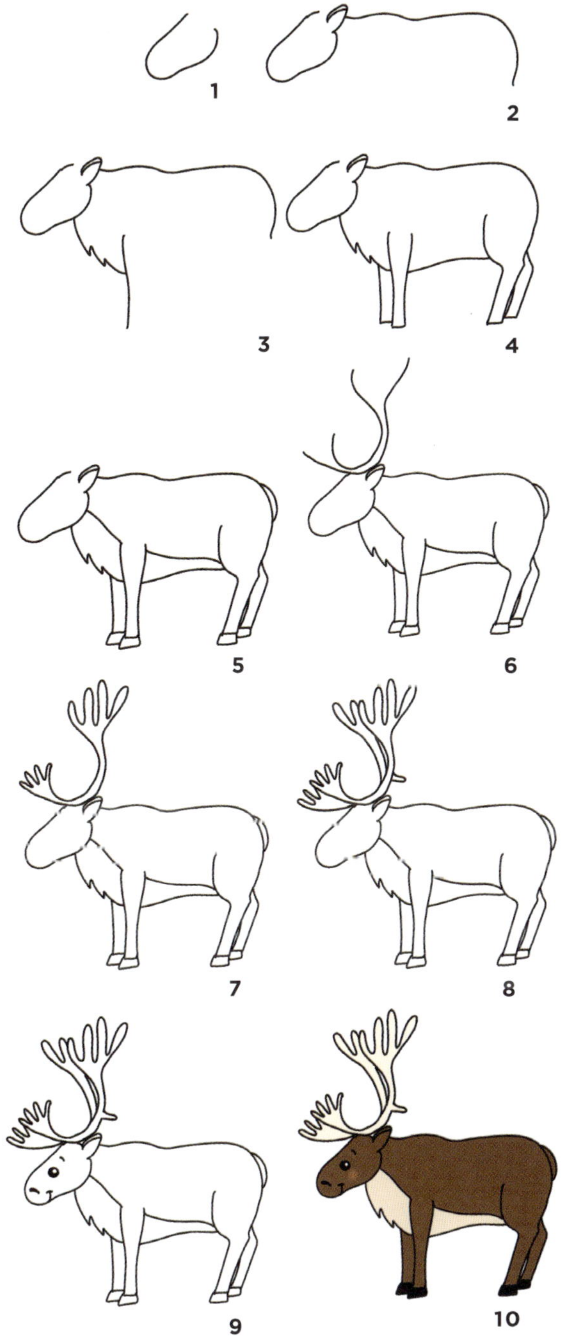

practice here

LEMMING

Lemmings are small rodents that have adapted amazingly well to the arctic environment. Unlike other rodents, they don't hibernate. Instead, they stay active burrowing through the snow and staying underground where the temperatures are actually warmer than the open air. Like our homes, lemming burrows are divided into rooms for specific purposes, like resting rooms, nesting rooms and bathrooms!

The first step for drawing a lemming is to sketch a curving "v" shape for the head. Next, draw a curving line to start shaping the body. Add a "c"-shaped back leg and a foot and draw a tiny, rounded ear inside the head. Sketch a short front leg and draw lines to connect it to the head and back leg. Give your lemming a small, thin tail. Add an eye and nose. Divide the body into several sections, including the top of the face and head, the lower part of the body and a rounded rectangle area on the back. Finally, give your drawing some color!

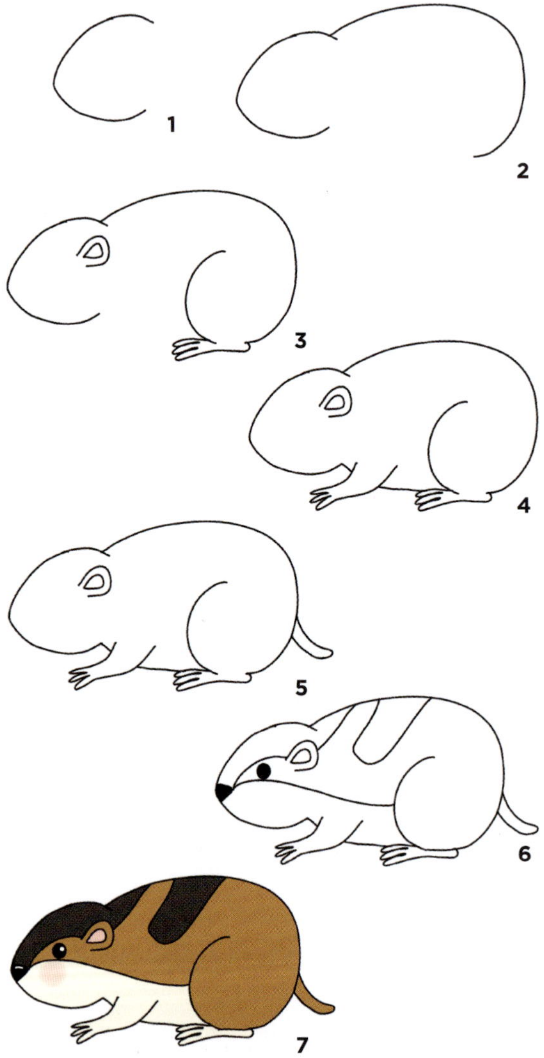

IN THE HABITAT

GLACIER

Glaciers are large masses of ice formed by compressed snow. They form on land, then constantly move under their own weight. Most glaciers in the United States are located in Alaska, but there are also some in other states. Glacier National Park in Montana is a great place to view these spectacular natural wonders.

The good news about drawing ice formations is that it's not an exact science! They can take on all kinds of shapes and sizes, so let your imagination take the lead. To doodle one like mine, start with a jagged line that forms a rough mountaintop. Then, draw another line behind it to indicate a second peak. Draw a third peak, overlapping the center one, then connect them all across the bottom with a wavy line. Add any detail lines you like to show a bit of texture, then color your glacier.

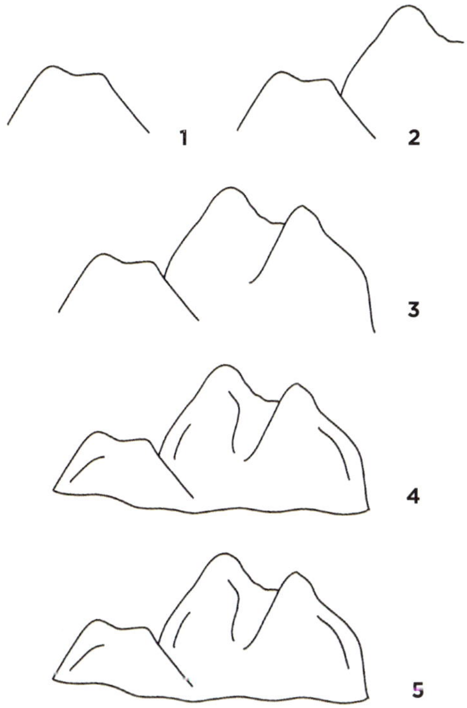

ICE

In an ice field, there are chunks of ice in all shapes and sizes that break away from the main glaciers and ice caps. To create an Arctic scene, all you need to do is sketch a glacier and add some of these smaller pieces of ice floating in the water around it.

Begin your ice doodle by drawing basically any shape you like. It can have wavy edges or jagged ones. The only thing to keep in mind is that real ice chunks have broken away; therefore, they aren't perfect or symmetrical. Next, draw a line below the front edge of your shape and connect it to the sides of the shape to create depth. Add a few detail lines for texture and dimension, then color your ice cap. This is a great place for one or more of your Arctic animals to hang out!

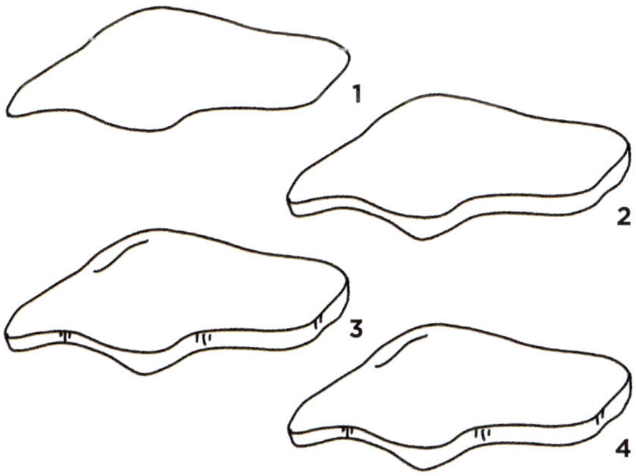

ACKNOWLEDGMENTS

Dan, Nathan and Noah—You are three of my greatest blessings. I'm incredibly grateful for you, and for your patience and understanding while I finished this book. Love you most.

The Page Street team—Thank you for paying me to sit on my couch and draw animals. Best job ever. Sarah, your enthusiasm, ideas and patience are much appreciated. I wouldn't want to do this with anyone else.

Mom and Dad—There aren't enough words to thank you for your constant love and support. I love you.

You, my friend and reader—Thank you for the opportunity to be part of your creative journey. I hope this book inspires you and brings you joy!

ABOUT THE AUTHOR

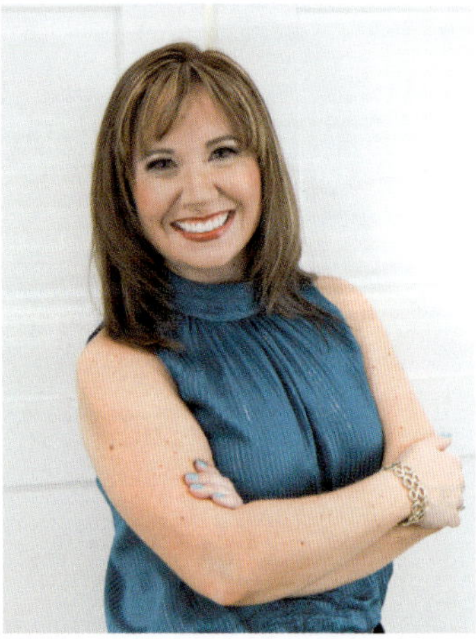

Amy Latta is passionate about inspiring others to explore and embrace their creativity. On her award-winning blog amylattacreations.com, you'll find hand-lettering tutorials, along with craft and DIY projects anyone can create. She also loves teaching in-person and virtual workshops all across the United States through Michaels Community Classroom, Pinners Conference and other venues. Amy also shares creative tips through regular craft segments on lifestyle television shows nationwide. And, of course, you can learn from Amy by reading one or all of her books, the most popular of which, *Hand Lettering for Relaxation*, has sold more than 100,000 copies. Amy is happiest when crafting, and when she's not covered in paint, you can find her working on hand-lettered art and professional design collaborations. Her original lettered designs have been featured nationally in Gap stores and Starbucks commercials. Amy is a Maryland girl who runs on iced coffee and loves spending time with her husband, their two sons and their furry friends, Pumpkin, Peanut and Flynn.

INDEX